Robertson County Tennessee

MARRIAGE RECORDS

VOLUME 1

1839–1861

WPA RECORDS

Heritage Books
2024

HERITAGE BOOKS

AN IMPRINT OF HERITAGE BOOKS, INC.

Books, CDs, and more—Worldwide

For our listing of thousands of titles see our website
at
www.HeritageBooks.com

A Facsimile Reprint
Published 2024 by
HERITAGE BOOKS, INC.
Publishing Division
5810 Ruatan Street
Berwyn Heights, MD 20740

Originally published
December 16, 1936

International Standard Book Number
Paperbound: 978-0-7884-8505-3

Marriage Records

Robertson County Tennessee

1839-1861
1829-1860.

(1) Ephraim Farthing   To   Polly Parsons   Oct. 29, 1839
                             Solemnized   Robert Green J P

     David Williams   to   Barbary E Gunn   16 Oct. 1830
                             Solemnized   .   J M Gunn J P

     Azariah Henly   to   Polly Howard   26 Oct. 1839
                             Solemnized   Benjamin Gambill J P

     John H Read   to   Nancy Morgan   13th Oct. 1839
                             Solemnized   Benjamin Gambill J P

     John M. Chambers   to   Mary E Seal   27 July 1839
                             Solemnized 28th. July 1839 Richd, W Mantlo J P

     James B Hallum   to   Lucy Ventress   17 April 1839
                             Solemnized 18th. April 1839, Thos. W Felts J P

(2) Robert S Sanders   to   Elizabeth Roberts   2 May 1839
                             Solemnized   J M Gunn J P

     Absalum Patterson   to Mary Chapman   May 1st. 1839
                             Solemnized 2nd. May 1839 Robert Green J P

     John Bothink   to   Nancy Carr   25 June 1839
                             Solemnized Isaac Steel

     George S Jones   to   Thites Morgan   10 June 1839
                             Solemnized   Geo. Childress J P

     John Grisham   to   Sophia Shanklen   25 August 1839
                             Solemnized   Uriah Young J P

     James Jones   to   Sally Ely Jones   7 Oct 1839
                             Solemnized 9 Oct. 1839, James Sprouse J P

(3) Archd. D Jones   to   Elizabeth Dorris   21 Sept. 1839
                             Solemnized 26 Sept. 1839 J Sprouse J P

     Samuel McMurry-   to   Elizabeth Ann Adams 18th. Sept. 1839
                             Solemnized 19 Sept. 1839 J Sprouse J P

     Stephen Kirby   to   Lucinda Browning   12 April 1839
                             Solemnized   A B Young J P

     Caswell Crutcher   to   Serona Stanley   1 August 1839
                             Solemnized 8th Aug. 1839 James Sprouse J P

     John Crutcher   to   Keziah Stanley   15 July 1839
                             Solemnized 17 July 1839, James Sprouse J P

Meredith Dorris   To   Highly Robins   23 March 1839
                    Solemnized 27th. March 1839, James Sprouse J.P.

(4) William H Adams   to   Sarah McMurry 18 Sept. 1839
                        Solemnized 20th Sept. 1839, J. Sprouse J.P.

Joseph C Barbee   to   Elizabeth Scoggin 15 March 1839
                    Solemnized 15 March 1839, Geo. Childress J.P.

William Evans   to Martha Nelms 1st. July 1839
                  Solemnized Geo. Childress J.P. for Robertson Co.

Wilson Pitt   to   Mary Ann Porter 16 March 1839
                Solemnized 17th March 1839, Jas. Woodard

Buswell J. Crain   to   Harriet Tucker 7 March 1839
                     Solemnized, Geo. Childress, J.P.for Robertson Co.

Nathaniel Russell   to   Ann Bailey 12 November 1839
                      Solemnized Novr. 14th 1839 W. Hollard J.P.

(5) William Huddleston to   Elizabeth H Harper 26 May 1839
                       Solemnized 26 June 1839. Richd. W. Mantlo J.P.

Asa Dobbs   to   Amy Bartlett Io August 1839
              Solemnized 11th Aug. 1839 Richd. W. Mantlo J.P

Thomas H. Farmer   to   Catherine Martin 22 Aug. 1839
                     Solemnized John Sherrill

Lewis Thomas   to   Elizabeth Henning 9 Lujy 1839
                 Solemnized Geo. Childress J.P.

Bryan Doughtry   to   Lydia Dotson   3 June 1839
                   Solemnized 12th June 1839, Isaiah Warren J.P.

(6) Dabney Jackson   to   Dorothy Dynn 11 May 1839
                       Solemnized 12 May 1839   John Bell J.P.

Peter Stanly   to   Martha Warren   27 June 1839
                 Solemnized Isaiah Warren J.P.

Lewis W. Merrit   to Mary Ann Stark   12 Oct. 1839
                    Solemnized 13th Oct 1839 Geo. Childress J.P.

Meredith Blackburn to   Amanda M Binkley 16 August 1839
                   Solemnized August 17 1839 A. Justice J.P.

Henry G. Williamson to   Eliza A Stone   11 August 1839
                    Solemnized Benjamin Gambill J.P.

Arthur Woodard   to   Polly Hall 17 June 1839
                   Solemnized 20th June 1839 Benjamin Rawls

James H Terrell   to   Elizabeth B Townly 20 Decr. 1839
                    Solemnized 23 Decr. 1839, Robt. Williams

(7)   Larken W. Willis   to   Mary K Willis 7 August 1839
                               Solemnized 8th August 1839, W. S. Boldry G.M.

       Manuel Hutchings   to   Jane Crawford 2 Septr. 1839
                               Solemnized 4th. Sept.1830 Robert Green J.P.

       Fountain S Allison   to   Maris L Emmit 12 May 1839
                               Solemnized Uriah Young J.P.

       David Browder   to   Mary E Evans 16 April 1839
                               Solemnized John P Moore

       James G Holemen   to   Martha Ann Mathews 3rd. August 1839
                               Solemnized 4th August 1839 Robert Green J.P

       Joseph Anderson   to   Martha Crafford 13 March 1839
                               Solemnized 14 March 1839 Isaiah Warren

(8)   Samuel Bray   to   Mary Langford 3rd. January 1840
                               Solemnized Jany.4th 1840 Lewis Adams, M.G.

       Abram Baldwin   to   Martha Ann McMurry 28th Novr. 1839
                               Solemnized Tho. Cook,Justice of the Peace

       Lemuel J. Henry   to Sally A.L.Pope 1 Nov. 1839
                               Solemnized 3 Novr. 1839, Jas. Woodard J.P.

       Henry M Rose   to   Nancy W. Benson 30 Decr. 1839
                               Solemnized Robert Green J.P.

       Willie L Norfleet   to   Sarah Woodard 14 Decr. 1839
                               Solemnized 15th Decr. 1839, Robt. Williams G.M.

       Memucan Allen   to   Martha Edward 28 Novr. 1839
                               Solemnized Robert Grenn J.P.

       William P Dorris   to   Amanda Bagget 3 Decr. 1839
                               Solemnized 10th Decr. 1839 Thos. Cook J.P.

(9)   Isaac Farmer   to Elizabeth H Mason 23 Sept. 1839
                               Solemnized 26 Sept. 1839 Jeremiah Batts J.P.

       William Holleway   to   Martha Sherrod 26 Decr. 1839
                               Solemnized Jeremiah Batts J.P.

       James Crockett   to Nancy W Menees 12 Novr. 1839
                               Solemnized J. W. Ferguson J.P.

       James T. Harris   to   Charlotts Lewis 3 June 1839
                               Solemnized 6th June 1839 W. H. Hudgins J.P.

       John Pepper   to   Matilda Browning 23 Oct. 1839
                               Solemnized Jas Woodard, J.P.

       Robert Russel   to   Ann Dalton 26 Novr. 1839
                               Solemnized 28th Novr. 1839 W. Holland J.P.

(10)   Edwin B Williams   to   Mary J Long 10 Oct 1839
                             Solemnized   Robert Green

       Lewis V. Adams   to   Mary S Sand   10 Oct. 1839
                             Solemnized L. Ayre J.P.

       Geo. A Smith   to   Rachel Johnson 29 Nov 1839
                             Solemnized Dec. 1st 1839 W. Holland J.P.

       John Jones   to   Celantha V Dunn 5 Nov 1839
                             Solemnized Robert Green J.P.

       Ale Lawrence   to   Creesy Beckham 24 Sept. 1839
                             Solemnized 25 Sept. 1839 W Holland J.P.

       Joseph Barnet   to   Elizabeth Sand 14 Decr. 1839
                             Solemnized   L. Ayres J.P.

       Clayton Lockert   to   Mary G Gunn 9 Nov. 1839
                             Solemnized Novr. 10, 1930 [1839]   James Gunn E.M.C

(11)   Henry Pool   to   Pelina Johnson 27 July 1839
                             Solemnized August 1. 1839 Tho. W. F. A

       William Nave   to   Ruth Carter 13 Novr. 1839
                             Solemnized L. Ayres   J.P.

       Larry S. Barnes   to   Beady M Batts   20 Feby. 1840
                             Solemnized 21st of Feby. 1840 Robert Green J.P.

       Reuben Griffin   to   Temperance Rose   25 Jany 1840
                             nSolemnized 27th. Jany. 1840 Benjamin Gambill J.P.

       Willie Holland   to   Amanda E. Dean   28 Jany. 1840
                             Solemnized Jany 30. 1840 Cabb Darden

       Joshua Blackard   to   Louisa Dorris   7 March 1840
                             Solemnized 8th March 1840   Jas. Sprouse J.P.

(12)   Flemming G Plaaters to   Martha L. M. Blick   Feb. 9th 1840
                             Solemnized   Jas. Gunn E.M.C

       William Mason Jr.   to   Elizabeth Chapman   8th Jany 1840
                             Solemnized Jany. 16th 1840 W. Holland

       Thomas Teragen   to   Araminta Wimberly   9 March 1840
                             Solemnized 28th March 1840 Robt. Williams

       William W Britt   to   Permelia A Small   16 Jany. 1840
                             Solemnized U. Young J.P.

       James Williams   to   Elizabeth A JcWate 27 Feby. 1840

Wm Brakefield   to   Elizabeth Vance   27 Feby. 1840
Solemnized U. Young J.P.

James H. Burney   to   Purahan Jernigan   16 Decr. 1839
Solemnized 18th Decr. 1839   E.J. Williams P.C

Jas. J Jones   to   Cinthia Babb   27 Feby 1840
Solemnized   Benjamin Gambill J.P.

(13)   Geo. C Murphy   to   Martha Adams   30 Novr. 1840
Solemnized 9th Feby. 1840   James Sprouse J.P.

Lemuel Warren   to   Nancy England   30 Jany. 1840
Solemnized 9th Frby. 1840   James Sprouse J.P.

Robert D. Felts   to   Nancy M Burnet   19 Feby. 1840
Solemnized 27th Feby. 1840   J.W. Hunt J.P.

S. E. Douthett   to   M.B. Edwards   17 Feby 1840
Solemnized Feby. 27th 1840   E. A. Williams P.G

John E Garner   to   Elizabeth A F Thomas   18 Jany 1840
Solemnized   Geo. McNelly Minister of the Gospel

(14)   William Adamse   to   Henrietta Payne   20 Jany. 1840
Solemnized 21 Jany. 1840   W. B. Burdess J.P.

Alexander Petty   to   Olive Benson   21 Decr. 1839
Solemnized 22 Decr. 1839   W. S. Baldry G.M.

Green Benton   to   Mary Morris   29 Jany 1840
Solemnized D. R. Harris G. M.

Thomas Savage   to   Nancy Baggat   5 Jany 1840
Solemnized 8th January 1840   Jas. Sprouse J.P

James Ryan   to Mary P Hunt   25 Jany 1840
Solemnized Jany. 26 1840   G. W. Dye

(15)   A. F. Hyde   to   Nancy Bobbett   14 Decr. 1839
Solemnized 17 Decr. 1839   J. W. Hunt J.P.

Elbert Williams   to   Lucinda Ferrel   2o Jany. 1840
Solemnized 23 Jany. 1840   D. D. Mason M. G.

Wm. W Stack   to   Elizabeth Burgess   18 Feby. 1840
Solemnized   Geo. McNelley Minister of the Gospel

William H. Farmer   to   Elizabeth Couts   23 Feby, 1840
Solemnized Feby. 24 1840   D. R. Harris M.G.

Lewis Inscore   to   Rebecca Williams   4 Jany. 1840
Solemnized 7th. Jany. 1840   J. M. Gunn J.P.

(16) Jacob Keeler   to   Susan T Cothan   28 Aug. 1839
                          Solemnized 29th. August 1839 J. W. Hunt J.P.

      Charles Kilgore   to   Rebecca Crabtree   11 Jany 1840
                          Solemnized 12 Jany. 1840   Wm. Haley J.P.

      Jeremiah Moore   to   Sally Moore   14 Jany. 1840
                          Solemnized Jany 16, 1840   J. W. Ferguson J.P.

      Leroy Fletcher   to   Marina T Ayres   25 March 1840
                          Solemnized J. W. Ferguson J.P.

      Benj. W. Bradley   to   Harriet Williams   31 Jany. 1840
                          Solemnized Feby. 14, 1840 J. W. Hunt J.P.

      Bailey Boren   to   Polly Herals   5th April 1840
                          Solemnized James Woodard   J.P.

(17) James Woodard   to   Amanda Porter   25 March 1840
                          Solemnized 26th March 1840 Jas. Woodard J.P.

      R. W. Bell   to   Susan Gunn 9 April 1840
                          Solemnized L. Adams M.G. M.E.church

      Garrett Holland   to   Elizabeth Ivy   March 2nd 1840
                          Solemnized 5 March 1840 Lewis Adams M. G. M.E.Churh

      Henderson Cole   to   Malinda Cole   March 30 1840
                          Solemnized 31st March 1840 William Haley J.P.

      Fisher Richd.   to Louisa Whitehead   May 1st. 1840
                          Solemnized George Childress J.P.for Robertson Co.

(18) Boling J Burgess   to   Rachel C Terry   January 30th 1840
                          Solemnized Jeremiah Batts J.P.

      James Knight   to   Miss Nancy Harrington April 9 1840
                          Solemnized J. W. Hunt   J.P.

      Joseph W Flood   to   Miss Elizabeth Boren   April 8th 1840
                          Solemnized Robert Green J.P.

      Joseph Eddings   to Miss Nancy Freeman   March 28th 1840
                          Solemnized Robert Green J.P.

      Calvin Benson   to   Miss Polly Harris   May 24th 1840
                          Solemnized Robt. Green J.P.

(19) Jonathan Addison   to   Nancy Emeline Harbeson Dec. 27 1839
                          Solemnized Jas. Woodard   J.P.

      A. J. White   to   L.B.M.Nicholls   June 2 1840
                          Solemnized Robt. Braughon J.P.

      Edmond H. Shaw   to   Huldah Holmes June 3rd 1840
                          Solemnized June 4th 1840 William Shaw M.G.

John A Strickling   to   Elizabeth Stark   23 May 1840
Solemnized June 7th 1840   Jas. Woodard   J.P.

Andrew West   to   Frances A Maize   30 April 1840
Solemnized   Isiah Warren J.P.

John Holland   to   Parmela A Babb   6 June 1840
Solemnized 8th June 1840   G. Childress J.P.

(20) Patrick P Martin   to   Martha Farmer   Dec. 12, 1839
Solemnized   Thos. Martin

Robinson T Dorris   &   Rebecca Beasley   Aug. 2 1839
Solemnized Aug 8th 1839   John G Balarcy   M.G.

Joseph H Fiser   &   Sarah B Davis   July 4th 1840
Solemnized Jule 5th 1840 Geo. Childress J.P.

John Hutchison   &   Nancy Young   July 27th 1840
Solemnized July 1st 1840   F.G. Ferguson   M.E.
                               chruch

Willis Hyde   &   Marina Shaw   Jany. 28th 1840
Solemnized 4th Feby. 1840   Nathan Morris J.P.

John Thomas Durham   &   Gueinaa Shaw   Jany. 28th 1840
Solemnized Feby.4th 1840   Nathan Morris J.P.

James W. Lawler   &   Sebrina A Cox   June 14th 1840
Solemnized   Benjamin Gambill J.P.

(21) Iredell M Cain   &   Nancy Johnson   Aug. 4th 1839
Solemnized   E. Edwards M.E.C.

Ellis P Cook   &   Louisa X Stother   Oct.16th. 19
Solemnized Oct. 16th, 1839   E Edwards M.E.C.

Nicholas Stone   &   Mary Perrett   Jany. 18, 1838
Solemnized Jany. 20, 1838 Edward Edwards M.E.C

James Edwards   &   Jemima Braves   August 2nd. 1838
Solemnized   Edward Edwards M.G.

David West   &   Mary Wright   Nov. 7th. 1839
Solemnized   E Edwards M.G.

Alfred McAdams   &   Rachel Woodard   Jany 12, 1839
Solemnized 15th. Jany. 1839 E Edwards M. Gospel

James B Wright   &   Susan Taylor   March 3rd. 1840
Solemnized   E Edwares M.G.

Harrison D Sisk   &   Eliza Moss   July 13th 1840
Solemnized 15th July 1840   E. J. Williams M.G.

(22) Lemuel Fiser   &   Julia Ann Dean   August 8th 1840
Solemnized 9th Aug. 1840 Robt. Green J.P.

John W Newton   &   Jane Harris   August 8th 1840
                       Solemnized 10th Aug. 1840 Robt. Draughan J.P.

Edward Porter   &   Cordelia Henry August 14th 1840
                       Solemnized Jas. Woodardon J.P.

Lewis Clinard   &   Haldah Justice Nov.2nd 1839
                       Solemnized 3 Nov. 1839 T. M. Felts

William A. Nicholls   &   Mary N Langford   June 4th 1840
                       Solemnized Thos. W Felts

G. F. Neill   &   Amanda M Hart   July 28th 1840
                       Solemnized July 29th 1840 George W. Dye

(23) William McPheinon &   Katherine Shepherd 3rd Day Sept 1840
                       Solemnized George Childress J.P. for the said Co.

James Boyd   &   Mariah Dumumbrahe   3rd Sept. 1840
                       Solemnized George Childress J.P. for said county

Burmell Ragsdale   &   Olive Foots   28th June 1840
                       Solemnized Geo. Chilress J.P. for said County

Charles Whitisearves &   Katherine A Dunn   28th June 1840
                       Solemnized Warren M Pitts M.G.

James H. Smith   &   Cyntha Beasley   19th June 1840
                       Solemnized 19th June 1840 Geo. Childress J.P.

(24) Robert Williams   &   Mary Hyde   June 1, 1840
                       Solemnized June 4th 1840 J. W. Hunt J.P.

William B. Nicholl   &   Martha A Cockran   28th Sept. 1840
                       Solemnized 1st of Oct. 1840 J. W. Hunt J.P.

John A Duer   &   Mary A Bigbee   20th day of Aug. 1840
                       Solemnized A. B. Young J.P.

William E Bibb   &   Katherine Hightower 4th Oct. 1840
                       Solemnized James Woodard J.P.

G. W. Shaw   &   Dicey A Hunt   22 Sept. 1840
                       Solmenized 22nd. Sept. 1840   Jas. Woodard J.P.

Jesse Grimes   &   Elizabeth Stark 22nd Sept. 1840
                       Solemnized Jas. Woodard J.P.

Jesse Sadler   &   Sarah Sadler   5 Oct. 1840
                       Solemnized 8th Oct. 1840 James Gunn E.M.C.

O.G.Tucker   &   Martha J. Sprouse Oct. 5 1840
                       Solemnized Edmd. Baldwin Minister of the Gospel

(25) William McCarley   &   Almyra Winfield   23rd. Oct 1840
                       Solemnized Thomas Cook J.P.

James W. Draughon   &   Nancy Huey 7 Nov 1830
                               Solemnized Geo. Childress J.P.

Jno. W Ashabraner   &   Maryett Willis 11 Dec. 1839
                               Solemnized Geo. Childress J.P.

James L. Strickling   &   Nancy Harmon 17th August 1840
                               Solemnized 18th Aug. 1840 William L. Baldry
                                                       Gospel Minister

Joel Jenkins   &   Martha Tooley 29 Oct. 1840
                               Solemnized George Childress J.P.

(26) James Kelton   &   Mary Randolph 21st Oct. 1840
                               Solemnized 22nd. Oct 1840 J. W. Judkins J.P.

Linch T Mantlo   &   Sarah Zech 21 Oct. 1840
                               Solemnized Oct. 22nd. 1840 Jas. Woodard J.P.

James Brake   &   Manda Doyal   Dec. 5th 1840
                               Solemnized D. R. Harris G. M.

James J Wilson   &   Mary C Nicholls 20 Oct 1840
                               Solemnized 22 Oct. 1840 N. Morris J.P.

John T Simmons   &   Permelia Randolph 5 Nov. 1840
                               Solemnized J.W.Judkins J.P.

George B Barbee   &   Nancy C Chapman 8 of Decr. 1840
                               Solemnized William L Baldry G Minister

Daniel Chapman   &   A. P. Thompson 9 pf Decr. 1840
                               Solemnized 10th Decr. 1840 J. M. Gunn J.P.

(27) William Boyd .   &   Martha Berget 40 Decr. 1840
                               Solemnized Isaac Steel G. M.

Shadrick Gunn   &   Mahaley Emmery 18 Of Decr. 1840
                               Solemnized Isaac Steel G. M.

A C Pace   &   Mary Suter   24 Decr. 1840
                               Solemnized N. Morris J.P.

William Verbam   &   Mary Connell 10 Nov 1840
                               Solemnized John Lamaster M.G.

John T. Batts   &   Mary Price 31st. Decr. 1840
                               Solemnized Williamson Burgress J.P.

John Choat   &   Barbary Bell Jany 23rd 1841
                               Solemnized Jany 24, 1841 L Adams Min.of the Gos

(28) Azariah B Boon   &   Mary A. Johnson   12th Oct 1840
                               Solemnized   U. Young J.P.

Nicholas T Ring   &   Nancy T Dancy   29th Decr. 1840
                               Solemnized   Thomas Gunn M. G.

John M Myres   &   Caroline Rolin 14th fo May 1840
                      Solemnized Robt. Williams Gos. Min

Alfred Jones   &   Polly Farthing 10 Sept. 1840
                      Solemnized 18 Sept. 1840 Robt. Green J.P.

Elbert Woodard   &   Harriet Moore   28 Nov. 1840
                      Solemnized 30th Nov. 1840 Robt. Green J.P.

Jeremiah Fyke   &   Beady Lellan   25th. Jany 1841
                      Solemnized 28th Jany 1840 Robt. Green J.P.

(29) William R Doss   to Mary Morris   Nov 13 1840
                      Solemnized 15th Nov 1840 R B Mitchell P

Jonathan Cagle   &   Elizabeth Miles   23rd Jany 1841
                      Solemnized 28th Jany. 1841 Charlew Crafford P

Richd. Swift   &   Sarah Robertson   3 rd Aug. 1840
                      Solemnized 6 Aug. 1840 Charles Crafford P

Champ T Cole   &   Polly Covington   1st Oct. 1840
                      Solemnized 8 Oct 1840 W Hailey   P

James Stewart   &   Nancy Simmons   21st Decr. 1840

(30) Bartholemew Egmon &   Paulina Kelly   2 Feby 1841
                      Solemnized Elisha House M of Gospel

Stephen Roberts   &   Virginia Forb   30 July 1840

Wm Roland   &   Lucina McNeill 22rd. Decr. 1840
                      Solemnized Jeremiah Batts   P

Varary Boren   &   Kerziah Boren 17 Decr. 1840
                      Solemnized R. B. Mitchell

John T Read   &   Susannah J Moore 31st Decr 1840
                      Solemnized Wm T Baldry G.M.

John B Parsons   &   Syntha A Powell   24 February 1841
                      Solemnized 25 Feby 1841 J.M.Gunn Justice Peace

J.H.W.Baker   &   Mary March 27th Feby 1841
                      Solemnized J.W.Ferguson J.P.

(31) William Felts   &   Sarah Hastins   19 March 1840
                       Solemnized

Thomas H Drain   &   Malinda Summer   2 April 1840
                      Solemnized Isaac Steele

Clabown Reeder   &   Sarah Brumbelow   12 Nov. 1838
                      Solemnized Nov. 14, 1838 Charles Croffard J.P.

John Roberts   &   M. R. Brashear   31 Decr. 1840
                      Solemnized Isaac Steels

John T Harris   & Susan Tisdale   14 Feby 1841
                       Solemnized Isaac Steele

Charles Howard &   & Eliza Conaway   16 February 1841
                       Solemnized   Isaac Steele M.G.

Berry Pennington   & Nancy Caudle   16 February 1841
                       Solemnized Isaac Steele

(32) Abner Edwards   & Sally Maxey   25 Jany 1840
                       Solemnized William Felts M of the G

J.M.Pintron   & Avy G Price   9 of Jany 1841
                       Solemnized 15 Jany 1841 Isaac Steele

Henry Talley   & Mary Gambill   8 Sept. 1840
                       Solemnized 9 Mayt, 1840   Isaac Steele

James Leake   & Sarah Ann Howard   28 Decr. 1840
                       Solemnized Isaac Steele

James M Holland   & Eliza Ann Turner   6 Decr. 1840
                       Solemnized Isaac Steele

James M Lawrence   & Sarah Plumer   15 Nov 1840
                       Solemnized Isaac Steele

Isaiah Hampton   & Ann Bernard   27 of Oct. 1840
                       Solemnized Isaac Steele

Noah Good   & Syntha MaesFykel8 March 1841
                       Solemnized   Jas, Gunn E.M.C.

(33) Thomas Ragsdale & Nancy Townsend   22nd Decr. 1840
                       Solemnized 24 of Decr. 1840 Warren M Pitts M.G.

Samuel F Mitchell   & Mary E Limebaugh 14 day April 1841
                       Solemnized 15th April 1841   James Gunn E.M.C.

Charles Murrah   & Nancy H Hudgins   29 of Nov 1840
                       Solemnized 20 Decr 1840 J. W. Hunt J.P.

F F D Ward   & Catherine Brown   18 April 1841
                       Solemnized Jas. Woodard J.P.

Alvis Pitts   & Mary C Gregory   2 of March 1841
                       Solemnized 4 day of March 1841 James Woodard J.P.

John Zech   & E. P. Walton   8 Nov. 1840
                       Solemnized Jas. Woodard J.P.

James Hall   & Nancy Holland   25 March 1841
                       Solemnized William T Baldry G.M.

John Minnick   & Sarah Taylor   15 May 1841
                       Solemnized Benjamin Gambill J.P.

(34) John C Benson   & Sally Traughber   19 May 1841
                             Solemnized Benja. Gambill J.P.

      J.E. Vaught   & Luvecea Daubs   22 May 1841
                             Solemnized J. B. Pitts J.P.

      Byram Brakefield   & Ann Benton   7 May 1841
                             Solemnized Tho. E. T. McMurry Justice of the
                                                                  peace

      James K Caudle   & Mary E Alsbrook   5 June 1841
                             Solemnized 6th June 1841 J. W. Ferguson J.P.

      Richard Paraise   & Sarah Smiley   14 April 1841
                             Solemnized 15 April 1841 Charles Crafford J.P.

      Jesse M Davis   & Sarah C E Featherston 29th March 1841
                             Solemnized Jeremiah Batts   J.P.

      Fielding Stark   & Nancy Heatle   26 April 1841
                             Solemnized 27 April 1841 M Haley J.P.

      Gabriel Choat   & James Brewer   16th Oct. 1841
                             Solemnized 17 Oct 1841 Richd. Chowning J.P.

(35) Phillip L. Raley   & Rachel Hickman   18 April 1841
                             Solemnized 19 April 1841 Wm Holland J.P.

      William H Posey   & Sally Wilson   31. May 1841
                             Solemnized A Justin J.P.

      Wesley H Hyde   & Martha L Pilant   24 May 1841
                             Solemnized A Justin J.P. for said County

      John Crafford   & Sally Pepper   19 June 1841
                             Solemnized 20 June 1841 Isaiah Warren J.P.

      William Gentry   & Anney Brewer   6 August 1841
                             Solemnized Richd Chowning J P

      Thomas J Hightower   & Addline Featherston   24 Sept. 1841
                             Solemnized Richd. Chowning J. P.

      James Moss   & Martha Chowning 21 May 1841
                             Solemnized Richd. Chowning J P

      Samuel May   & Sarah Mitchell 14 April 1841
                             Solemnized 15 May 1841 R. B. Mitchell J O

(36) George W Lovel   & Eliza Dorris   22 May 1841
                             Solemnized 26 May 1841 William D Baldin M.G.

      John G Dowlen   & Rachel Carter   30 June 1841
                             Solemnized A Justice J P

      Thomas Alsbrook   & Lucina Daubs   17 July 1841
                             Solemnized H Forey J P

      James T Craig   & Nancy A Reasing 15 July 1841
                             Solemnized Reverend Thomas Martin

William B Farmer   &   Julia A M White   24 July 1841
Solemnized   25 July 1841   H Frey J.P.

Robert Moore   &   Elizabeth Alley   13th Jany 1836
Solemnized Jay. 15, 1836   William Shaw G M

John Hughan   &   Hannah Hunt   1st. June 1841
Solemnized   William Shaw   G M

Larkin Gower   &   Rhapsy X Grimes   7 July 1841
Solemnized July 18, 1841   William Shaw G M.

(37)   E G Murphy   &   Nancy G Williams   9 August 1841
Solemnized H Frey J P

John A Swann   &   Mildres Yates   August 2 1841
Solemnized Aug. 5 1841   J W Judkins J P

John A Griffin   &   Sarah I Hardy   13 August 1841
Solemnized 14 August 1841   Lewis Adams M G

James A Shaw   &   Mahalia Robins   31st August 1841
Solemnized Sept 1st 1841   Wm D Baldwin M of G

John G Hollaway   &   Susan Sory   11 Sept 1841
Solemnized 12 September 1841   Robt. Williams

William L Colemen   &   Lucy I Bryant   2 Sept 1841
Solemnized   Robert Green P

(38)   Charles Simpson   &   Virginia Chastene   9 August 1841
Solemnized   Benj. Gambill J P

John Goon   &   Lovey Etherage   1St Day Aug. 1841
Solemnized   Benja. Gambill J P

David V Sanders   &   Susan May   2 Sept 1841
Solemnized   U Young J P

William Miles   &   Susannah Haley   31 March 1841
Solemnized   Isaiah Warren J P

Samuel Smith   &   Marthy Rice   26 June 1841
Solemnized   W Hollard J P

Robt. C Patterson   &   Elizabeth McMurry   2 Oct 1841
Solemnized 3rd Oct 1841   J W Judkins J P

James H Bealsey   &   Polly B Procter   19 Sept. 1841
Solemnized   Benjamin Gambill J P

(39)   John Griffin   &   Sarah J Hardy   13 August 1841
Solemnized 14 August 1841   Lewis Adams M G

George L Blewitt   &   Nancy D Harris   23 Sept 1841
Solemnized   R D Harris G M

Tolbert L Dalton   & Angeline Mathews   13th Sept 1841
                      Solemnized Robt. Draughon J P

William L Barry   & Malinda Jernigan   22nd Sept. 1841
                      Solemnized 23 Sept 1841 W L Payne J P

Jackson Amos   & Elizabeth Musick   31st. Aug 1841
                      Solemnized W L Payne J P

William P Barry   & Eleanor Wright   3rd. Oct 1837
                      Solemnized 2nd Nov 1837 W L Payne J P

(40) J L Holland   & Martha Bigbee   2rd Oct 1841
                      Solemnized 3 Oct 1841 W L Payne J P

Anderson Johnson   & Mary R B Pack   16 August 1841
                      Solemnized 19 Sept 1841 W L Payne J P

Berry Wilson   & Perniece Williams   30th August 1841
                      Solemnized 31st August 1841   W L Payne J P

John W Woodall   & Nancy Sulam   20th June 1841
                      Solemnized 22nd June 1841   W L Payne J P

Marley Dorris   & Susan Brumbelow   15 September 1841
                      Solemnized Wm. D Baldwin M of the Gos.

Anderson Mathews   & Susan Powell   14 Oct. 1841
                      Solemnized Robt, Draughon J P

(41) Gustin Noe   & Malinda Corbwin   15 Aug 1841
                      Solemnized Jas. Woodard J P

Henry Butt   & Emeline Fiser   21st Oct 1841
                      Solemnized 24 Oct 1841   Robt Draughan N P

William H Haggard   & Elizabeth Holman   19 Oct 1841
                      Solemnized Jas. Woodard J P

James T Browning   & Elizabeth Crafford   7 Sept. 1841
                      Solemnized Isaiah Warren J P

William Agee   & Syntha Wynn   29 Sept. 1841
                      Solemnized 30 Oct 1841 Charles Crafford J P

Bradford Clinard   & Nancy Justice   23 Oct 1841
                      Solemnized 24th Oct 1841 William D Baldwin
                                               Minister of the Gospel

(42) John T Davis   & Eliz McNeilly   31 Oct 1841
                      Solemnized D R Harris G M

W L Foster   & Susan L Cheatham   28th Oct 1841
                      Solemnized D R Harris G M

Christopher White   & Mary A Shreevis   23rd Oct 1841
                      Solemnized W L Payne J P

Daniel Cothern   & Martha Nimro   5 August 1841
                        Solemnized Isaac Steele G M

James G Murphy   & Lucinda Howard   9th July 1841
                        Solemnized 13 day of July 1841   Jeremiah Batts
                                                                    J P

L L Williams   & Ann Boatright   23rd Sept 1841
                        Solemnized Isaac Steele G M

D D Holman   & Mary A Polk   3rd OCt. 1841
                        Solemnized Mitton Raney Misinter of the Gospel

(43) Joseph Grant   & Harriet A Atkins   7 July 1841
                        Solemnized Mitton Raney Minister of the Gospel

Thomas B Marshall   & Mary Ann Browning   11th. Nov. 1841
                        Solemnized Jas. Woodard J P

John Morgan   & Leura Gorham   18 Nov 1841
                        Solemnized J B Pitts J P

Edward C Garrett   & Susan Taylor   23rd. Decr 1841
                        Solemnized Wm. T Baldry G M

Thomas Frey   & Jane Farthing   14 Decr. 1841
                        Solemnized 20 Decr. 1841 Wm T Baldry   G M

James M Stroud   & Oylann Givvins   24 Decr 1841
                        Solemnized Wm. T Baldry G M

(44) Saml H Elliott   & Nancy Hyde   L2 Sept. 1841
                        Solemnized J W Hunt J P

Thos G Sprouce   & Malinda Beasley   24 Decr 1841
                        Solemnized 26 Decr 1841 Wm D Baldwin M G

Saml. Fuqua   & Malinda Clinard   17 Nov 1841
                        Solemnized 18th Nov 1841   Benja. Rawls G M

Robert Sory   & Elizabeth Adams   13 Nov 1841
                        Solemnized 15 Nov 1841 John Bell J P

Thomas Hunt   & Susan Shiven   28 June 1841
                        Solemnized July 8 1841   J W Hunt   J P

(45) John R Stricklin & Katherine Campbell   8 Nov 1841
                        Solemnized Benja Gambill J P

Wm W Graham   & Francess Woodall   14 July 1841
                        Solemnized 15 July 1841   Benja Gambill J P

James M Shelton   & Sarah Hetterbram   23rd. Decr 1841
                        Solemnized Wm L Baldry M.G.

Abel O Babb   & Juleit Straughn   10 Oct 1841
                        Solemnized Benja Gambill J P

16   Robertson Co., TN - Marriage Records - Volume 1 - 1839 - 1861

****

S. W. D. Scott   &   S A Adcock   22 April 1841
no certificate

Rawls Maxey   &   Rebecca M Edwards   22 April 1841
Solemnized 8 August 1841   William Fitt   M. G

(46)   J G Mason   &   Mary Roberts   7 Decr. 1841
Solemnized   Robt. Green   J P

Charles Person   &   Sarah Breakfield   9 July 1841
Solemnized 11 of July 1841   Charles Crafford J P

Richd Cannon   &   Malinda Young   23 Decr 1841
Solemnized   A Justin Justice of the peace for
            R County

Wm Newtin   &   Charlotte Anderson   1st Decr 1841
Solemnized 3rd Decr 1841   Charles Crafford J P

Meredith Long   &   Nancy Roberts   14 Decr 1841
Solemnized   Jas Warren   J P

William B Porter   &   Dliva A Newton   28 Decr 1841
Solemnized   Robert Draughon   J P

R W Thompsom   &   Rachel Roberts   21st Decr 1841
Solemnized   Jas. Woodard J P

(47)   Jesse Roberts   &   Elizabeth Williams   9 Decr 1841
Solemnized Jas. Woodard J P

James P Bivins   &   Martha D Stewart   14 Oct 1841
Solemnized   A Justin Justice of the peace for
            said R C

Samuel A Graves   &   Mary A Farmer   6 Jay 1842
Solemnized   D R Harris   G Minister

W P Blick   &   Ann Camelay   4 Jay 1842
Solemnized   Jas Woodard J P

Hiram R Murphy   &   Nancy Winters   3rd Jay 1841
Solemnized 6 Jay 1842   Robt. Draughon   J P

Dempsy House   &   Polly Johns   28th Octd1842
Solemnized   Robt. Green   J P

Charles W Beaumont   &   Nancy Bradley   2nd Sept 1841
Solemnized   Call A Slater

(48)   Elisha Binkley   &   Harriet J McCormack   6 Aug 1841
Solemnized 8 Aug 1841   John Forbes J P

Alpheus Elliott   &   Mary Eliz. Barbee   28 Oct 1839
Solemnized Oct 29 1839   John Forbes J&P

Williard Everett   &   Barbary Maxey   11 Decr 1841
Solemnized 19th Decr 1841   John Forbes J P

Charles Ghurt   &   Mary Sanders   18th Feby 1840
                                Solemnized 23 February 1840   John Forbes J P

(49) Mathew V Fyke   &   Sally A Mathews   28 Feby 1842
                                Solemnized   Robt. Green J P

Daniel Hudgins   &   Nancy Do Durham   23 Dec 1841
                                Solemnized   Robt. Green J P

Hiram Rice   &   Nancy Roland   20 Oct 1841
                                Solemnized   Robt. Green J P

John B Farthing   &   Martha Farthing   27th Jay 1842
                                Solemnized   Thomas Gunn M G

John Brewer   &   Nancy A Forister   25 Sept 1841
                                Solemnized 26 Sept 1841   W Haley J P

(50) Crawford Cole   &   Elizabeth Whitemill   23rd Decr 1841
                                Solemnized   Benja Gambill J P

Hall Willie   &   Nancy Babb   17 Feby 1842
                                Solemnized   Banja Gambill J P

Cook, Alexander C   &   Sally A Stark   12 Decr 1841
                                Solemnized   Benjamin Gambill J P

Tillman, J Ray   &   Sarah Dark   12 Decr. 1841
                                Solemnized   Banja. Gambill J P

Jesse Reasons   &   Wilmouth A Wattson   26th Aug 1841
                                Solemnized   R B Mitchell J P

(51) Thomas W Bracy   &   Martha P Alsbrook   25 February 1842
                                Solemnized Feb 27th 1842 A Justin Justice of the
                                                                    peace
James L Shettan   &   Drusilla Woodard   20th Jay 1842
                                Solemnized   W L Baldry G M

John Matthews   &   Sally Harrison   24th Jay 1842
                                Solemnized   R B Mitchell J P

Joseph W Fort   &   Susan M Whitfield   7th Jay 1842
                                Solemnized   R B Mitchell J P

William England   &   Mary Savage   8 Jay 1842
                                Solemnized 9 Jay 1842   James Sprouse J P

A L Smith   &   M M Long   8 March 1842
                                Solemnized   W L Baldry   G M

(52) John C Blankenship   &   Eliz Murphy   30 Nov 1841
                                Solemnized   Benjamin Rawls G M

David L Alsbrooks   &   Adaline A Green   9 May 1840
                                Solemnized 10th May 1840   Benjamin Rawls   G M

Drury Easley   &   Cassander Farley   14th March 1842
                      Solemnized   W L Payne   J.P.

Pitts Lynn   &   Polly L Miles   13 Jany 1842
                      Solemnized   Joseph B Pitts J.P.

Benjamin F Holland   &   Angeline Menees   20 Jay 1842
                      Solemnized   Benja. Rawls G M

Charles F Miller   &   Weathly I Ventress 28 March 1842
                      Solemnized Benja. Rawls G M

(53) Albrittian M Drake   &   Eliz A Hancock   20 Oct 1841
                      Solemnized   26th Decr. 1841   U Young J.P.

George W Stone   &   Matilda Cole   19 Jay 1842
                      Solemnized   Wm D Baldwin G M

Wesley W Moulton   &   Cyrene Stark   4 April 1842
                      Solemnized Jas. Woodard   J P

Kindred Wilson   &   Martha Choat   5 Feby 1842
                      Solemnized 10 February 1842 Tho. Cook J P

J H Hull   &   Martha Walton   26 March 1842
                      Solemnized Tho. Cook   J P

James Brewer   &   Nancy A Frey   18th Oct. 1841
                      Solemnized April 4th 1842 Richard Chowning

(54) Redick Rose   &   Lucy Clayton   7 February 1842
                      Solemnized 8 February 1842 THo. W Felts Minister

Jackson Rust   &   Sarah Traughber   3 March 1842
                      Solemnized 6 March 1842   T W Felts Min.

Mansfield Jenkins   &   Rachel Warren   9 March 1842
                      Solemnized   J B Pitts J P

Reuben Ellimore   &   Julia Crawford   18 Sept 1842
                      Solemnized Richd. Chowning J P

Milton Ramy   &   Phebe C Gunn   3rd May 1842
                      Solemnized James Gunn E M C

William Draughon   &   Martha J Ruffin   24 February 1842
                      Solemnized Robert Draughon J P

(55) John Cook   &   Sarah T Brewer 14 Jay 1842
                      Solemnized 4 April 1842   Richd Chowning J P

Reuben Lawrence   &   Eliza Tanner   23rd May 1842
                      Solemnized Benjamin Rawls G M

Thomas M Martin   &   Marina C Glover   18 March 1842
                      Solemnized 20 March 1842 Thomas Martin G M

John Lawes   & Zelphy J Ellis   20th April 1842
                      Solemnized   H Frey J P

George W Perkerson   &   Emiley A Roach   31st Decr 1840
                            Solemnized Robt. Williams Gospel Minister

Millington Easley   &   Eliz Ann Davis   6 June 1842
                            Solemnized   W Seal Justice of the Peace

(56) Thomas Gunn   &   Mary A Newton   28 Decr 1841
                            Solemnized   Jeremiah Batts Justice of the peace

Josephus C Marchal   &   Juanith A Spain   7 June 1842
                            Solemnized   James Gunn E M C

James Benton   &   Mary Dickerson   4 June 1842
                            Solemnized 5 June 1842 Jesse L Ellis J P

Thoman J Payne   &   Eliz Roney 14 June 1842
                            Solemnized W L Payne J P

Josiah Biggs   &   Nancy Redfern   27 June 1842
                            Solemnized W L Payne   J P

Samuel Baley   &   Mariah Adcock   28 Nov 1838
                            Solemnized B Rawls M G

(57) George Forde   &   Emeline Love   4 Oct 1839
                            Solemnized

James J Chambers   &   Sally Ann Seal   6 Aug 1840
                            Solemnized Benjamin Rawls   G M

J D Dover   &   Jane Gentry   2 March 1841
                            Solemnized 3rd March 1841 Benja. Rawls G M

Eli Reavis   &   Eliz Smith   14 April 1841
                            No Return

Carroll W Hyde   &   Martha Manlove   18 March 1841
                            No Return

Joel Chaudion   &   Martha A Felts   31 August 1841
                            Solemnized Sept 2 1841 Benjamin Rawls G M

Solomon Fiser   &   Matilda Crockett 10 Oct 1839
                            Solemnized Benjamin Rawls G M

William C Rawls   &   Mary A M Green   26 Sept. 1839
                            Solemnized Benjamin Rawls G M

(58) Alexander Ally   &   Rachel Binkley   6 August 1842
                            Solemnized 7th August 1842 S Brewer

William H Heath   &   Caroline Ayres   11 July 1842
                            Solemnized 12 July 1842 Richd. W Bell J P

James M Johnson   &   Emily T Ayres   21 July 1842
                            Solemnized Richd. W Bell J.P.

Benjamin Crabtree   &   Sally Brewer   L4 May 1842
                           Solemnized   Thos. Cook J P

Geo. W Featherston   &   Patsy Redfern   29 March 1842
                           Solemnized Benja. Gambill J P

(59) Henderson Fletcher   &   Emeline Benton * 3rd 1842   Thos T McMurray
                                                                        J P

Henry Turner   &   Beersheby Holland 14 Decr 1841
                           Solemnized   W Holland J P

H. M. Martin   &   Eliza Redfern 16 August 1842
                           Solemnized W L Payne J P

Mary J Powell   &   Lewis Powell   March 1842
                           Solemnized W Holland   J P

Richd. B Rose   &   Clarissa Mason   4 May 1840
                           Solemnized W Holland J P

John A Walker   &   Lucy Gibson   3rd July 1842
                           Solemnized A L P Green M G

William THG Stoval   &   Nancy B Holland   21 Oct 1842
                           Solemnized   W Holland   J P

John Chapman   &   Eliz C Thompson   March 1842
                           Solemnized W Holland J P

(60) John Chapman   & Elizabeth Thompson   5 March 1842
                           Solemnized W Holland

Abraham Broadrick   &   Louisa Krisles   8 October 1842
                           Solemnized   James Woodard J P

(61) John Flood   &   Mary A Stark   30 December 1842
                           Solemnized January 1st 1843 James Woodard J P

Jackson Crockett   &   Eliz Fiser   29 Decr 1842
                           Solemnized   W Seal J P

Joseph T Taylor   &   Mary J Darden   3 Nov. 1842
                           Solemnized   James L Adams J P

Edmond W Hughes   &   Nancy Mason   17 November 1842
                           Solemnized 22 November 1842 Thomas Gunn M G

Richd. Wilks   &   Martha Sneed   5 November 1842
                           Solemnized   Thomas Gunn M G

James W Williams   &   Malvina Carter   27 December 1842
                           Solemnized. James Sprouse J P

(62) Eldnage W Dorris   &   Louisa England   27 Sept 1842
                           Solemnized 28 September 1842 James Sprouse J P

Withbaler Branson   &   Jane Hardison   L January 1843
                           Solemnized D G Baird J P

William W Vaughan   &   Martha A Bailey 19 October 1842
                           Solemnized 20 October 1842 Tho W Ruffin J P

John Pace   &   Ruthia Darden   28 November 1842
                           Solemnized R Pennington J P

W W Ayres   &   Nancy Johnson 25 October 1842
                           Solemnized 25 1842 Richd. W Bell J P

H C Larkin   &   Susan Frey   1st April 1841
                           Solemnized 4th April 1841 M Parks V D M

Jesse M Spright   &   Sarah T Bryan   1st April 1841
                           Solemnized 4 April 1841 H Parks V D M

Wm W Burnett   &   Martha Dowlen   3rd Aug 1842
                           Solemnized 4 August 1842 J W Hunt J P

(63)   William Sherrod   &   Mary Reed   3rd of August 1842
                           Solemnized Lewis Minister of the Gospel

Westley W Pepper   &   Penny Young   12 November 1842
                           Solemnized 13 November 1842 D R Harris G M

John A Dudley   &   Katherine Haydon 30 August 1842
                           Solemnized   U Young J P

John C May   & Mary A M Mitchell 4th July 1842
                           Solemnized 5th July 1842 Jas. L Adams J P

R K Hicks   & Ann R Greer   18 October 1842
                           Solemnized Thomas Farmer J P

Sherrod Hunter   &   Lydia Hunter 10 October 1841
                           Solemnized

James Babb   & Annus Jones   9 Nov 1842
                           Solemnized 10th Nov 1842 Greenberry Kelly

(64)   Joseph Babb   &   Eliz Rose   13 April 1842
                           Solemnized Isaac Steel

Geo. Wright   &   Elena Hunt
                           Executed

Greenberry Greer   &   Katherine Hide   1st September 1842
                           Executed

Richd. P Winn   &   Eliz Richeson   26 June 1841
                           Solemnized 27 June 1841 W L Baldry G M

Alvin Berry   &   Agness Haley 16 September 1842
                           Solemnized Sept 21st 1842 David Jones J P

George Hazle   &   Milly Wheeler   5 November 1842
                    Solemnized   W L Payne J.P.

(65)   John B Schenck   &   Caroline A Beeknell   6 Oct 1842
                  Solemnized   12 October 1842 Thos Wheat
                           Rector of Christ Church Nashville

Arthur L Burk   &   Matilda M Henry   3 Octl 1842
                  Solemnized 5 Oct. 1842   Wm. L Baldey M G

Geo H Johnson   &   Louisa Smith   14 Sept. 1842
                  Solemnized 15 September 1842 Thomas Farmer J P

L J Truman   &   Martha Pennington   13 Oct. 1841
                  Solemnized Robt. Williams

William F Gullege   &   Pheby Dorris   220 August 1842
                  Solemnized W L Baldry Gospel Minister

Mary J Powell   &   Lewis Powell   13 March 1842
                  Solemnized   W Holland J P

John E Reed   &   Harriet E Sherod   3 August 1842
                  Solemnized   Lewis Adams

(66)   John C Bigbee   &   Harriet E Clark   13 Aug. 1842
                  Solemnized   Greenberry Kelly

Alford Dolton   &   Eliz Borders   31st May 1842
                  Solemnized \ U Young J P

Willie Heiflin   &   Emily Adams   5 Sept 1842
                  Solemnized 8th Sept 1842 Jas. L Adams J P

James Cook   &   Martha J Overstreet   20 Sept 1842
                  No return

Geo. E Draughon   &   Tabitha Couts   8th Nov 1842
                  Solemnized   W Seal J P

James Randolph   & Eliz Jones   23 Oct 1842
                  Solemnized   25 Oct 1842 J W Judkins J P

Jesse Sawyers   &   Melissa A Winters   22nd Oct 1842
                  Solemnized 29 Oct. 1842 J L Ellis J P

(66)   William A Holman   &   Ann Mason   12th January 1843
                  Solemnized   Jas. Woodard J P

Geo Murphy   &   Rebeca F White   3rd May 1843
                  Solemnized May 4 1843 Jesse L Ellis J P

John Pepper   &   Mary Cannon   23 Feby 1843
                  Solemnized A Justice, Justice of the peace for
                                  R County

Isaac Robertson   &   Julia Cannon   9 July 1843
Solemnized Thomas Farmer Justice of the peace
for Robertson County

Joseph A Tucker   &   Louisa V Rowe   21st March 1843
Solemnized 25 March 1843 James Sprouse J P

Samuel Tucker   &   Martha Ellmore   17 Feby 1843
Solemnized James Sprouse J P

(67)   Archor S Dorris   &   Nancy Ellmore   1st March 1843
Solemnized 2nd March 1843 James Sprouse J P

James W Gower   &   Milly Head   12 Nov 1841
Solemnized Nov 16, 1841   William Shaw G M

Ardra H Gooche   &   Martha J Johnston   4 June 1843
Solemnized   Joel Whitton

Albert Byram   &   Eliz. McGuire   24 Decr 1842
Solemnized 27 Decr. 1842   C Woodall J P

William Johnson   &   Louisa Ayres   16 Oct 1841
Solemnized   T W Felts Min.

Jonathan Batts   &   Mary M Bandy   4 Feby 1843
Solemnized 5 Feb. 1843   J L Adams   J P

Wm H Mosely   &   Hariet Bagby   4th Feb. 1843
Solemnized   D G Baird J P

(68)   W L Dorris   &   Martha Johnson   5 March 1843
Solemnized   J L Adams J P

Coleman Farthing   &   Mariah Jones   2 Jay 1843
Solemnized   Robt. Green J P

Henry Shaw   &   Martha A Sherron   3 January 1843
Solemnized 4 January 1843   John Forbes J P

Plummer W Teasley   &   Eliz. Miles   31 January 1843
Solemnized 1 Feby 1843   John Forbes J P

John Saunders   &   Nancy Saunders   11 Oct 1843
Solemnized John Forbes J P

(69)   Benard Brickles   &   Hepsey B Shaw   1st Decr 1841
Solemnized   William Shaw G M

John Rosse   &   Eliz. Smith   23 March 1843
Solemnized   W L Payne J P

John Satterfield   &   Sarah Bowers   23 March 1843
Solemnized   W L Payne J P

Allen H Wingo   &   Nancy F Shaw   1st Decr 1841
Solemnized William Shaw G M

Samuel Horton   &   Lucinda Martin   2 January 1843
                                Solemnized W L Payne   J P

William L Davis   &

(70) Henry Stone   &   Susan K Frey   27 July 1842
                                No return

Edward Newton   &   L M J Winn   1 April 1843
                                Solemnized 13 April 1843   Richd W Bell J P

Robin Bartlett   &   Jane M Gunn   15 April 1843
                                Solemnized 16 April 1843   J M Gunn J P R C

Napolean B Neal   &   Martha Bobbett   17 April 1843
                                Solemnized 18th April 1843   W W Williams J P

Reason S Porter   &   Ann E Shackleford   8 Jany 1843
                                Not Return

J T Durrett   &   E J Patton   3 Aug 1842
                                No return

James McCasland   &   Matilda Pike   19 Sept 1842
                                No return

(71) Marcus Hall   Sarah Crawford Nov. 23 1842
                                Solemnized 8 Decr. 1842   W L Payne J P

Andrew Bell   &   Mary Frey   2nd January 1843
                                No return

Anderson Adcock   &   Terry Wilson   16 November 1843
                                Solemnized 20 November 1842 Wm D Baldwin M G

Grandville J Denning   &   Malvina Cooper   18 Nov 1842
                                Solemnized   C Woodall J P

J E McMurry   &   Malone Edwards   28 January 1843
                                Solemnized 30 Jay 1843 Joel Whitten

David O Guerin   &   Emeline Taylor   23 January 1843
                                Solemnized 24 Jan. 1843   James Sprouse J P

(72) Franklin Warren   &   Ann E Amos   23rd Decr 1842
                                Solemnized 29 Decr 1842 Isaiah Warren J P

Harry B Winters   &   Sarah J True   13 July 1842
                                Solemnized 14 July 1842 Wm D Baldwin M G

John N Frey   &   Lucinda Dean   31st January 1843
                                Solemnized D G Baird J P

John M Henry   &   Harriet B Woodard   10 Decr 1841
                                Solemnized 12 day of Decr 1841 Robt Green J P

John A Williams   &   Sarah Williams   15 Jau 1843
                                Solemnized D D Mason

(73)   David C Briggs   &   Sarah M Whitscarver   3rd April 1843
                                    Solemnized U Young J P

        John Boren   &   Mary A Wells   14 December 1842
                                    Solemnized U Young J P

        John Graham   &   Adaline Knight   17 Nov 1842
                                    Solemnized U Young J P

        Tho. M Herendon   &   Mary M Mart   11th May 1843
                                    Solemnized U Young J P

        John Clevenger   &   Harriet Steel   8 March 1842
                                    Solemnized   T W Felts Minister

        John W Gorham   &   Lydia Traughber   21 May 1843
                                    No return

        Robert Frizzle   &   Nancy McCloud   27 March 1842
                                    Solemnized   Thos. W Felts Minister

(74)   David Browder   &   Eliz. Irvin   7 Nov. 1842
                                    Solemnized 8 Nov. 1842 A H Redfern

        James T Williams   &   Caroline Steel   25 Decr 1842
                                    Solemnized Tho W Felts

        Wm. H Mosely   &   Harriet Bagly   4 Feby 1843
                                    Solemnized D G Baird J P

        Lewis Thomas   &   Sarah Mantlo   20 July 1843
                                    Solemnized Thomas Farmer J P

        James M Finlay   &   Mary Holland   13 June 1843
                                    Solemnized 15 June 1843 Greenberry Kelly

        Wm. A Bernard   &   E I Mc Millin   25 June 1843
                                    Solemnized   June 26 1843 John M Nolen

(75)   Henry G Bibb   &   Sarah Adams   30 July 1843
                                    Solemnized   U Young J P

        John W Goddard   &   Rebecca Johns   28 August 1843
                                    Solemnized   W L Payne J P

        Bowling L Poor   &   Sarah Ann Adams   29th Oct 1843
                                    Report probally on the Bond

        John C Curd   &   Mary E Price   17 July 1843
                                    Solemnized   U Young   J P

        Dave Grant   &   Tibitha J Y Hutchison   9 August 1843
                                    Solemnized   G W Dye

        Wm W Thomas   &   Martha Smith   3rd August 1843
                                    Solemnized   Robt. Draughan J P

        James V Roy   &   Ann Virginia Harbison   16 Decr 1843
                                    No trturn

(76)   Elijah Deen   &   Penelope Taylor   28 Decr 1843
                            Solemnized   28th 1843   Jas Woodard J P

       George Barnes   &   Caroline C McNeil   21st Nov 1843
                            No return

       Charles Howard   &   Mary Randolph   20 Nov 1843
                            Solemnized   Greenberry Kellu M G

       D C Sanders   &   Sarah A Duke   14 Decr 1843
                            Solemnized Thomas Martin Minister of the Gospel

       James Rose   &   Martha Taylor   10 Jany 1844
                            Solemnized   Robert Green J P

       Mitchell G Thurman   &   Mary R Worsham   20 May 1843
                            Solemnized James Sprouse J P

       Miles A Jackson   &   Sary A G Spears   28 Nov 1843
                            Solemnized   Lewis Adams Minister of the Gospel

(77)   M D L Williams   &   Luoisa Jane Adams   23 Decr 1843
                            Solemnized 28 Decr 1843 Jesse L Ellis J P

       Moses J Rowe   &   Sarah D Dorris   4th Decr 1843
                            Solemnized 5 Decr. 1843 Wm D Baldwin, Minister
                                                           of the Gospel
       Ambrose D Owen   &   Elizabeth Grimble   24 Decr 1843
                            Solemnized   D G Baird J P

       Stephen Rodden   &   Jane F Adcock   11th Decr 1843
                            Solemnized   Isaac Steel G M

       Giles A Saunders   &   Phebe Simmons   5th June 1843
                            Solemnized   John Forbes   J P

       Geo W Easley   &   Mahala Miller   19Oct 1843
                            Solemnized 20th October 1843 A Justice
                                                     Justice of the Peace
       Thomas Foster   & Harriet Williams 8th November 1843
                            Solemnized 9 November 1843 W.L.Baldry
                                                        Gospel Minister
(78)   Wilford C Jackson   &   Susan E Barnes 23 Decr 1843
                            Solemnized Decr. 24 1843 Jas Turner E M C

       Clabourn Derrett   &   E J Long   25 Oct 1843
                            Solemnized   David Jones J P for said County

       Meredith Stark   &   Martha Pope   4 Nov 1843
                            Solemnized 5 Nov 1843 W L Baldry Gospell Minister

       Wm R Seal   &   Mary Ann Frey   6th September 1843
                            Solemnized Richd Chowning J P

       Perry M Peesly   &   Amanda Price   14 December 1843
                            Solemnized D Young J P

Wm. M Adams   & Mary A Seymore   2nd November 1843
                            Solemnized   U Young J P

Alfred Hodges   & Mary Russell   17 August 1843
                            Solemnized   U Young J P for Robertson County

(79) John Vick   & Susan J Allison   17 Decrmber 1843
                            Solemnized U Young J P

William Tyner   & Semantha Newton   28 Decr. 1843
                            Solemnized   U Young J P

Richard N Foote   & Eliza M Denton   11th Jany 1844
                            Solemnized

James M Townsend   & Matilda E Farmer   28 September 1843
                            Solemnized W M Pitts M G

William H Boyder   & Louisa J E Hanson   24 Oct 1843
                            Solemnized

Robert I Baker   & Frances A Boyers   31 August 1843
                            Solemnized U Young   J P

James C Porter   & Susan Richison   20 Aubust 1843
                            Solemnized D G Bairds J P

Obadiah Stone   & Sally Stark   24 Oct p843
                            Solemnized   Richard Chowming J P

(80) Thos. J Shaw   & Sally A Veal   3rd Sept 1843
                            Solemnized Jas Gunn E M C

   William Merrit   & Sarah Powell   4 Sept. 1843
                            Solemnized Sept 6 1843   W M Pitts M G

William Pike   & Lucy Choat   19 Sept. 1842
                            Solemnized 22nd September 1842 C Crafford J P

John Hardyman   & Anny Stanley   1st Jany 1842
                            Solemnized 5 day od Jany 1842 Charles Crafford
                                             J P for Robertson County

Thomas Willis   & Susan Holland   28 July 1843
                            Solemnized 8 August 1843 D G Baird J P

Wm R Deen   & Harriet Aiken   17 July 1842
                            Solemnized July 18 1843 Jas Woodard J P

Squire Mozee   & Louisa Adams   26 Sept 1843
                            Solemnized   James Woodard J P

Thomas Newman   & Patience Hope   16 September
                            Solemnized Jas Woodard J P

(81) Sterling W Sherain & Eliza Harris   10 August 1843
                            No return

Wm O Gilbert   &   Martha Ann Carr   3rd Sept 1843
                       Solemnized D G Baird J P

John Henderson   &   Zelah Nanny   6 March 1843
                       Solemnized Isaac Steel G M

William Rice   &   Susan Fykes   2nd Feby 1843
                       Solemnized   W L Baldry Gospel Minister

Fanning J BEasley   &   Joannah Williams   9 November 1843
                       Solemnized W L Baldry Gospel Minister

Thomas Starke   &   Winny Stone   9 Oct. 1843
                       Solemnized Richd. Chowning J P

Cornelius Hase   &   Katherine Dick   11 Feb 1843
                       Solemnized Isaac Steel G M

Geo B Sprouse   &   Martha A Crafford . 27 Decr 1843
                       Solemnized Wm. L Baldwin Minister of the Gospel

(82) Henry L Farmer   &   Mary E Gooche   27 Decr 1843
                       Solemnized R W Bell J P

Jesse Davis   &   Hernietta Vick   3 Decr 1843
                       Solemnized 4 Decr 1843 Lewis Adams M G

Alexander E Rayan   &   Deland Pitts   23rd Jan. 1844
                       Solemnized D. G. Baird J P

Franklin R Gooch   &   Nancy C Hubbard   30 Decr. 1843
                       Solemnized 2nd Jany.1844 Robt Draughon J P

John M Copeland   &   Lourinda Eatherly   2nd Decr 1843
                       Solemnized 6 Decr. 1843 J W Judkins J P

Joel Vaughon   &   Rebecca C Gooch   7th Sept. 1843
                       Solemnized Thos W Ruffin, Justice of peace for
                                                said County
Geo. H Whitehead   &   L A Gardner   24 Nov 1843
                       Solemnized Jas L Adams J P

D Neely   &   Jude Overstreat

(83) James Reneer   &   Susan Bowling   15 Jany 1844
                       Solemnized   James Woodard   J P

Lilburn M Jackson   &   Martha P Gunn   12 Feb 1844
                       Solemnized March 6 1844 Lewis Adams minister of
                                                the gospel
Wm. H Smith   &   Ann Eliz. Dobbs   4 March 1844
                       Solemnized 5 March 1844 Robert Draughon J P

Joshua W Featherston   &   E M P Jackson   27 Feby 1844
                       Solemnized G W Twell Minister of the Gospel

Thomas Randolph   &   Loucinia Doss   31st Jany. 1844
Solemnized 6 Feby. 1844   Greenberry Kelly M G

Wm Meguire   &   Rebecca A Williams   11th Jany 1844

Thomas O Bryan   &   Rebecca L Cothran   3rd Jany 1844
Solemnized 10 Jany 1844   J W Hunt J P

Andrew Traughber   &   Sarah Bailey   1st March 1844
Solemnized 3 March 1844   Hiram Rice J P

(84)   Mark Chambless   &   Mary V Alley   28 Feb 1844
Solemnized 2 March 1844   J W Hunt J P

Aaron Maner   &   Mary A Hubbard   27 Feby 1844
Solemnized   Robert Darughon   J P

William Adcock   &   Sarah Joiner   6 Feby 1844
Solemnized   Benja. Rawls M Gospel

Wm L Adams   & Mary E Batts   30 Jany 1844
Solemnized   1 Feby 1844   Jas L Adams J P

Rober H Clurane   &   Mary Gullege   23rd March 1844
Solemnized   25th March 1844   D G Baird J P

Henry Cummings   &   Martha A Henley   27th of Decr 1844
Solemnized   J M Garland   Min of the Gos.

Saml Gilbert   &   Susan L Young   8 May 1844
Solemnized March 10th 1844   Benja Rawls G.M.

Benjamin W Kelly   &   Susan Dorris   8 March 1843
Solemnized 10th March 1843   Thos. W Felts Min.

(85)   James H West   &   Jane Bobb   18th March 1844
Solemnized 19th March 1844   Thomas W Felts
                                Minister

Sampson Moore   &   Narcisse Cox   18 March 1844
Solemnized   W L Payne J P

Thomas L West   &   Mary A Vahhook   4 March 1844
Solemnized   Greenberry Kelly   Minister Gos.

Abraham Lyons   &   Eliza, M Shark   8 February 1844
Solemnized   D G Baird J P

Elijah H Whitinghill   &   Sarah E Hall   19th Oct 1843
Solemnized   W L Payne J P

Wm. J McKissick   &   Milly Doss   29 March 1844
Solemnized 31st March 1844   Greenberry Kelly
                              Mins of the Gospel

James Humphrey   &   Mary J Bailey   13 March 1844
Solemnized   W L Payne J P.

(86)   Wm C Mills   &   Mona Louisa Brooks   24 March 1844
Solemnized   D G Baird J P

John J Adair   & Maragret G Holeman   25 Oct 1843
                         Solemnized   W L Payne J P

Robert E Mays   & Nancy Bell   23rd April 1844
                         Solemnized 24 April 1844 Lewis Adams M G

Jesse D Nicholson   & Anna Walker   14 Nov 1843
                         Solemnized 16 Nov 1843 W W Williams J P

William P Jernigan   & Ann Covington   20 April 1844
                         Solemnized 21 April 1844 Lewis Adams M G

Jesse W White   & Emily Pace   14 March 1844
                         Solemnized R Pennington J P

James Lee   & L D Madox   5 Feb 1844
                         Solemnized 7 Feb 1844   W W Williams J P

(87) Oliver Edwards   & Elizabeth Sherrod   22 November 1843
                         Solemnized W W Williams J P

Ebenezer Guest   & E E Evans   20th Oct 1843
                         Solemnized Isaac Steel   G M

Thomas Howell   & W J Robertson   1st March 1844
                         Solemnized Isaac Steel   G M

Wm. Lewis   & Lucy Fresh   19 April 1844
                         Solemnized Isaac Steel M G

John L Parris   & M J Starks   27 April 1844
                         Solemnized Isaac Steel M G

Theodore Hermans   & M M Lucas   27 April 1844
                         Solemnized 30 April 1844 W L Payne J P

Wilson Brankley   & Elizabeth Walker   9 April 1844
                         Solemnized 11th April 1844 R Pennington J P

Ephriam Moize   & Della Cold   13 July 1844
                         Solemnized 14 July 1844 Robt. Green J P

(88) James H House   & Syntha McClenden   19 May 1842
                         Solemnized   Isaac Steel G M

John Bowie   & Susan Redfern   22 Oct 1842
                         Solemnized Isaac Steel G M

Gideon Franklin   & Nancy Dorris   3 May 1844
        Leonard   No return

Little J W Ivy   & Virginia Thompson   22 April 1844
                         Solemnized   G W Sneed Minister of the Gospel

Chasteen Coursey   & Elizabeth J Crabtree   14 Feby 1844
                         Solemnized U Young JP

John Stratton   &   Martha Smith   16 Feby 1844
             Solemnized   U Young J P

Bazel Boren   &   Agness Huddleston   31st May 1844
             Solemnized June 2 1844   A Justice, Justice of
                                 the peace for said County

Thomas McKey   &   Milly Farthing   23rd May 1844
             Solemnized   U Young J P

William Cherry   &   Charlotte Ettinage   28 Oct 1842
             Solemnized   Isaac Steel G M

(89) Jo A Stewart   &   Tabitha Creekmore   16 February
             Solemnized 8 June 1843   Isaac Steel G M

Albert G Jones   &   Martha J Odle   8 June 1843
             Solemnized   Isaac Steel   G M

J L Maginnis   &   Elizabeth Bowls   18 Oct 1843
             Solemnized   Isaac Steel M G

Presley Neil   &   M O Burgg   29 August 1842
             Solemnized   Isaac Steel   G M

Bennett Groves   &   Jane E Turner   9 June 1844
             Solemnized   W L Payne J P

James A Stinson   &   Sarah J Chappel   3 March 1844
             Solemnized   U Young J P

Wm G Cow   &   M J Herndon   11th April 1841
             Solemnized   Isaac Steel G M

Joseph Kirk   &   Alse Campbell   14th Sept. 1843
             Solemnized   Isaac Steel   G M

Jordan W Hall   &   A Eliza. Wittson   23 June 1844
             Solemnized   Isaac Steel   G M

(90) Wm Cox   &   Salina Bannon   18 June 1844
             Solemnized   Isaac Steel   G M

David Vance   &   Harriet Brakefield   23 May 1844
             Solemnized   Hiram Rice J P

Herman H Dick   &   Caroline R Allen   22 May 1844
             Solemnized   Isaac Steel G M

John W Abner   &   Kerziah Daughorty   4 March 1844
             Solemnized   C Woodall   J P

W J Barnes   &   Lucinda Draughon   1st August 1844
             Solemnized   R W Bell   J P

John L Shannon   &   Louisa M M I Heath   31 March 1844
             Solemnized   C Woodall J P

Wm Hancock   & Mary A Morgan   28 July 1844
Solemnized   James Woodard   J P

Alexander Gorden   & Nancy Balance   12 July 1844
Solemnized   G W Felts   M G

(91) Samuel Sales   & Susan Boyd   10 August 1844
Solemnized   Thomas W Felts Minister

James McDonal   & Mary Smiley   18 July 1844
Solemnized 19 July 1844   A Justice J P

Saml. S Ireland   & J A Jackson   14 Decr 1842
Solemnized Decr 15, 1842 Robert Williams G M

Geo W Carter   & Lucinda Gillaspy   1st July 1844
Solemnized   Lewis Adams M G

Silas Tucker   & Martha A Choat   5 June 1844
Solemnized   James Sprouse   J P

John Bourne   & Mary Hitt   30 Decr 1843
Solemnized 1st Jan. 1844   Thomas W Ruffin J P

Thomas Traughber   & Nancy Ivy   16 July 1844
Solemnized   D G Baird   J P

(92) Herman Traughber   & Rebecca Nelms   3 July 1844
Solemnized 4th July 1844   D G Baird J P

John Clark   & Armildrice Rountree   22 August 1844
Solemnized   Robert Green   J P

P J L Flours   & Mary Corbin   7 July 1844
Solemnized   D G Baird   J P

Joseph Laurance   & Eliz. Jones   10th of May 1844
Solemnized   D G Baird   J P

Andrew Elleson   & Milly Swift   3 May 1844

Solemnized 4 May 1844   James Sprouse
                       Justice of the peace
Robert C Tate   & M L Covington   28 August 1844
Solemnized August 29th 1844   Lewis Adams M G

Robt. Head   Mary J Green   3 Frb 1845
Solemnized 9th Feb 1845   W L Baldry G M

(93) Patrick Coney   & Mary Bryant   9 June 1844
Solemnized   James Woodard   J P

John W Warren   & Martha J Holeman   11 Feb 1845
Solemnized 16 February 1845   Charles Crafford
                (16)   J P for Robertson County

Granberry Baggett   &   Mary J Crawford   14 January 1845
                         Solemnized 16 January 1845 Charles Crafford
                                                              J P

Samuel Hardyman   &   Katherine Brakefield   13 Feb 1845
                         Solemnized 15 February 1845 Wm D Baldwin
                                              Minister of the Gospel

John M McHenry   &   Virginia Bailey   3 Feb 1845
                         Solemnized James Woodard J P

Andrew J Rhinehart   &   Sarah A Edmond   5 Decr 1844
                         Solemnized James L Adams J P for Robertson Co.

Isaac Brasier   Pricilla Travathan   2 January 1845
                         Solemnized David Hening Justice of the peace

Jacob McMurry   &   Hannah Cook   2nd Jany 1843
                         Solemnized Jan. 5 1843 Wm D Baldwin M G

(94) John D May   &   Emilea H Jones   6 June 1842
                         Solemnized 16 June 1842 Wm D Baldwin M G

James Crafford   &   Nancy Brumbelow   11 Decr 1844
                         Solemnized 15 Decr 1844 Wm D Baldwin
                                              Minister of the Gospel

Wm H Bell   &   Nancy Tate   6 Feb 1845
                         Solemnized 9th Feb 1845 David Jones J P

James L Procter   &   Mary A Ashburn   6 January 1845
                         Solemnized 16 Jan 1845 D G Baird J P

Vincent D Rose   &   Jane Winn   16 January 1845
                         Solemnized James Woodard J P

John W Edward   &   Malvina Stark   18 January 1845
                         Solemnized Jany 19th 1845 Jas Woodard J P

Galbreath F Neill   &   Carline Hart   1sr Feb 1845
                         Solemnized Feb 3 1845 Jamesd Woodard J P

Allen Jones   &   Susan J Baggett   19 Decr 1842
                         Solemnized Dec 22 1842 Wm D Baldwin
                                              Minister of the Gospel

(95) Henry Porter   &   Martha Clark   8 March 1845
                         Solemnized 9 March 1845 Thomas Farmer J P

James B Simpson   &   Martha Ann Bough   19 Sept 1844
                         Solemnized   Isaac Steel

Ambrose G Coghill   &   Jomima Fuquay   19 Sept 1844
                         Solemnized Isaac Steel

Richd L Clayton   &   Elizabeth Willis   24 Sept 1844
                         Solemnized 26 Sept 1844 D G Baird J P

Wm D Payne   &   Eliza Turner   24 Sept 1844
                         Solemnized 28bJuly 1844 J W Judkins J P

Alfred Robb   &   M E Conrad   9 Oct 1844
                         Solemnized M Harshall V D M

Robert Ring   & Mary Chilton   18 Sept 1844
Solemnized   Jas L Adams J P

James L Crawford   & Lutendy Kelly   19 Sept 1844
Solemnized   D G Baird J P

Jacob Good   & Emeline E Ruffin   29 August 1844
Solemnized   R W Bell J P

(97) Wm L Parker   & Mary A Watson   9 Oct 1844
Solemnized Oct 10 1844 Benjamin Rawls

Benjamin Harper   & Deletha Glover   28 Oct 1844
Solemnized 29 Oct 1844 Patrick Martin

Joel M Jones   & Mary Elizabeth Lowe   5 Decr 1844
Solemnized   D G Baird J P

Dempsey Hunter   & Mary Ann Jones   16 Nov 1844
Solemnized Nov 19 1844 Rev Wm Randle

Mathew Hunt   & Sampiar L F Hudgins   28 Sept 1844
Solemnized 29 Sept 1844 Rev Wm Randle

Wm R Alsbrook   & Lucinda Webb   27 Nov 1844
Solemnized 28 Nov 1844 P Martin M G

Geo T Holeman   & Mary May   7 Nov 1844
Solemnized James Sprouse J P

Thomas H Boyles   & Delila England   1st Oct p844
Solemnized 6 Oct 1844 Thomas Farmer J P

(98) Mary Ann Hutchins   & Daniel G Dishman   6 July 1843
Solemnized W C Richmond acting Justice of the
                                          Peace

John G White   & Mary Winters   28 Nov 1844
Solemnized Jesse L Ellis J P

John W Stratton   & Polly Frathing   1st 1844
No return

Lewellyn Phipps   & Eliz. Robbins   2 Jan 1844
Solemnized William D Baldwin Minister of the
                                          Gospel

Jesse Robertson   & Eliz. Dorris   1st Oct 1844
Solemnized 3rd Oct 1844 William D Baldwin
                             Minister of the Gospel

Henry Warren   & Elizabeth Choat   15 of July 1844
Solemnized 16 July 1844 Charles Crafford J P

James Gullage   & Arrilla L Clinard   16 March 1844
Solemnized 20 March 1844 W L Baldry
                             Gospel Minister

(99)   John F Hudgens   &   Rosey M King   17 Decr 1844
Solemnized 19th 1844   Rev Wm Ranals

Wm Ayres   &   Martha Ann Trice   2nd Decr 1844
Solemnized 3rd Decr 1844   Charles Crafford J P

Wm T Chowning   &   Sarah A Frey   24 Decr 1844
Solemnized 26 Decr 1844   David Jones J P

John Babb   &   Lucy A Goulding   4 Sept 1844
Solemnized 5 September 1844   D G Baird J P

Pleasant C Hooper   &   Rebecca J Winn   21st Decr 1844
Solemnized 22nd 1844   R W Bell J P

Harmon Capbell   &   Rebecca Clenton 8 Sept 1844
Solemnized   D G Baird

George P Dawson   &   Mary J Overstreet   16 Decr 1843
Solemnized   W C Richmond acting Justice of the
                                               peace

(100)   Richd Jones   & Emily Pepper   2 Decr 1844
Solemnized   M powell   Justice peace

Frances Armstrong   &   Maranda Stolts   16 Sept 1844
Solemnized 19 Sept.   James Sprouse J P

Joseph L Chastain   &   Eliz. A Hill   10 Sept 1844
Solemnized   U Young J P

John A Finn   &   M B Duval   25 Jany 1845
Solemnized 27 Decr 1845   Y Schenlat

Benj West   &   Sarah J Bell   28 Oct 1844
Solemnized   Lewis Adams Minister of the Gospel

John Merrit   &   Susan Shelly   5th Oct 1844
Solemnized 6 Oct. 1844   David Jones J P

(101)   Azariah Ingram   &   Jermimah Mc Murry   28 Sept 1844
Solemnized 1st Oct 1844   Thos Gunn M G

Benjamin O Crenshaw   &   Mary E Gunn   21st 1844
Solemnized   Joel whitten

Wm F Sutton   &   Rebecca Fitzhough   1st Aug 1844
Solemnized   U Young   J P

Wm Moore   &   Hannah Sharp   22nd Jany 1844
Solemnized   U Young J P

Elli Graham   &   Priscilla J Fortune   23 Oct 1844
Solemnized 25 Oct 1844   U Young   J P

Alexander L Williamson   &   E F McDaniel   17 July 1844
Solemnized   U Young   J P

John C Richard   &   Emily K McMillen   24 Oct 1844
Solemnized   Greenberry Kelly M G

Wm B Harrison   &   Amanda Niell   7 Nov 1844
Solemnized   D G Baird

(102)   James Dorris   &   Anny Ivey   17 Sept 1842
Solemnized 28th Sept 1842   W C Richmond J P

James L Jones   &   Mary Brooks   5th August 1844
Solemnized 8th Aug. 1844   R Chowing J P

Thos. Ivey   &   Jane Shannonn   27th July 1844
Solemnized   Richd. Chowning J P

Martin Abbott   &   Mary Reynolds   3rd Oct 1844
Solemnized   Thomas Farmer J P

John Bowers   &   Sarah J Gossett   27 May 1845
Solemnized May 28th 1845   L Brewer Minister of
the Gospel

Simon Farthing   &   Elizabeth Crane   16 Feby 1845
Solemnized   U Young J P

Wm B Hunt   &   Nancy A Huntaana   1st March 1845
Solemnized   U Young J P

John Moore   &   Nancy Moore   12 Jany 1845
Solemnized   U Young J P

(103)   Armstrong B Wells   &   Ann Bagby   12 Jany 1845
Solemnized   U Young J P

Richard C Mays   &   Martha A Mays   3rd day of May 1845
Solemnized 4th May 1845   Thomas Stanley J P

William Crutcher   Martha Cagle   15 April 1845
Solemnized 17 April 1845   Charles Crafford J P

Epraim M Pence   &   Nancy Harper   30 of April 1845
Solemnized   Jas Woodard J P

Joseph F Knight   &   Locky L Merryman   15 March 1845
Solemnized 16 March 1845   William D Baldwin
Minister Gospel

Jesse Strickling   &   Susan McMurry   11 March 1845
Solemnized 13 March 1845   William D Baldwin
Minister Gospel

George W L Justen   &   Rebecca White   6 March 1845
Solemnized   Jesse L Ellis J P

(104)   A L Lipscomb   &   M A Langford   25 of March 1845
Solemnized 27 March 1845   Jesse L Ellis J P

Benjamin F Townsond   &   Mary G Lockard   7 day of Nov 1844
Solemnized   J M Stemmons

Solomon B Mize   & Elviney Adcock   10 August 1844
                         Solemnized   Jas Woodard   J P

J B Roberts   & Maranda Henry   17 Decr 1844
                         Solwmnized 18 Decr 1845   Jas Woodard J P

Geo T Herandon   & Martha F Walton   17 say march 1845
                         Solemnized   Jas Woodard J P

James Rice   & Martha A Williams   2nd of Feby 1845
                         Solemnized   James Woodard

James W Herandon   & Permelia Zech   3rd February 1845
                          Solemnized Jas Woodard J P

James M Shelton   & Martha Benson   15 day Feb 1845
                         Solemnized Jas Woodard   J P

David Cook   & Sarah Patten   21 March 1845
                         Solemnized   David Jones J P for said County

(105) John Woodard   & Carline Woodard   31st day of May 1845
                         Solemnized   R Green Justice of peace

Jack A Justice   & Susannah M Riser   19 may 1845
                         Solemnized   Jesse L Ellis J P

Howell Fraiser   & Sally Wall   19 Decr 1843
                         Solemnized 21st Decr 1843   William Tate minister
                                                     of the Gospel

Spiva Sivols   & Margaret Trimble   22 Decr 1844
                         Solemnized Tho. W Felts minst.

John Shepherd   & Julian Grason   6 Decr 1844
                         Solemnized   Tho W Felts Minst.

Eli T Cook   & Luoisa Fletcher   3 May 1845
                         Solemnized 4 May 1845   R W Bell J P

(106) Wm Woodard   & Martha Green   25 Jany 1844
                         Solemnized 26 Jany 1844 Wm Felts Minister of
                                                     the Gospel

Granberry B Jones   & Martha A Suter   5 February 1844
                         Solemnized Feb. 8th 1844 Thos N Lankford
                                                  Minister of the Gospel

Donald McClean   & Emeline Leptrick   31st July 1845
                         Solemnized H Frey   J P

Jesse Brakefield   & Elizabeth Brakefield   7 June 1845
                         Solemnized 8 June 1845 R B Rose J P

Wm White Sr.   & Mildred James   28 May 1845
                         Solemnized 30th May 1845   H Frey J P

Thos J Choat   & A J Williams   20 July 1845
                         Solemnized David Jones   J P

James N McMillin   &   Louisa Ellia   11 July 1845
Solemnized   R Green

(107)   David W Jernigan   &   Mary A Gilbert   3rd Feb 1839
Solemnized   Ed Edwards   6 Feb 1839

Geo W Bigee   &   Lucinda Inman   30 July 1840
Solemnized 2nd August 1840   Ed Edwards

James Jernigan   &   Debby S Stricklen   25 Nov 1835
Solemnized 27 Nov 1835   Ed Edwards

Pleasant H Anderson   &   Catherine Cheek   13th 1829
Solemnized 14 Oct 1829   Ed Edward

William Smith   &   Jane Leek   13 Sept 1839
Solemnized 16 Sept 1839   Ed Edward

Mosely Holland   &   Anna Park   21 Oct 1829
Solemnized   24 Oct 1829   Ed Edward

Richd B Smith   &   H S L Hadett   21st Decr 1838
Solemnized 24 Decr 1838   Ed Edwards

James Glidewell   &   Huldah Armstrong   8 Aug 1830
Solemnized 10 August 1830 Ed Edwards

A M Blain   &   Martha Dinning   23 July 1840
Solemnized   Ed Edward

(108)   Saml. Leak   &   Sarah Houston   4th Oct 1841
Solemnized 16 Nov 1841   Ed Edward

David Lambert   &   Frances Norman   14 Aug 1830
Solemnized   Ed Edward

James Groves   &   M A Bryam   25 August 1840
Solemnized   Ed Edwards

Joseph Williams   &   H Strain   18th July 1839
Solemnized Elisha Car

John P Martin   &   M A Neil   26 Sept 1842
Solemnized   E Edwards

Jesse Long   Minerva Wright   12 July 1845
Solemnized   Thomas West Minister

Crafford Strickling   &   Elily Long   27 August 1845
Solemnized   David Jones J P for said County

Willie B Allsbrook   &   Francis W Connell   2 Sept 1845
Solemnized   Sept 3rd   Thomas Martin

(109)   James W Inom   &   Maleda Sawyers   4 August 1845
                                        Solemnized   7 Aug 1845 Thomas Stanley J P

        Josephus Armstrong   &   Sarah Williams   15 Sept 1845
                                        Solemnized 18 August 1845 Jas. Woodard J P

        W C Gosset   &   Emely Stout   19 March 1845
                                        Solemnized   James Woodard J P

        P M Fisher   &   Elizabeth Bourne   5 June 1845
                                        Solemnized   James Woodard J P

        Benj. F Hunt   &   Lucy W Farmer   22rd Aug 1845
                                        Solemnized   James Woodard J P

        John M Deen   &   Minerva Barbee   31st Aug 1845
                                        Solemnized Wm T Baldry Gospel Minister

        Edward Brewer   & Nancy Choat   3 September 1845
                                        Solemnized 4th October 1845 James Sprouse J P

(110)   James Smith   &   Nancy D Simmons   21 February 1845
                                        Solemnized 26 Feb 1845 W W Williams G S

        Henderson Lipscomb   &   Elizabeth James   10 September 1845
                                        Solemnized   Jesse L Ellis   J P

        Josiah Rutherford   &   Carline Hannam   3 Sept 1845
                                        Solemnized   Thos Cook J P

        Norfleet Pool   &   Elizabeth Clark   8 Nov 1845
                                        Solemnized W L Baldry Minister Gospel

        E M Reynolds   &   J A Couts   30th Sept 1845
                                        Solemnized   Benjamin Rawls

        Saml Sneed   & Ally Henry   10 June 1845
                                        Solemnized J M Gunn (Seal) Justice of the
                                                                peace for R C

        Wm M Shirves   &   Martha J Easley   14th Aug 1845
                                        Solemnized J M Gunn (Seal) Justice of the peae

(111)   W J Procter   &   Melissa Morgan   20 Sept 1845
                                        Solemnized 21 Sept 1845 D G Baird J P

        John W James   &   Malinda J Reed   20 Sept 1845
                                        Solemnized 25 Sept 1845 Jesse L Ellis J P

        P P Babb   &   G Ann Hight   10 June 1845
                                        Solemnized   D G Baird J P

        Green W Cohee   & Martha F Fort   29 Oct 1845
                                        Solemnized Thomas Martin

        Allen Warren   &   M J England   2 Sept 1845
                                        Solemnized 3rd Sept Sept 1845 Thos. Stanley J P

Jas Fyke	& A Chilton	20th Oct 1845
	Solemnized Jas L Adams J P of Robertson County	
Wm Price	& Marinda Ayres	24 Oct 1845
	Solemnized 26 Oct 1845 H Frey J P	
Franklin Moore	& Lydia Barbee	17th Nov 1845
	Solemnized 27 Nov 1845 W L Baldry Gospel Minister	
(112) Geo W Caudle	& Middy Ally	8 March 1845
	Solemnized 9 March 1845 J W Hunt	
Ed. Brewer	& Nancy Choat	3 Sept 1845
	Solemnized 4th Sept 1845 Jas Sprouse J P	
Henderson Lipscomb	& E James	10 Sept 1845
	Solemnized 11th Sept 1845 Jesse L Ellis J P	
Benj F Walker	& Anny Durham	15th March 1845
	Solemnized 18 March 1845 W W Williams J P	
Frank L Young	& Missoure Bigbee	6 Nov 1845
	Solemnized J W Judkins J P	
Jephtahah Pilant	& Amanda Ventress	18 Nov 1845
	Solemnized 20th day Nov 1845 W L Baldry Gospel Minister	
W W Wall	& Henrietta Maxey	29 Decr 1845
	Solemnized W W Williams J P	
Levi A Chilton	& Frances C E Sartin	25 Nov 1845
	Solemnized R W Bell J P	
John W Adams	& E Adams	30 Decr 1845
	Solemnized R W Bell J P	
(113) R Chowning	& Milly Brewer	24 Feby 1845
	Solemnized though not certified	
Henry Wells	& Nancy Woodcome	23 Oct 1845
	No return	
Archer Whiting	& M A McCasland	11th Aug 1845
	No return	
Wm H Pope	& M H Benson	23rd Decr 1845
	Solemnized 23rd 1845 Jas Woodard	
John Temerline	& Penelope Williams	4 Sept p845
	Solemnized W L Baldry Gospel Minister	
Ainsey C Herring	& H B Shaw	11th Oct 1845
	Solemnized Thomas Farmer J O for Robertson County	
John Sanders	& Phebe Sanders	23 July 1845
	Solemnized 30 July 1845 W W Williams J P	

(114) John Houtchan   &   Susan Ellison   27 Nov 1845
                             3rd Dec 1845 Solemnized R G Cole J P

       Geo Walker   &   Lucinda Head   10 Sept 1845
                             Solemnized 11th Sept 1845   Jesse L Ellis J P

       Francis Pride   &   Mary E Farmer   12th July 1845
                             Solemnized 'J M Gunn J P

       Kenchen Bassford   &   Minerva Lancaster   30th 1845
                             Solemnized 2nd Oct 1845 R Pennington J P

       James Smith   &   Nancy D Simmons   21 Feby 1845
                             Solemnized 26 Feb 1845 W W Williams J P

       Levi Davis   Patsy Caudle   26 Sept 1845
                             Solemnized ⅄ A Justice Justice of the peace for
                                                                      R C

       William Woodring   &   Piety Ann Ragsdale   20 August 1845
                             Solemnized 21st Augts 1845 _____

(115) Stephen H Daniel   & Elizabeth Daniel   10 November 1845
                             Solemnized 13 Nov 1845 U Young

       Walter M Thomas   &   Martha E Gill   3 December 1845
                             Solemnized 4 Dec. 1845 U Young J P for Robert-
                                                                      son Te

       Eli Vaughan   &   Mary M Winters   9 Oct 1845
                             Solemnized   Jesse L Ellis

       William C Sharp   &   Susan Jane Mathis   2 March 1846
                             Solemnized 6 March 1846 H Frey J P

       James R Woodall   &   Elizabeth Williams   5th February 1846
                             Solemnized Thomas West Preacher

       Silas M Thomas   &   Frances Fletcher   14 December 1844
                             Solemnized   U Young J P

       Robert Armstrong   &   Dorothy H Inman   9 September 1844
                             No return

(116) James Harris   & Polly Ann Liles   27 July 1845
                             Solemnized   U Young J P

       Reuben Farthing   & S E Ragsdale   6 March 1845
                             Solemnized   U Young J P

       Ephram Moize   &   Huley Mikey   8 July 1845
                             Solemnized E W Green

       Jesse Bandy   &   Martha Daub   1 April 1846
                             Solemnized Jas L Adams J P

       Jacob Miles   &   Martha A Smith   8 May 1846
                             Solemnized 10 May 1846 U Young J P

Richard B Felts   & Margaret Murrah   5 March 1846
Solemnized 8th day of March 1846

George Farmer   & Susan Langford   8 April 1846
Solemnized 9th April 1846   Jesse L Ellis J P

Thomas Wells   & Sally A Moore   27 January 1846
Solemnized 29 Jan 1846   B B Rose J P

(117) Calvin Hart   & Jane A Watson   13 August 1845
Solemnized 14 August 1845   R R Rose J P

Leanard Frazier   & Susan Maxey   31 January 1846
Solemnized 3 February 1846 W W Williams J P

Alfred P Jones   & Sarah D Follis   31 December 1845
Solemnized D Bolswin Min of the Gospel

George Crutcher   & Mary Brumbelon   26 January 1846
Solemnized   _____

Benjamin F Bagget   & Susan Porter   15 December 1845
Solemnized   Tho. Cook J P

Alfred Chapman   & Martha Edward   24 January 1846
Solemnized   _____

Isade Green   & Carline Strater   27 December 1845
Solemnized 29 Decr. 1845 James Sprouse J P

George Q Kingly   & Elisabeth Elnon   18 October 1845
Solemnized   James Sprouse Justice of the
                                            peace

(118) Samuel Warren   & Mary G Holemen   15 December 1845
Solemnized   James Sprouse J P

Wesley Mastin   & Mary L Ledbetter   31 January 1846
Solemnized 1 Feb 1846   Robert Draughon J P

W M Gardner   & Pamelea Adline Powell   23 March 1846
Solemnized + Richd W Bell J P

William A Loulbs   & Saley L Phipps   18 March 1846
Solemnized march 24 1846 Thomas Standley J P

Lewis Parks Jernigan   & Katherin Jane Senner   28 February 1846
Solemnized 1 March 1846   James Sprouse J P

John C Staughn   & Selcheat Holland   31 January 1846
Solemnized 5 Feb 1846   W S Baldry J P

Ephraim Berry   & Minerva Martin   9 January 18
Solemnized 11 Jan 1846   R G Cole J P

George W Daugherty   & _____   10 March 1846
Solemnized 11 March 1846 Jas L Adams J P

Henry D Featherson   &   Mary Draughon   7 April 1846
                            Solemnized   Thomas Farmer J P

(119) Emanuel Traughber   &   Elisabeth Crawford   13 January 1846
                            Solemnized   Jas Woodall J P

William T Nelson   &   Arness H Traughber   18 February 1846
                            Solemnized 19 February 1846 W L Baldry, Minister
                                                       of the Gospel

A L Hutchison   &   Sarah Griffeth   4 June 1846
                            Solemnized Thos. Gunn J P

Asa Banfield   &   Amand Linch   22 September 1842
                            Solemnized   William L Perry J P

Alexander Traughber   &   Rebecca Summons   19 January 1846
                            Solemnized 22 Jan 1846 W C Hickmon

Samuel A Doss   &   Mary J Farmer   22 January 1846
                            Solemnized 23 June 1846 T W Felts

James Doss   &   Martha Bell   18 Aug 1845
                            Solemnized 20 Aug 1845 _____

John P Fyke   &   Elizabeth Solomon   21 Jany 1846
                            Solemnized   Robt Draughon J P

(120) Elija Mc Intosh   &   Adline Buren   30 December 1845
                            Solemnized ____ J.P. For Sd. County

William H Blackburn   &   Elizabeth Menees   14 May 1846
                            Solemnized Thomas Martain

William H Pace   &   Mary A E Husky   23 September 1844
                            Solemnized 26 September 1844 Williams S Perry
                                                                    J P

James Baker   &   Choischana Watson   11 February 1840
                            Solemnized   W S Perry J P

Richard James   &   Judith Higgs   15 May
                            Solemnized 31 May 1838   William J Perry J P

Elisha P Fort   &   Martha Ann Gardener   20 December 1835
                            Solemnized   William L Perry J P R C

Kinchen Barford   &   Nancy Maddox   5 November 1838
                            Solemnized William L Perry J P R C

Samuel H Northington   &   Elizabeth Grant   4 January 1839
                            Solemnized William L Perry J P R C

James A Alsey   &   Elizabeth A Hooper   23 Aug 1841
                            Solemnized   William L Perry J P R C

(121) John Duke   &   Elizabeth Bobb   23 January 1838
                          Solemnized William L Perry J P

       William J Walon   &   Martha J Adams   23 December 1841
                          Solemnized William L Perry J P

       John R Elliott   &   Frances A BObo   15 July 1838
                          Solemnized William L Perry J P

       William Reiley   &   Harriet Wynn   25 Oct 1841
                          Solemnized 28 Oct 184b William L Perry J P

       William A Hall   &   Elizabeth Robertson 13 March 1839
                          Solemnized   William L Perry J P

       John Byrns   &   Elizabeth Long   10 December 1844
                          Solemnized 11 Dec 1844 William L Perry J P

       Joseph T Massey   &   Permelia Bigbey   30 January 1838
                          Solemnized O B Monroe Minister of the Gospel

       Thomas H Gardner   &   Frances Whitehead   15th __ 1841
                          Solemnized 16 __1841 William L Perry J P R C

       William Picking   & Nancy Connell   15 Novenber 1840
                          Solemnized William L Perry J P   R C

(120) William Stroud   &   Nancy Rosson   29 Oct 1841
                          Solemnized   William L Perry J P R C

       Isiaeh Eidson   &   Harriett Adams -   4 October 1843
                          Solemnized   William L Perry J P

       Jesse B Hall   &   Louisa Wyne   30 July 1842
                          Solemnized William L Perry J P

       Jno W Crafford   &   Celia Tinson   3 Feby 1846
                          Solemnized   Wm D Baldwin Minister of the
                                                              Gospel

       Saml H Bracy   &   Mary E Marlon   21 Aug 1846
                          Solemnized   N H Ryan J P

       Jabus L Roberts   &   Eliz. Roberts   16 June 1846
                          Solemnized 18 June 1846 R GReen J P

       D Smiley   &   E Robertson   23 April 1846
                          Solemnized   Wm D Baldwin G M

(121) Lewellyn Phipps   &   H Dorris   6 March 1846
                          Solemnized 8th March 1846 Wm D Baldwin M G

       Benj. P Bracy   &   N A Alsbrook   18 I July 1846
                          Solemnized July 19th 1846 A Justice J P
                                                      Robt. County

       Benj F Nelms   &   Nancy A Bailey   23 Decr 1845
                          Solemnized 30 Decr 1845   D G Baird J P

       Andrew Rhinehart   L J Connelly   21 Jany 1841
                          Solemnized W L Perry J P

John Hudgins   &   Delila Farmer   Aug 31st 1846
Solemnized 2 Sept 184b   W L Perry J P

Daniel H Holland   &   Sarah H Willis   3 March 1846
Solemnized 9th April 1846   D G Baird J P

John W Walker   &   Martha W Cheatham 1st Sept 1846
Solemnized   Benja Rawls

E J Harrell   &   A Allsbrook   4 July 1846
Solemnized + Wm L Baldry Gospel Minister

(122) Elijah Benson   &   G L AL Baldry   2o Aug 1846
Solemnized   Wm L Bardry Gos. Minister

Hyram Johes   &   Nancy A Broadrick   7 Sept 1846
Solemnized Robt. Draughon   J P

John Fredrick   &   S A Frederick   14 June 1846
Solemnized Robt Draughon   J P

RichD Jones   &   R E Huddleston   17 Aug 1846
Solemnized 20 Aug 1846   Robt Green J P

Thomas Crutcher   Caoline McMurry   9 Dec 1846
Solemnized Wm D Baldwin   J P

Joshua Hall   &   Surdna A Dowlen   14 Nov 1846
Sole nized   Wm D Baldwin G M

Mills H Lanaster   &   Lucy A L Craffors   10 Dec 1846
Solemnized   Wm D Baldwim M G

(123) Randolph R Petts   &   Jane Murry   21 Oct 1846
Solemnized Wm D Bladwin

John Kelton   &   M M Simmon   5 Jany 1847
Solemnized   R G Cole J P for Robertson

Jessa S Miller   &n. Elizabeth B Porter   15 Dec 1846
Solemnized   R W Bell J P

D M Hooper   &   Temperance Eddinga 9 Oct 1846
Solemnized   R W Bell J P

Sollomon Fiser   &   Zelicha Hutcherson   31 Decr 1846
Solemnized   R B Rose J P

John W Dean   &   Sarah M Cook   19 No 1846
Solemnized 19 Nov 1846   R B Rose J F

R H Williams   &   E R Bailey   30 March 1846
Solemnized   R B Rose   J P

John Bill   &   Elisa L Cook
Solemnized 22 Sept 1846 Hugh C Read M G

(124)   Henry A Readmon   &   Nancy Armstrong   8 Nov 1846
                                 Solemnized   L Hoste

        William A Cobbs   &   Nancy J Dunn   26 June 1846
                                 Solemnized   Thomas Martin   J P

        Henry L Covington   &   Mary M B Tate   30 Deer 1846
                                 Solemnized   Rev Russel Eskew

        Robt. Baxter   &   Sarah J Connell   8 July 1846
                                 Solemnized Rbt. Williams   M G

        John Bobbell   &   Lucy Jones   3 Oct 1846
                                 Solemnized Joseph Pitt

        William D Graves   &   Eliza R Eidson   24 Sept 1846
                                 Solemnized James Sprouse   J P

        Phillip Harrington   &   Elizabeth Howell
                                 Solemnized 1 May 1846   L W Hunt J P

(125)   Augustus Marklin   &   Parthena Webb   22 Jany 1846
                                 Solemnized   J W Hunt J P

        J S Whitehead   &   Sarah M Dunn   25 June 1846
                                 Solemnized   J M Garland   M

        Russel Warren   &   M J Bryan   24 Sept 1846
                                 Solemnized   24th Sept James Sprouse J P

        John A Winters   &   Mary E Burns   6 Nov 1846
                                 Solemnized   Jesse L Ellis   J P

        Edward Choat   &   Martha Ann Shannon   16 August 1846
                                 Solemnized R G Cole J P

        Philip R McCormack   &   Rebeca M Daniel
                                 Solemnized 16 August 1846   R G Cole J P

        John Campbell   &   Susan Ann Luadth   22 Sept 1846
                                 Solemnized D G Baird   J P

        Reason Pool   &   Mary Ann Lands
                                 Solemnized Sept 30 1846 Jas Woodard J P

(126)   Andrew Casey   &   Polly Cagle   2 Aug 1846
                                 Solemnized Charles Crafford J P

        Newton M Langen   &   Harriette E Henderson   18 Dec 1846
                                 Solemnized   Robert Gunn J P

        John Chowning   &   Caroline Cannon   5 Oct 1846
                                 Solemnized   J W Judkins J P

        Thomas Pike   &   Drusilla Choat   23 July 1846
                                 Solemnized 12 Nov 1846 Wm D Baldwin Minister
                                                of the Gospel

****

Joshua Hall   &   Lurana A Dowlen   10 November 1846
Solemnized 12 November   Wm. D Baldwin
Minister the Gospel

Edward Choat   &   Martha Ann Shannon   15 Aug 1846
Solemnized 16 August 1846   R G Cole J P

Philip R McCormack   &   R. McDanniel
Solemnized 5th Sept 1846   Joseph D Darrowe

(127)   John Campbell   &   Susan An Suddoth   22 Sept. 1846
Solemnized   D G Baird   J P

John L Whitehead   &   Sarah M Dunn   24 June 1846
Solemnized June 25 1846 J M Garland Minister
of the Gospel

William D Graves   &   Eliza R Eidson   24 Sept. 1846
Solemnized   James Sprouse J P

Philip Harrington   &   Elisabeth Howell   1 May 1846
Solemnized   J W Hunt J P

Augustus Marklin   &   Pathena Webb   22 May 1846
Solemnized   J W Hunt J P

John Krisle   &   Nancy Shelton   15 April 1847
Solemnized David Herring J P

Jackson Morrus   &   Amanda Newton   24 April 1847
Solemnized   David Herrington   J P

(128)   Milton Wells   &   Mary Stark (Myram)   26 Sept 1846
Solemnized   David Herrington J P

William Tatum   &   Harriet Freeman   25 Nov 1845
Solemnized   David Harrington   J P

William Renfro   &   Mary Easley   18 Nov. 1846
Solemnized   David Herringto J P

Henry L Covington   &   Margarat N Tate   30 December 1846
Solemnized   Rev. Rassel Eskew

Meredith L Edwards   &   Eliza Newton   12 November 1846
Solemnized   David Herring   J P

Joel R Doss   &   Carline Jones   16 June 1847
Solemnized Jas. W Woodard   J P

(129)   Wesley Easley   &   Nancy Blachburn   28 Feby 1846
Solemnized   David Herring   J P

William Hudleston   &   Mary Kiger   10 June 1847
Solemnized P Martain M.

Thomas Pike &   &   Drusilla Choat   21 July 1846
Solemnized 23 July 1846   Charles Crafford   J P

John A Winters	& Mary E Burnes	5 Dec 1846
	Solemnized 6 Nov 1846 Jesse J Ellis J P	
Reason Poll	& Mary Ann Langanas	29 Sept 1846
	Solemnized Sept 30, 1846 Jas. Woodard J P	
Andrew Casey	& Polley Cagle	19 Aug 1846
	Solemnized on 22 August 1846 Charles Crafford	
	J P for Robertson County	
John Chowning	& Caroline Cannon	5 Oct 1846
	Solemnized J W Judkins J P	
(130) Joseph Brain	& Ann Brown	26 May 1846
	Solemnized Thos. W Ruffin J P	
Archer B Couts	& Martha J Couts	7 June 1847
	Solemnized June 8 Benjamin Rawls M G	
John Gambill	& Lacy F Burr	21 May 1847
	Solemnized 23rd May 1847 D G Baird J P	
William C Huddleston	& Elizabeth Jones	30 May 1847
	Solemnized T B Matthew J P	
William N Cherry	& Malinda Head	22 Feb 1847
	Solemnized 25 Feb 1847 James M Cherry M G	
William Ramon	& Lucinda Chaudion	22 Oct 1846
	Solemnized Wm Barton M G	
John M Deen	& Minerva Barbee	3 July 1845
	Solemnized 31 July 1845 W L Baldry M G	
(131) William Traughber	& Mary A Edward	20 Feb. 1847
	Solemnized James Woodard J P	
Burgess Shearing	& Elizabeth R Edwards	19 January 1847
	No return	
George W Snowdy	& Aisley S Wingo	8 January 1847
	Solemnized 10 January 1847 Charles Crafford	
	J P R C	
David J Fort	& Mary B Farmer	1 Feby 1847
	Solemnized 4 February 1847 William L Perry M G	
Patterson T Williams	& Nancy A Whitehead	23 Sept. 1846
	Solemnized 25 Sept. 1846 William L Perry M G	
John A Morris	& Elvira Brinton	1 Dec 1846
	Solemnized Charles Crafford J P R County	
Roberts Felts	& Susan Carter	3 October 1846
	Solemnized 7th October 1846 W L Baldry M G	
Townley Redfearn	& Martha Crawford	17 Nov 1846
	Solemnized James Woodard J P	

(132)   James H Harris   & Nancy Ann Dinning   30 July 1846
                              Solemnized Aug. 2 1846   J D Darrow

        James A Reley   & Mary A. Rose   19 Sept 1846
                              Solemnized 1 Oct. 1846   J. W.

        Geo. F Fisher   & Margaret E Griffin   19 Dec 1846
                              Solemnized 22th Dec. 1846 _____

        Joshua Fyke   & Louisa Lipscomb   25 Jan 1847
                              Solemnized 26 Jan. 1847 Robert Green J P

        Peter Farthing   & Elisabeth Holland   9 January 1847
                              Solemnized 10th Jan. 1847 Robert _____ J P

        Benjamin F Russell   & Sarah A E Angel   22 Sept. 1846
                              Solemnized 24 Sept. 1846 D.G.Baird J P

        John Clinard   & Malinda C Hollis   16 April 1847
                              Solemnized 21 April 1847 A Justice J P

        Benjamin E Williams   & Rebecca Draughon   13 May 1847
                              Solemnized   Isaac Steel

(133)   William A Sandefur   & Minerva Sandefur   21 Feb. 1846
                              Solemnized   Isaac Steel

        Walter A Chism   & Mary E Caudill   23 Nov 1846
                              Solemnized   Isaac Steel

        William L Mallory   & Sarah Ann Johnes   30 Dec 1846
                              Solemnized   Isaac Steel

        Hugh Taylor   & Mary Ann Carter   29 Nov 1846
                              Solemnized   Isaac Steel

        William Edwards   & Nancy D Price   12 August 1846
                              Solemnized   _____

        James M. Maguire   & Malinda Caudle   1 July 1846
                              Solemnized 2 July 1846 Isaac Steel

        William F. Brown   & Martha Hiser   2 May 1847
                              Solemnized T. W. Ruffin J P

        Josh M. Jones   & Minerva A. Conrad   22 Feb 1847
                              Solemnized G. G. Elle Minister of the M.E.
                                                          church
        Henry Wells   & Myram Starke   24 April 1847
                              Solemnized 25 April 1847   David M Wells J P

(134)   Joseph Farmer   & Olive Fletcher   12 April 1847
                              Solemnized   R. W. Bell J P

        Joseph Inscor   & Clarrinda Yong   14 March 1847
                              Solemnized 15 March 1847 R Green J P

James Rossen   &   Lucretia Vanhook   3 March 1847
                       Solemnized 4 March 1847 Robt. Williams   G M

John Mauzy   &   Hannah Harrison   13 May 1847
                       No record of return

Harrison W Akin   &   Mary A. Sanders   20 March 1847
                       Solemnized 23 March 1847 James Woodard

Allen J Shannon   &   Sally A Williams   1 May 1847
                       Solemnized 2 May 1847   R.G.Cole J P

Thomas Crabtree   & Mary A Morgan   27 January 1847
                       Solemnized 28 Jan. 1847 W.B.Richmon J P

Reece Johns   &   Judith Larkins   22 March 1847
                       Solemnized 23 March 1847 W. B. Richmond J P

(135) Sterling Walker   &   Rosanna Harris   2 Jan 1847
                       Solemnized 7 Jan. 1847 W.W.Williams J P

Carrol Hughey   &   Carline Walton   17 April 1847
                       Solemnized 18 April 1847 James Woodard J P

Anderson Erwin   &   Martha Ann Warren   2 January 1847
                       Solemnized 2 Jan. James Sprouse J P

Green B. Goodwin   &   Aurelis D. Graves   1 March 1847
                       Solemnized 4 March 1847 R.W.Ja   M J

Harrey Chapman   &   Nancy Chapman   27 Feb. 1847
                       Solemnized   James Woodard J P

William F. Morrow   &   Mary E. Denton   19 Dec. 1846
                       Solemnized 22 Dec. 1846 D.C.Stevens Minister of
                                                        the Gospel

John W Teasley   &   Sarah A Nicholson   31 Oct. 1846
                       Solemnized 5 Nov. 1846 W. W. Williams J P

Abraham Ashabrannah   &   Margarett Pitts   9 Dec. 1846
                       Solemnized 17 Dec. 1846   D.G.Baird J P

(136) Samuel Gettlebeel   &   Susan Adams   2 Nov 1846
                       Solemnized 19 Nov. R. Moody Minister of the
                                                        Gospel

Joseph Felts   &   Fransec J Moon   2 Nov. 1846
                       Solemnized 5 Nov. 1846 R. Moody Minister of
                                                        the G P

Samuel King   &   Nancy L Hudgens   24 Oct. 1846
                       No record of return

John H Lacey   &   Elizabeth Sumpter   9 Oct 1846
                       Solemnized W. R. Turner

Newton Sawyers   &   Harriette E Henderson 18 Dec. 1846
                       Solemnized   Robert Green J. P.

Leonard Page   &   Frances Russel   8 December 1846
Solemnized 10 Dec. 1846   D. G. Baird J P

John Flood   &   Pricilla Chapman   2 November 1846
Solemnized   James Woodard

William Miller   &   Sarah Holens   17 Dec 1846
Solemnized   W. L. Baldry   M. G.

(137)   Iredell White   &   Almariena Pitt   16 August 1846
Solemnized   Aug 18 1846   W. C. Ricmond J P

Daniel Latimer   &   Nancy Long   24 Nov. 1846
Solemnized   David Jones   J P

John Chapman   &   Rachel Morris   25 Decr. 1846
Solemnized   David M Wells J P

James M Kenton   &   Nancy Jane morris   24 Decr 1846
Solemnized 25 Decr. 1846   James Sprouse J P

James W. Walker   &   Sarah Bobbett   22 Sept. 1846
Solemnized   24 Sept. 1846   W. W. Williams J P

Noah Booker   &   Lewesa Payne   21 Nov 1846
Solemnized   Nov. 22 1846 A. Justice   J P

Jeremiah Rice   &   Elizabeth Jordan   20 May 1838
Solemnized   Joel Moore J P

(138)   Britton Stark   &   Viney Smith   8 Dec. 1845
Solemnized Dec. 9 1845

Shelly Langston   &   Nancy A Briton   12 Sept 1846
Solemnized 13 Sept. 1846   Thos. W. Ruffin J P

Edwin Stainback   &   Sarah E Cunningham   18 Nov. 1846
Solemnized Nov. 19, 1846 Thos. W. Ruffin J P

Wm. R Sadler   &   Rhoda A Gunn   24 July 1847
Solemnized   July 27 1847 J.I.Ellis   M G

J F Ragsdale   &   Martha A. Warden   16 March 1847
Solemnized   R. D. Rose

Bennett L Holland   &   Eliz. Mason   24 April 1847
Solemnized 25 April 1847   R. B. Rose

Francis Samapher   &   Fanny Young   3rd March 1847
Solemnized 5 March 1847   R. B. Rose

John Porter   &   Pricilla Morris   14 July 1847
Solemnized 15 July 1847   Thomas Farmer J P

(139)   Wm. Mason   &   Margart Chapman   24 July 1847
Solemnized 25 July 1847   R. B. Rose

William Couts   &   Martha Moon   28 Aug 1847
                              Solemnized 29 Aug. 1847 Jas. Woodard J P

John Ashworth   &   Rhoda Benton   5 Sept. 1847
                              Solemnized   Thos. B. Mathews J P

James Hatchell   &   Eliz. R. Adams   1st July 1847
                              Solemnized   Joshua W Featherston Minister of
                                                        the Gospel

James H. Murphy   &   Amanda E Crabtree   15 Sept.1847
                              Solemnized 16 Sept 1847 R. G. Cole

Edward L Coleman   &   M. C. Small
                              Solemnized 29 Oct 1846   N. B. Lewis M G

(140) Joel E Bell   &   Rebecca Williams   15 Sept. 1847
                              Solemnized   James Woodard Esq.

Thomas W Lipscomb   &   A M N Toler   11th Aug 1847
                              Solemnized   James Woodard,Esquire

Peter Noe   &   Lucinda Borin   25 Sept. 1847
                              Solemnized 26 Sept. 1847 David M. Wells J P

Henry Harrison   &   Martha Holland   18 Sept 1847
                              Solemnized   R. W. Bell J P

Wm Orand   &   Susan Starke   28 July 1847
                              Solemnized   Jas. Woodard

G. W. Baird   &   M. E. Traughber   7 Oct 1847
                              Solemnized Thomas Farmer Justice of the Peace
                                                for Robertson County Tennessee
Wm. W Johnston   &   Martha L Nichols   17 Aug 1847
                              Solemnized   R. W. Bell J P

(141) Bartlett Pitts   &   Ruth Burnes   12 Aug 1847
                              Solemnized   Thomas Farmer J P

David J Younger   &   Emily Keller   18 Oct 1847
                              Solemnized Thomas Farmer J P

R. M. Roe   &   Winny Morris   4 Aug 1847
                              Solemnized 6 Aug. 1847 Charles Crafford J P

William J Dunn   &   Mary E Lawrence   16 Nov 1847
                              Solemnized Nov 18th 1847 R W Bell J P

James Maxey   &   Rachel Dowlen   6th Decr. 1847
                              Solemnized 9th Decr. 1847 H Frey J P

James Fiser   &   B Bartlett   29 Decr 1847
                              Solemnized 30 Decr 1847 T B Mathews J P

George Dunn   &   Angeline Robertson   23 Decr 1847
                              Solemnized   T. B. Mathews J P

(142) Stephen Cole   &   Dosha Turner   15 Jany 1848
                               Solemnized 18 Janu 1848 J. W. Judkins J P

       J. N Howard   &   M J Strain   23 Nov 1847
                               Solemnized Wm B Kelly M G

       Geo W Gill   &   S A Dunn(Susan A)
                               Solemnized 27th June 1846 Thos. Watts M G

       A D Barker   &   L Simmons   29 July 1847
                               Solemnized Jas. Woodard J P

       H Pitt   &   N M Cole   23rd Decr 1847
                               Solemnized R G Cole J P

       E Chapman   &   C Redfearn   27 Nov 1847
                               Solemnized 28 Nov 1847 W B Kelly M G

(143) Willis Pepper   &   Mandy McHenry   27 Nov 1847
                               Solemnized   David   M Wells J P

       William A Shannon   &   Lucy Simmons   14th Aug 1847
                               Solemnized 15 Aug 1847 Thos Cook J P

       Elias C Vick   &   R T Dunn   12th October 1847
                               Solemnized 22 Oct. 1847 Thomas Farmer J P

       F E Dycas   &   Mary F Featherston   1 January 1848
                               Solemnized 2 Jan. 1848 R W Bell J P

       Robert Savage   &   Amanda Tucker   11th August 1847
                               Solemnized 12 Aug. 1847 James Sprouse J P

       J. M. Cole   &   E Henry   2 Decr 1847
                               Solemnized   James Sprouse J P

(144) Stephen Jones   &   Martha Porter   21 Oct 1847
                               Solemnized James Sprouse J P

       Marcus Jernigan   &   Mary A Lewis   6 Decr 1847
                               Solemnized   James Sprouse J P

       John Johnson   &   Mary J Elmore   19 August 1847
                               Solemnized 23 Aug. 1847 James Sprouse J P

       Mathew Keller   &   Ider Bodine   18 Oct. 1847
                               Solemnized David M Wells J P

       Wm. J Lawrence   &   Frances Sory   18 Decr 1847
                               Solemnized R. W Bell J P 19 Decr 1847

       W H Jones   &   Amanda Baldry   22 Decr 1847
                               Solemnized 24 Decr 1847 Robert Green

(145) James W Powell   &   Jane Taylor   30th Oct 1847
                               Solemnized   Robert Green J P

****

John Ellison   & Mary Gaines   22 Nov 1847
Solemnized   R G Cole J P

Wm H Adams   & Margaret Crafford   24 April 1847
Solemnized 25 April 1847 Wm. D Baldwin M G

Stephen J Dorris   & Elizabeth Brumbelow   5 August 1847
Solemnized   Wm D Baldwin Minister of the Gos.

Jo Piles   & L I Reader   30th Oct 1847
Solemnized 31st Oct. 1847   Wm. D Baldwin M G

E Benton   & E Draughon   9 Decr 1847
Solemnized   P Martin

John Showmaker   & Rebecca Booker   8 Decr 1847
Solemnized   Wm K Turner Judge

(146) Miles A Jackson   & Permelia L Jackson   28 Decr 1847
Solemnized 30 Decr 1847   R W Bell J P

Jacob Myres   & Mary A Wade   6 Jany 1848
Solemnized   James Gunn E. M. C

Thomas C Cobb   & Martha M Darden   15 Nov 1847
Solemnized 18 Nov. 1847   J L Ellis J P

H. A. Holmes   & Nancy Morgan   22 Decr 1847
Solemnized 23rd Decr 1847   Jesse L Ellis J P

William M Bennett   & Mary J Thompson   22 Decr 1847
Solemnized dec. 23 1847   Isaac Steel

Asburry Will   & Eliza J Hall   5 April 1848
Solemnized   Isaac Steel

Jno L Crafford   & Margaret Bennett   8th Nov 1847
Solemnized   Isaac Steel

Fielding M Wright   & Carline Brabtree   26 Decr 1845
Solemnized 27 Decr. 1845   Isaac Steel

(147) Elijah Turner   & Matilda Moon   24 March 1847
Solemnized   Isaac Steel

Jacob Connell   & Mary Kirby   10 Sept 1847
Solemnized 11 Sept. 1847   Isaac Steel

Geo. Crewdson   & Eliza I Thompson   22nd Decr1847
Solemnized Dec. 23 1847   Isaac Steel

John Borthick   & Eleanor Pond   9 Decr 1847
Solemnized   Isaac Steel

Thomas Curenberry   & M J Sears   6 November 1847
Solemnized Dec. 23 1847   Isaac Steel

John A Thomas   &   Nancy Ruffin   16th June 1848
Solemnized   Robt. Draughon   J P

James W Holmes   &   Frances Miller   12th Feby 1848
Solemnized 13 Feb. 1848 W L Baldry Gospel
                                Minister

F G Traughber   &   Mary Ivens   18 Nov 1847
Solemnized   Jas. Woodard

John T Green   &   S A James   20 January 1848
Solemnized   Jesse L Ellis   J P

(148)   Edward G Clark   &   Mary C Felts   18 Decr 1847
Solemnized 23 Decr. 1847   Jas. Woodard

Hanzey Redfearn   &   Dicey Hutchings   11 January 1848
Solemnized 13 Jan. 1848 W B Kelly M G

William Cox   &   Elizabeth Harris   20th January 1848
Solemnized   Robert Green   J P

James B Rose   &   Wilmouth B Smith   10 January 1848
Solemnized 11 Jan. 1848   Robert Green J P

James C Goodmon   &   Mary Rolson   3rd January 1848
Solemnized 6 Jan. 1848 Robert Williams M G

Thomas L Campbell   &   Martha Jones   21st Feb 1848
Solemnized 22 Feb. 1848 W B Kelly M G

William Russel   &   Ann Traughber   21st Dec 1847
Solemnized 26 Decr. 1847 D G Baird J P

William Randolph   &   Elizabeth Babb   22nd 1848
Solemnized 26 Jan. 1848 W B Kelly M.G.

(149)   Alexander Bourn   &   Harriet Newman   8 January 1848
Solemnized 13 Jan. 1848   Thos. W Felts

Armstead Justice   &   E L White   24 Decr 1848
Solemnized   25 Decr. 1847 W L Bakdry G M

Thomas F Jones   &   Martha Boyd   26 Feb 1848
Solemnized   27 Feb. 1848 Greenberry Kelly M G

P J Bailey   &   Tabitha Cumie Earl   11 March 1848
Solemnized on 12 March 1848   E M Gunn M G

A D DAvidson   &   Tabitha Rosson   22nd January 1848
Solemnized 23 Feb. 1848   Robert Williams G M

Ambrose Porter   &   G A Tanner   27 October 1847
Solemnized   James Woodard

Thomas Carter   &   Louisa T Hawkins   8 June 1848
Solemnized **11, June, 1848   W.L. Baldry G.M.**

Graves Gunn   &   Jane Sneed   15 May 1848
Solemnized G M Gunn Justice of peace for
                           Robertson County

(150) Charles Bradley   &   Rebecca Bobbitt   30th July 1847
Solemnized 10 Aug. 1847 J W Hunt J P

James Lanaster   &   Mary Tucker   6th day of March 1848
Solemnized 8 March 1848 J M Nolen M G

Francis P Easley   &   Sarah Doss   13 March 1848
Solemnized 16 March 1848 D G Baird J P

Anthony L Binkley   &   Mary Benton   27 January 1848
Solemnized   Thos. Martin L E

Jack E Turner   &   Elily A Darden   1 May 1848
Solemnized 3 May 1848 Robt. Williams G M

William G Tucker   &   Susan Baseford   13 Jany 1848
Solemnized Jan. 14 1848 W Ramey M G

Washington Ogg   &   M A Pittman (Martha)   23 Feb. 1848
Solemnized 24 Feb. 1848 R W Bell J P

Michael Rose   &   Mary M Steel   5 January 1848
Solemnized 6 January 1848 W B Kelly M G

(151) Geo. W. Bailey   & Sarah W Bell   26th June 1848
Solemnized June 29 1848 James Gunn E. M. C.

Wesley Stovel   &   Dosha White   1st August 1846
Solemnized O H Morrow, A Minister of the Gospel

J H Davis   &   E A Villines   22 June 1848
Solemnized 25 June 1848 Jno. M Harry J P

Daniel Henry   &   H McMurry   3rd April 1848
Solemnized 5 April 1848 Jno M Harry J P

Wm W Felts   &   S A Mc Allen   13 day of June 1848
Solemnized 15 June 1848 J W Hunt J P

A L Moore   &   S A Couts   7 June 1848
Solemnized D G Baird J P

Presely E Holland   &   Carline Taylor   3rd July 1848
Solemnized 23 July 1848 G D Baird J P

Hyram Beach   &   F B Smith   29 July 1848
Solemnized 30 July 1848 Robert Green J P

(152) James C Griffin   &   M K Fisher   8 July 1848
Solemnized 9 July 1848 A B Randolph J O

L M Johnson   &   M A Moon   3 August 1848
Solemnized W B Mathews J P

B G Hooper   &   M E Bishop   5 Oct 1847
Solemnized Alex Lowe Minister

Robert N Myres   &   Cornelius Darden   18 May 1848
Solemnized Alex Lowe Minister

John C Mathews   &   Sarah E F Manlow   1st Decr. 1846
Solemnized Alex Lowe Minister

James T Rawls   &   Mariah J Binkloy   30th day of Jay 1846
Solemnized Alex Lowe Minister

A T Binkley   &   S J Reaves   5 Jany 1849
Solemnized Alex Lowe Minister

B C Clinard   &   N P Rawles   3 Nov 1847
Solemnized Ales Lowe Minister

L D Bowers   &   Julia Pepper   3 June 1846
Solemnized Alex Lowe Minister

(152) P Payne   &   L JL Darden   24th June 1846
Solemnized Alex Lowe Minister

Thomas Campbell   &   Rachel Moon   3 August 1848
Solemnized James Sprouse J P

Wm Mehaffy   &   Carline M. Amos   4 August 1848
Solemnized 6 Aug. 1848   James Sprouse J P

John G White   &   Martha M Winters   18 July 1848
Solemnized 19 July 1848   D C Stephens G M

Sidney Campbell   &   Martha Rigsby   18th Junr 1848
Solemnized Thos. West, Minister of the Gospel

William Kirby   &   Lina Camoll   20 May 1848
Solemnized 25 May 1848 Thomas West, Minister

Augustine Bryant   &   Mahala A May   22nd March 1848
Solemnized 23 March 1851 J M Stemmons

(153) Lewis Stratton   &   E A Gibson   10 June 1848
Solemnized 18 June 1848 J M Stemmons

John Wells   &   M A Huey   17 Feby. 1848
Solemnized   J M Stemmons

Thomas Debauport   &   Carline Turner   16th day August 1848
Solemnized 17 Aug. 1848 Thomas Farmer J P

Waddy Jones   &   Eliz. Worsham   5th of July 1848
Solemnized Thomas Farmer Justice of the peace
                                        for Roberston County

James L Kiger   &   Ann Violet   11 August 1848
Solemnized Thomas Farmer J P for R C

Elisha Whiting   &   Susan Phipps   30 June 1848
                        Solemnized   John Crafford   a J P

(154) Nathaniel Farmer   &   S C B inkley   17 Oct 1848
                        Solemnized J W Hunt Justice of the peace

      W. E. Falts   &   M J Walker   6 Decr 1848
                        Solemnized 7 Decr 1848   J W Hunt J P

      W H Grayon   &   Mary J Shepherd Dec. 21st 1848
                        Solemnized 25 Decr 1848 D G Baird J P

      John Mc Intosh   &   E M Gillim   22 Decr '48
                        Solemnized 26 Decr 1848 D G Baird J P

      F Patton   &   Mary Woodard   4 Sept. 1848
                        Solemnized 7 Sept 1848   J M Henry J P

      H P Robertson   &   A Lanaster   11 Nov 1848
                        Solemnized A Akins an acting Justice for Robert-
                                                          son County

      Sandy Jones   &   Elizabeth Cole   26th Oct 1848
                        Solemnized   James Sprouse J P

(155) Samuel Volner   &   S A Harper (Syntha) 26 November 1848
                        Solemnized   W H Bugg J P for R. C.

      Wm Draughn   &   Mary Murphy   3o November 1848
                        Solemnized   T B Mathews J P

      Samuel McMurry   &   Mary Escue   15 November 1848
                        Solemnized 16 November 1848 Eli Baggett J P

      James Carter   &   M E Carter   6 Nov 1848
                        Solemnized 9 Nov 1848   G W Martin G. M.

      E T Stoltz   &   M L Batts   22 Oct 1848
                        Solemnized J L Ellis Minister of the Gospel

      Burket Mahan   &   Emily Foster   24 May 1848
                        Solemnized Thomas Farmer Justice of the Peace

      William Engler   &   S A Hunsacker   27 Aug. 1848
                        Solemnized   James Woodard

      J J Bradley   &   E Holmes   5 Sept 1846
                        Solemnized 7 Sept. 1848   J W Hunt J P

(156) J G F Spears   &   Rebecca Ring   28 August 1848
                        Solemnized   U Lawrence J P

      Jno. W Cordel   &   B A Gossett   28 August 1848
                        Solemnized   W M C Barr J P for Robertson Co.

      Thomas Randolph   &   Catherine Darke   21st August 1848
                        Solemnized 24 Aug. 1848 W H Rife J P for Robert-
                                                             son County

****

R. Ogg	&	Martha Ann Adams	26 July 1848
	Solemnized 27 July 1848 Thos. W Ruffin J P		

Samuel Gillum	&	Martha Beasley	4 Sept 1848
	Solemnized John Crawfford J P for said County		

Henry Burchett   &   Editha Stratton   12 May 1848
     Solemnized 18 May 1848   David M Wells J P

John W Vestal   &   M J Mallory   6 Nov 1848
     Solemnized Milton Ramey Minister of the Gospel

(157)   Saml. Price   &   M J Bostic   31st Decr 1848
     Solemnized Wm C Vannester Minister of the Gospel

Meredith Woodard   &   S Woodard   22nd Decr 1848
     Solemnized   R Green

John Long   &   Nancy Harrison   17 Oct 1848
     Solemnized   Jeremiah Batts J P for Robertson Co.

S R Stoltz   &   M A Cobb   16 Oct 1848
     Solemnized 17 Oct. 1848   Jeremiah Batts J P

Thos. Ruffin   &   Eleanor Broadrick   6 Decr 1848
     Solemnized 8 Decr. 1848 J Batts J P

Rheid. A Boren   &   Leatha Newton   7 Decr 1848
     Solemnized   F R Gooche S L

W D Alfred   &   G Menees   23 Sept 1848
     Solemnized 24 Sept. 1848 Jeremiah Batts J P

John W Ivey   &   E A Chapman   27 Decr. 1848
     Solemnized 28 Decr. 1848   Jas Woodard J P

(158)   Charles R Browning   &   L L Gorrell   28 Nov 1848
     Solemnized   Jas. Woodard

D Henry   &   E Ewing   8 Decr; 1848
     Solemnized Decr. 7 1848   Jas Woodard

H D Featherston   &   M E Davis   25 Nov 1848
     Solemnized Nov. 26 1848 Milton Ramey M G

Robert Watson   &   M D Adams   30 Decr 1848
     Solemnized 31 Decr. James Burnes Justice of the
                                                    peace

John L Yates   &   P Gorham   10 Jany. 1849
     Solemnized Thomas Farmer Justice of the peace

G W Moake   &   Sally Harris   28 Oct 1848
     Solemnized Nov. 8 1848   J C Nowlim

Robert D Mays   &   Martha A Ward   23 Decr 1848
     Solemnized   J W Featherston

James A King   &   E A Bell   21 Oct 1848
Solemnized 24 Oct 1848 D G Baird J P

(159) H Pool   &   E A Smithwick   18 Oct 1848
Solemnized 19 Oct. 1848 A B sayers J P

Daniel Clayton   &   Nancy P Willis   7 Sept. 1848
Solemnized   D G Baird J P

James W Swann   &   Martha J Jernigan   8 January 1849
Solemnized 11 Jan. 1849 Moses F Earhart M G

E L Durrett   &   M A Clark   6 July 1846
Solemnized Robt. L Tate M. G.

John A Horton   &   S A Groves   13 Jany 1849
Solemnized 14 Jan. 1849 Will C Barr J P

Jacob H Darden   &   S E Polk (Sarah)   3rd Feb 1849
Solemnized 4 Feb. 1849 Jas. Burns acting Justice
             of the pease for said County

Edmons L Roberts &   Martha Chapman   23 Decr 1848
Solemnized 24 Decr. 1848 G B Mason J P

J C Shannon   &   Carline Shelly   4 November 1846
Solemnized 5 Nov. 1846 Robt. L Tate M G

(160) J Hays   &   Lucy Ray   30 Jany. 1849
Solemnized   James Woodard

Thos. C Brown   &   S A Bennett   16 January 1849
Solemnized   James Woodard

W H F Ligon   &   S Pope   24 Oct. 1848
Solemnized Thos. N Langford Minister of the Gos.

Lemuel Warner   &   Charity Winn   16 Decr 1848
Solemnized Decr 20th 1848 Jno M Nolen M G

Thos. Lipscomb   &   Polly Edwards   14 January 1849
Solemnized Thomas Farmer Justice of the peace

Bluford J Miller &   M J Chasteen   28 Decr 1848
Solemnized J H Smith

William Sterry   &   Martha A Hudgins 19 April 1848
Solemnized 20 April 1848 John M Vestal M G

H A Rock   &   M B Parker   15 July 1848
Solemnized Jas Woodard

(161) James B Morris &   Eliz. Murrah   2nd January 1849
Solemnized 4 Jan. 1849 B W Bradley J P

C C Williams   &   A P Hyde   3rd Jany. 1849
Solemnized 4 Jany. 1849 J W Hunt J P

Mathew Foreman   &   C S Appleton   1st Sept 1848
                        Solemnized   Jas Woodard

Leonard Page   &   M A L Page   4 Decr 1848
                        Solemnized 5 Decr 1848 James Lamb Gospel Minister

J J Bradley   &   E F Justice   5 Feb 1849
                        Solemnized 6 Feb 1849 J W Hunt J P

Young Babb   &   Martha Freeman   22nd August 1848
                        Solemnized Greenberry Kelly M G

B W Edwards   &   A Moon   Jan.21st 1849
                        Solemnized D G Baird J P

W A Johnson   &   M E Grainger   2nd Jany 1849
                        Solemnized 4 Jany 1849 D G Baird J P

(162) P B Johns   &   M A Taylor   28 March 1849
                        Solemnized Jas. Woodard

J Ennis   &   Eliz. Clinard.   3 Feb 1849
                        Solemnized 11 March 1849 W H Bugg

Russelle Shoemaker   &   Nancy Panson   24 Feb. 1849
                        Solemnized 2 March 1849 W H Bugg

Jacob Zech   &   Clarissa Cook   13 Jany 1849
                        Solemnized 16 Jany. 1849 Greenberry Kelly M G

J A Bottom   &   E F Sandofer   5 April 1849
                        Solemnized Jas. Woodard

M Phillips   &   Emily Boleyjack 21 Jany. 1849 Greenberry
                                                         Kelly M.G.

William Phelps   &   Prudence Draughon   9 March 1849
                        Solemnized 11 March 1849 T B Mathews J P

W L Mathews   &   V Purkerson   12 March 1849
                        Solemnized Thos. Farmer Justice of the peace

W P Wilson   &   Ann Dorris   26 March 1849
                        Solemnized W H Bugg Esq.

(163) James E Roberts &   Nancy Hughlett   28 Feb 1849
                        Solemnized 1 March 1849 Thos. West Minister

William H Blackburn   &   Carline W Menees   7 June 1849
                        Solemnized 10 June 1849 Patrick Martin M Gospel

Eli Boren   &   L A Baker   1st June 1848
                        Solemnized   Jas. Woodard

Daniel Henry   &   H McMurry   3rd April 1849
                        Solemnized 5th April 1848 J M Henry J P

W W Felts	&	S A McClain	13 June 1848
	Solemnized 15 June 1848 J W Hunt J P		
William Hunt	&	Mary A Nanny	2 July 1849
	Solemnized Thos. Farmer Justice of the peace		
Isaac B Walten	&	Louisa Cage	26 May 1849
	Solemnized John M Vestal M G		
Thos Staley	&	L I Amos	16 Sept 1845
	Solemnized _____		
W. A. Clark	&	E Mcguire	14 June 1849
	Solemnized , N M Henry J P		

(164)   Sandford West   &   Nancy Boyd   24 Day of April 1849
                           Solemnized April 26th 1849 B Randolph J P

        E Harris   &   Mary Jane Nichols   11 October 1848
                           Solemnized 15 October 1848 W W Williams J P

        Williams E Gower   &   Rosannah Durham   10 Feb 1849
                           Solemnized 13 Feb 1849 W W Willaams

        Simeon Frey   &   Mary J Deen   5 July 1849
                           Solemnized Robert Draughon J P

        Geo. McCauley   &   P L A Darden   31st day of Aug.1849
                           Solemnized 1Sept. 1849 M P Parham Minister of M. E
                                                              Church South
        David Sanders   &   Martha F Forbes   5 Jany 1849
                           Solemnized 18 Jan. 1849 W. W. Williams J P

        James W Shewron   &   Rebecca Maxey   9 July 1849
                           Solemnized 12 July 1849 W W Williams J P

        John Travis   &   M C Watson   22 Nov 1848
                           Solemnized 24 Nov 1848 W W Williams

        Washington Wall   &   Harriet Walker   27 March 1847
                           Solemnized 8 April 1847 W W Williams

(165)   S Watson   &   E A Johnson   29 October 1847
                           Solemnized W W Williams J P

        Benj. F Stewart   &   Emily Maxey   9 Decr 1848
                           Solemnized 23rd Decr. 1848 W W Williams J P

        A B Johnson   &   E G Bagget   23 April 1849
                           Solemnized 28 April 1849 S H Wills J P

        Isaac Walton   &   Louis Cage   26 May 1849
                           (page 163)

        B F Chandler   &   L P Cook   10 January 1849
                           Solemnized 11 Jan. 1849   James Sprouse J P

        David Cook   &   M A Chowning   22 Feb 1849
                           Solemnized   James Sprouse J P

****

(Note: p 62 is missing but no subject matter is missing.)

Robert Watson & Martha J Adams 30 Decr 1848
Solemnized   James Byrnes Justice of the peace

E S Small & J T Hill 13th Feby 1849
Solemnized   Tho. W Ruffing J P

(166) Sol. Jackson & Mary Howard 2 August 1849
Solemnized   T B Mathews   J P

William Robertson & Frances Elliott 4 July 1849
Solemnized   G B Mason J P for Robertson County

Anderson Adcock & Carlina Smiley 9 June 1849
Solemnized 14 June 1849   John Warren J P

Jos. E McGuire & M E Chism 10 January 1849
Solemnized   Isaac Steel

Aaron Caudle & Sarah Stringer 26 Oct 1849
Solemnized 27 Oct. 1849 Isaac Steel

W H Clayton & S E Willis 23 May 1848
Solemnized 24 May 1848   Isaac Steel

Elsey Jones & Martha Hampton 15 April 1849
Solemnized   Isaac Steel

Noah Draper & Charity Arnold 26 Oct 1848
Solemnized 27 Oct 1848   Isaac Steel

James Brown & Jane E Carpenter 20 Decr 1848
Solemnized   Isaac Steel

(167) William R Doyal & Harriet Choat 25th April 1849
Solemnized 29th April 1849 John Crafford J P

William A Adams & Susan Chapman 26th April 1849
Solemnized   G B Mason J P for Robertson County

John L Yates & P Gorham 10 January 1849
Solemnized   Tho. Farmer Justice of the peace

A C Gains & L L Norfleet(Louisa) 27 Decr 1849
Solemnized 28 Decr 1848 Robert Williams G M

John Walker & Nancy Wilson 25 of Aug 1849
Solemnized   B M Wm Bradley J P

C Payne & Ann Payne 25 of Aug 1849
Solemnized   J M Harry

Richd W Smith & Eliz Warren 10 Oct 1849
Solemnized   J M Gunn Justice of the peace

D M Hooper & E Roberts 17 Oct 1849
Solemnized   J M Gunn Justice of the peace

(168)   John G Bradley   &   E C Felts   4 Sept 1849
                               Solemnized 6 Sept 1849   A B Sayor

         Samuel W Page   &   Eliza Smith   23 Oct 1849
                               Solemnized 30 Oct 1849   James Lamb

         Moses Stanley   &   Mary J Warren   21st of Aug 1849
                               Solemnized James Sprouse J P

         W F Cobb   &   S M Darden   15 Sept 1849
                               Solemnized 16 Sept 1849 Robert Draughon J P

         Elias Volver   &   Wilmouth Ann Thomas 12 May 1849
                               Solemnized 13 May 1849   W H Bugg J P

         Asa Daub   &   Prudence Turner   27th Aug 1849
                               Solemnized 28 Aug 1849   W H Bugg J P

         J L Kirby   &   Mary G Cagle   27 April 1849
                               Solemnized 2nd May 1849 W H Bugg

         J Sullivan   &   Jane Bowers   6 Sept 1849
                               Solemnized   J Lawrence J P

(169)   C B Williams   &   A W Jernigan   21st Sept 1849
                               Solemnized 23rd Sept. 1849 B Randolph J P

         John A Likn   &   Martha Randolph   8 Sept 1849
                               Solemnized Sept 12th 1849 B Randolph J P

         Jordon T Judkins   &   E G Adkinson   5 Sept 1849
                               Solemnized 9 Sept. 1849 L M Taylor Minister of
                                                             the Gospel
         W J Harris   &   Sarah A Winn   18 January 1849
                               Solemnized Jeremiah Batts J P

         B F Stolts   &   Amanda Winn   13 Jay. 1849
                               Solemnized   Jeremiah Batts J P

         John J Moulton   &   Susan Cobb   11 Aug 1849
                               Solemnized 12 Aug 1849 Patrick Martin M Gospel

         John F Swann   & Martha Wilson   21st day of June 1849
                               Solemnized Robert Draughon J P

         C H Abernatha   &   N J Hollis   13 Jay 1849
                               Solemnized B Rawls M G

         W P Warren   &   M A Moizee   Aug. 21st 1849
                               Solemnized 22nd Aug 1849 James Sprouse

(170)   John D Huffman   &   Mary A Rawls   11 Oct 1849
                               Solemnized Benjamin Rawls

         James G Brynes   &   Aramiscia Dunn   1st Nov 1849
                               Solemnized Benjamin Rawls

Robertson Co., TN - Marriage Records - Volume 1 - 1839 - 1861   65

****

Elias Millican   &   Sarah A Redding   11 Oct 1849
                        Solemnized   Benja Rawls

Harrison Kelly   &   Nancy Rose   16 July 1849
                        Solemnized 19 July 1849 W B Kelly M G

William Jones   &   Martha Lucas   11 Sept 1849
                        Solemnized 13 Sept 1849 Eli Baggett J P

Isham Tredway   &   L J Gilbert   5 Oct 1849
                        Solemnized 7 Oct 1849 R G Cole J P

Thos. A Adams   &   Martha Gardner   2 of Aug 1849
                        Solemnized J Lawrence J P

Alex H Williams   &   Nancy A Shaw   19 Sept 1848
                        Solemnized   Sept 20 1849 Benj Rawls M G

Wm B Chambliss   &   Sarah A Chaudion   19 Decr 1848
                        Solemnized   Benja Rawls

(171) James M Pike   &   M A M Andrews   5 Jany 1847
                        Solemnized B Rawls

Amos G Felts   &   M L Coleman   16 Decr 1848
                        Solemnized B Rawls

Lewis Thomas   &   Mary Pool   27 May 1849
                        Solemnized Benj. Rawls

Geo. W Frey   &   Sarah B Beadwell   15 Nov 1849
                        Solemnized 16 Nov 1849 B Rawls

J K Milliken   &   L J Dowlen   25 Sept 1849
                        Solemnized Benj. Rawls

Wm N Foote   &   M B Walton   7 Feb 1850
                        Solemnized 10th Feb 1850 B Randolph J P

J Franklin   &   Amanda Harrison   22 Feb 1850
                        Solemnized Feb. 24 1850 G B Mathews

B Brakefield   &   A Aleom   25 Feb 1850
                        Solemnized   G B Mason

Simon P Knox   &   M A Nicholson   14 Janu 1850
                        Solemnized Jany. 17 1850 J Moore M G

(172) Joseph Wilson   &   Mahala E Baggett   7 Jan 1850
                        Solemnized 9 Jan 1850 Eli Baggett J P

Wm Dose   &   Nancy D Elmore   1st Jany 1850
                        Solemnized 2nd Jan 1850 W B Kelly M G

Banj. F Drake   &   Julina Green   22nd Jay 1850
                        Solemnized Benjamin Rawls M G

Eli T Herron   &   A Williams   3 Decr 1849
                      Solemnized 4 Decr 1849   Jorden Moon M G

Derias Gorham   &   S V Harrison   5 March 1850
                      Solemnized James Woodard J P

Levi Pitt   &   Hannah Dunn   11 Feb 1850
                      Solemnized Feb 12 1850   Lewis Adams Gospel Minis-
                                                                 ter

John Randolph   &   Harriet Randolph   21 Feb 1850
                      Solemnized JM M. Henry Justice of the Peace

Benjamin Hooper   &   Sary Sands   4 March 1850
                      Solemnized   James Woodard J P

Jesse Wright   &   E J Caudle   15 Decr 1849
                      Solemnized 16 Decr. 1849 W M C Barr J P

(173) John B Carter   &   M E Chowning   17 Jany 1850
                      Solemnized   J Sprouse J P

Carter Pearson   &   Lucy Ponds   23 Jany 1850
                      Solemnized 24th Jan. 1850 Wm M C Barr J P
                                              for Robertson County

John Glover   &   Tollsberry Harris   8 Jany 1850
                      Solemnized 9 Jan. 1850 A B Sayors J P

James Gilbert   &   Charlotte Brinain   26 Jay 1850
                      Solemnized   R G Cole J P

Wm Volner   &   Nancy Boren   3rd Oct 1849
                      Solemnized 4 Oct 1849 W H Bugg J P

Henry Chaudion   &   Luoretia Pool   25th Sept 1849
                      Solemnized 28 Sept. 1849 W H Bugg J P

G W Barr   &   Jane Cannon   30th Jay 1850
                      Solemnized W H Bugg J P

J C Jones   &   Augestine Burch   19 Decr 1849
                      Solemnized 26 Decr 1849 W H Rife J P

(174) Abner Keller   &   Sarah Stark   19 Decr 1849
                      Solemnized 20 Decr 1849 W W Mann

Samuel J Murphy   &   Eliza Traughber   26 Feb 1850
                      Solemnized 3 March 1850   D G Baird J P

Washington J Williams &   Louisa Brewer   26 Nov 1849
                      Solemnized 29 Nov. 1849 W B Kelly M F

G C Cummings   &   Mary T Johnston   29 Jay 1850
                      Solemnized   Lewis Adams Minister of the Gospel

James Bobbett   &   Julia A L Whetter   3rd Decr 1849
                      Solemnized 6 _____ 1850 B W Bradley J P

Daniel C Johnston   &   Elizabeth Holland   4 Feb 1850
Solemnized 5 Feb. 1850 Robert Green 1850

Jacob Mafford   &   Sally Traughber   27 Decr 1849
Solemnized D G Baird J P

Hillery Fisher   &   Elizabeth Flood   18 Nov 1849
Solemnized B Randolph J P

(175)   Ed M Richard   &   Bernecy Payson   6 Nov 1850 .
Solemnized 12 Nov 1849 J M Henry J P

Albert West   &   M A Wright   27 Nov 1849
Solemnized 29 Nov 1849 J M Henry J P

James A Williams   &   Mary C Allen   22 Decr 1849
Solemnized Decr 27 1849 Patrick Martin M G

James H Hall   &   Mary F James   6 of Decr 1849
Solemnized Decr 9 1849 Lewis Adams Minigter of th
                                     Gospel

Jno F Couts   &   Eliz. A Davis Decr 16 1849 Lewis Adams M G

John A Cannon   &   M M M Hamson   29th Oct 1849
Solemnized 2nd Nov 1840 Tho W Ruffin J P

F W Grubbs   &   R A Warren   31st Decr 1849
Solemnized 1 Jan. 1850 James Anderson J P

A H Briggs   &   Leethy Warren   14 Decr 1849
Solemnized Decr 18 1849 James Anderson J P

David Flood   &   L A Fisher   6 Jany 1849
Solemnized B Randolph J P

(176)   Greenberry Reddle   &   E F Summerville   9 Oct 1849
Solemnized 11 Oct 1849 Thos. West Bap. Minister

Tho. D Mathews   &   M McMurry   31 Decr 1849
Solemnized E Baggett J P

J M Chandler   &   Lutitia Wilson   10 Decr 1849
Solemnized 13 Decr. 1849 James Sprouse J P

Frederick Jones   &   Nancy Esura(?)   1st Oct 1849
Solemnized J Sprouse J P

Thos. B Polk   &   A E Long   2 Jany 1850
Solemnized Jay. 3rd 1850 L. Adams Minister of
                                  the Gospel.

Moses E Fortner   &   Martha Grow   24 Decr 1849
Solemnized D G Baird J P

S Murphy   &   F Elliotte   10 May 1848
Solemnized 12 May 1848 Thomas Farmer Justice of
                                  the peace

A. H. Herring   &   M. Stanley   10 Jay. 1850
Solemnized J. W. Hunt J.P.

(177) Henry F. White   &   Elizabeth Fort   25 March 1850
Solemnized 26 March 1850 R. W. Bradley J. P.

Jesse Clark   &   Sally Chambliss   13 June 1850
Solemnized 15 June 1850 J. W. Hunt J P

A. J. Lunsford   &   Martha Dorris   6 June 1850
Solemnized D. G. Baird J. P.

Luther Riggins   &   Nancy Trimble   25 June 1850
Solemnized J. E. Winfield Clk.

James R Rose   &   Mariah Coke   12 March 1850
Solemnized G. B. Mason J P

J. L.Gillem   &   M.C.Starke   22 Decr. 1849
Solemnized J.D.Barney, Minister of the M EM
                                      Church

M. L. Draughon   &   S. H. Murphy   3 Apr. 1850
Solemnized Tho. Farmer Justice of the peace

B. Bowlin   &   E. Newman   7 April 1850
Solemnized John W Hanner, Minister of the Gospel

(178) Robert Huddleston   &   Alabama Benson   27 March 1850
Solemnized 28 March 1850 B. Randolph J P

Jeremiah Franklin   &   Amanda Hamson   22 Feb. 1850
Solemnized Feb 24 1850 T. B. Mathews J P

Joseph Wilson   &   M. E.Baggett   7 January 1850
Solemnized 9 Jan 1850 E. Baggett J P

James Draughon   &   Avalina Frey   27 March 1850
Solemnized B. Randolph J P

Wm. N. Foote   &   Martha B. Walton   7 Feb. 1850
Solemnized 10 Feb. 1850 T. B. Mathews J P

W. Brakefield   &   A. Alcorn   25 Feb 1850
Solemnized G. B. Mason J P

T. P. Crutcher   &   J. A. Deadwell   13 Feb 1850
Solemnized Benj. Rawls M. G.

Lewis Warren   &   Mary Appleton   29 Jay 1850
Solemnized J. M. Gunn J P

(179) Joseph Turner   &   Sarah A Babb   18 Feb 1850
Solemnized 20 Feb. 1850 Greenberry Kelly M. G.

Turner, E. Knox   &   Martha A Nicholas   14 January 1850
Solemnized Jay 19, 1850 J. Moon M.G.

James Yates   &   Louesa Moon   4 May 1850
Solemnized May 5 1850 B. Randolph J. P.

	Wm H Roderick	& Martha J Burn 4 May 1850
		Solemnized 6 May 1850 Benjamin Rawls M G
	James Farthing	& Sereno Adams 6 April 1850
		Solemnized 7 Paril 1850 G B Mason J P
	W H Shepperd	& Margaret Franklin 13 May 1850
		Solemnized 16 May 1850 J M Stemmons
	James Wallace	& M H Jones 2nd June 1850
		Solemnized 4 June 1850 Eli Baggett J P
	James Sewell	& T Barrow 26 Feby 1850
		28 Feb 1850 Solemnized J M Stemmons
(180)	John Crafford	& Martha Brakefield 30 March 1850
		Solemnized 1 April 1850 W L Baldry Gospel Minister
	T M Nave	& M A Cobb 2nd May 1850
		Solemnized May 7th 1850 Tho. Martin L E
	G W Parker	& Martha J Carter 22 May 1850
		Solemnized P Martin M G
	Wm L Hudwall	& E Christmas 6 April 1850
		Solemnized 7 April 1850 J M Henry J P
	John C Adams	& Mary Benson 9 June 1850
		Solemnized D G Baird J P
	Albert Mays	& Mary Harrison 16 March 1850
		Solemnized 18 March 1850 John Crafford J P
	Andrew J Cole	& Ellen Villines 8 day June 1850
		Solemnized 9 June 1850 Wm H Rife J P
	Josiah M Dorris	& Amanda Hampton 13 June 1850
		Solemnized · D G Baird J P
(181)	Wm. Summers	& Jane Nichols 12 March 1850
		Solemnized John Crafford J P for R County
	Geo W Smith	& Milly Agee 11 Feb 1850
		Solemnized 12 Feb. 1850 John Crafford J P
	C Doyal	& E Phepps 21 Decr 1849
		Solemnized John Crafford J P
	Vincent Braswell	& Lucinda A Sick 5 Aug 1850
		Solemnized J W Featherston Minister of the Gospel
	Thos. Spain	& Martha L Davis 14 Aug 1850
		Solemnized Lewis Adams Minister of the Gospel
	Tho. Baird	& E T Cole 22 Aug 1842
		Solemnized 24 Aug. 1850 Isaac Steel

Calvin Wilson   &   Laundale Williams   10 Jay 1850
                         Solemnized 17 Jay 1850 Isaac Steel

Saml. W Sherrod   &   Susan Hames   10 April 1850
                         Solemnized J W Featherston

Wm K Stone   &   M J Samuel   30 Jay 1850
                         Solemnized Isaac Steel

(182)   Richard C Sprouse &   Mary A Carter   22 August 1850
                         Solemnized   James Sprouse J P

P M Carter   &   L A Carter   14 Oct 1850
                         Solemnized 15 Oct 1850 Tho. Martin L E

Willis Johnson   &   Mary Night   31st 1850
                         Solemnized Thos. Farmer Justice of the peace

Flivoas J Carter   &   Sarah E Parker   15 August 1850
                         Solemnized Patrick Martin L E

William Redfern   &   Mary Long   20 Aug 1850
                         Solemnized 21 Aug. 1850 W B Kelly M G

Zachariah Durham   &   Carline Winters   26 June 1850
                         Solemnized 3 July 1850 B W Bradley J P

Thimothy T Lasiter   &   Lucinda A Adams   19 August 1850
                         Solemnized 20-August 1850 J W Featherston G M

Elisha W Willis   &   Mary A R Roberts   15 Decr 1849
                         Solemnized 16 Decr 1849 E W Benson G M

E Baggett   &   A L Shannon   4 September 1850
                         Solemnized Eli Baggett J P

(183)   P B Holland   &   Carline Wells   3 August 1850
                         Solemnized 9th August 1850 W L. Baldry G M

Wm H Smith   &   Emily Standfield   29 Aug 1850
                         Solemnized Thomas Farmer Justice of the Peace

Ellis Nipper   &   Mary Sellers   26 Sept 1850
                         Solemnized T B Mathews J P

Absalum Vance   &   Nancy Raynolds   18 Aug 1850
                         Solemnized 20th Aug. 1850 David M Wells J P

James C Husley   &   Martha Dickerson   22 July 1850
                         Solemnized 23rd July 1850 Elisha Lutor

Noah Elks   &   Sary I Clark   20th Sept 1850
                         Solemnized 24 Sept. 1850 Tho West Baptist Minis-
                                                                    ter

Wm Brooke   &   Emeline Krisel   19 March
                         No record of return

H B Barnes   &   M E Chance   12 Oct 1850
                              Solemnized 13 Oct 1850 F R Gooch L O

Wm J Gambill   &   Mary E Johnson   10 Oct 1850
                              Solemnized Thos Farmer Justice pf the peace

(184)   Josiah Farmer   & Nancy Long   10 Aug 1850
                              Solemnized 11 Aug. 1850 Lewis Adams M G

C S Gooch   &   Mary J Watson   5 Oct 1850
                              Solemnized Oct 6th L850 Mark Sellers M G

J M Campbell   &   Mary A Fulton   Sept. 24 1850
                              Solemnized Sept 27, 1850 W B Kelly M Gospel

Asa Ledbetter   &   E N Anglin   26 Oct 1850
                              Solemnized 27 Oct 1850 T B Mathews J P

Jesse J Rawls   &   J C Gooch   3 Sept. 1850
                              Solemnized   Benjamin Rawls M G

R R Mayes   &   Elizabeth E Watson   1st Oct 1849
                              Solemnized 2nd. Oct 1849 Robert Williams M G

John Dickerson   &   Mary Compesry   8 March 1851
                              Solemnized 9 March 1851 Thomas B Mathews

William Adams   &   Jane Dickerson   3 March 1851
                              Solemnized   _____

Absalum A Tatum   &   Martha T Dunn   2nd March 1851
                              Solemnized Tho. Farmer Justice of the peace
                                 for Robertson County State of Tennessee
(185)   Wm P Sales   &   Elizabeth Randolph   12 Feb 1851
                              Solemnized Feb 18 1851 B Randloph

John C Howard   &   Nancy F Turner   14th January 1851
                               Solemnized 22 Jan. 1851 W H Rife J P

James E Lawrence   &   Sally Barnes   10 Feb 1851
                              Solemnized Joseph Gunn Minister

John Stewart   &   Nancy W Coats   18th Feb 1851
                              Solemnized   J M Henry J P

Richard M Winn   &   Martha Appleton   6 January 1831
                              Solemnized 9 Jan. 1851 J M Gunn J P

Paschal Haley   &   Eliz. B Smith   21st January 1851
                              Solemnized 22 Jan. 1851 Robert Draughon J P

Benjamin Stark   &   Jane P Hall   25 January 1851
                              Solemnized 2 Feb. 1851 B Randolph J P

James Fisher   &   Elsunda Doss   7 Jan 1851
                              Solemnized Jan 9 1851 B Randolph

	Thos. Winns	& Louisa Dickerson	21 Decr 1850
		Solemnized 22 Decr 1850 Tho B Mathews J P	
(186)	James D Hubbard	& Elizabeth Scott	18 February 1851
		Solemnized Robert Draughon	
	Willis Nichols	& Sarah E Harris	6 Feb 1851
		Solemnized J W Hunt J P	
	McCarney A Orman	& Dicy Dickerson	31st Decr 1850
		Solemnized 1st Jay 1851 J W Hunt J P	
	John S C Adams	& Mary Cochran	6th July 1850
		Solemnized 9 July 1850 A Rose M G	
	John W Cochran	& Nancy D Hudgins	15th May 1850
		Solemnized 16 May 1850 A Rose Minister of the Gospel	
	William Tatum	& Harriet Freeman	25 August 1850
		Solemnized 26 August 1850 D G Baird J P	
	Henderson J Crocker	& L E Doss	2nd Decr 1850
		Solemnized Decr 4, 1850 B Randolph J P	
	Lewis Warren	& Nancy J Webb	30 Nov 1850
		Solemnized 1 st Decr. 1850 O H Morrow, G M	
	Saml. O Cloud	& Martha W Roberts	4 Oct 1850
		Solemnized 5 Oct 1850 D G Baird J P	
(187)	Clayton T Edwards	& Pantha A Stark	26 Decr 1851
		Solemnized B Randolph J P	
	Wm. W Rainwater	& Rebecca J McDaniel	22 May 1850
		Solemnized Jas. Woodard J P	
	James W Welborne	& Susan Gooby	13 July 1849
		Solemnized July 13 1850 Jas. Woodard J P	
	John J Lowry	& R A Davis	23rd Oct 1850
		Solemnized Jas. Woodard	
	Armstead Aikin	& Nancy Hardy	2nd Sept 1850
		Solemnized Sept 5th 1850 James Woodard J P	
	Collin Adams	& Elizabeth W Gunn	19 Sept 1850
		Solemnized W H Adams M of Gos.	
	Stephen Smelser	& E A Dozier	16 May 1849
		Solemnized May 18, 1849 James Woodard	
	Robt. A Poor	& Sarah A Powell	12 Decr 1849
		Solemnized 13 Decr 1849 Jas Woodard J P	
	A Dorris	& A E Crawford	19 Now 1849
		Solemnized May 20th 1849 Jas Woodard J P	

	T W Arnold	&	E J Wheeler	4 July 1849

T W Arnold   & E J Wheeler   4 July 1849
                  Solemnized   Jas. Woodard J P

(188) Joseph Porter   & Martha Ritter   28 April 1850
                            Solemnized April 30, 1850 James Woodard J P

Joseph W Felts   & S A R Owen   30 Decr 1850
                      Solemnized Tho. W Felts January 1 1851

James A Duncan   & Mary J Browning   1st Aug 1850
                      Solemnized Jas. Woodard J P

George W Simmons   & M A Traughber   26 Oct 1850
                        Solemnized Thos. W Felts

Stephen A Ligon   & Susannah C Fort   15 Nov 1850
                        Solemnized 19 Nov 1850 Tho. Watts M. G.

George W Morris   & A J Morris   24 Decr 1850
                        Solemnized P Martin M G

Geo. E Thomas   & Mary J Thomas   28th Decr 1850
                      Solemnized 29 Decr 1850 J W Featherston M G

W G Baggett   & L A Clark   8 Nov 1850
                    Solemnized 10 November 1850 E Baggett J P

/189) Lemuel Chowning   & Amamda J Cole   30 Nov 1850
                              Solemnized 1 Decr 1850 O H Morrow Minister of the
                                                                            Gospel

(189) Drury Wilson   & Elizabeth Dorris   23 Decr 1850
                            Solemnized W L Barldry Gospel Minister

Mathew J Draughon   & Polly A Solomon   5 Decr 1850
                          Solemnized Thos. B Mathews

William Eddings   & Susan Samuel   24 Oct 1850
                        Solemnized 28 Oct 1850 G B Mason J P for Robertson
                                                                      County

James W Dorris   & Mary Powell   10 Oct 1850
                      No record of return

W C Young   & P A Hutchison   24 of June 1850
                  Solemnized John Wynn M G

E R Rose   & V A Green   19 Decr 1850
                 Solemnized Thos. Farmee J P

P M Leaton   & Mississippi Stone   23 Oct 1850
                   Solemnized R G Cole J P

H T Madin   & L A Gorden   19 Nov 1850
                  Solemnized 21 Sept. 1850 Thow. W Ruffin J P

S A Walls   & Martha Ayers   24 Sept. 1850
                  Solemnized Thos. Farmer J P

(190) M W Rose   &   Elizabeth G Kelly   7 June 1850
                             Solemnized 9 June 1850 W B Kelly M G

       J M Wines   &   L V Clark   14 Decr 1850
                             Solemnized 15 Decr 1850 Benjamin Rawls M G

       James I Coleman   &   Margaret J Harrison   23rd Nov 1850
                             Solemnized Benjamin Rawls M G

       W C Pepper   &   E L P Baldry   3rd Decr 1850
                             Solemnized 5 Decr 1850 W L Baldry Gospel Minister

       L B James   &   N A Cobb   9 Nov 1850
                             Solemnized Nov 10 1850 P Martin L D

       James L Pride   &   P E Porter   4 May 1850
                             Solemnized 23rd June 1850 Thos. W Ruffin J P

       W L Frey   &   Lucy J Fountain   9 Jay. 1851
                              Solemnized   _____

       John Allsbrook   &   Polly Booker   8 Jany. 1851
                             Solemnized M C Banks J P

       Vincent W Pitt   &   E A Willis   6 Jay 1851
                             Solemnized 8 Jay. 1851 Joseph Willis Minister of
                                                              the Gospel
(191) Cornelius Doss   &   Lucy Aiken   4 July 1851
                             Solemnized 8 July 1851 W L Baldry Gospel Minister

       William Burgess   &   Martha Murphy   8 May 1851
                             Solemnized 9 May 1851 R G Cole J P

       C W Campbell   &   Caroline Wilson   17 May 1851
                             Solemnized   Robert Green J P

     · James H Doyel   &   Polly Ann Choat   30 Decr 1850
                             Solemnized 3 Jan. 1851 John Crafford J P

       Griffin Gunn   &   Sarah A Winn   18 February 1851
                             Solemnized 20 Feb. 1851 J M Gunn J P

       James Brakefield   &   Susan Harris   11 January 1851
                             Solemnized   G B Mason a justice of peace

       Alfred J Rose   &   Martha A Harris   31st March 1851
                             Solemnized   G B Mason J P

       W H Green   &   Amanda Binkley   18th. Nov 1850
                             Solemnized Nov 20 1850 John Craffors J P

(192) C J Norris   &   E L Mc Henry   16 Oct 1850
                             Solemnized Oct 17, 1850 Mark Senter M. G

       John B Jackson   &   Mary Phipps   29 March 1851
                             Solemnized 31 March 1851 John Crafford J P

Robert J Green   &   Mary C Nave   26 Feby. 1851
                        Solemnized   Thomas Martin M G

Richard M Adams   &   Amanda Morris   29 April 1851
                        Solemnized   James Sprouse J P

Richard A Davis   &   L A Polk   21 April 1851
                        Solemnized J W Featherston

James B Bell   &   Virginia Thomas   12 May 1851
                        Solemnized 13 May 1851 Joseph Willis Minister of
                                                           the Gospel

Henry Keller   &   Martha Pitts   2nd April 1851
                        Solemnized 3 April 1851, Joseph Willis M G

Daniel Johns   &   Rebecca Holland   14 March 1851
                        Solemnized W H Rife J P for Robertson County

(193) Warren Price   &   P Babb   18th March 1851
                        Solemnized 20 March 1851 W H March J P

N Lawrence   &   Elizabeth Daughtery   9 July 1851
                        Solemnized 10 July 1851 James Anderson J P

John L Brown   &   M A Mccarty   30 June 1851
                        Solemnized Thomas Farmer J P

Henry Kirh   &   L V Bowers   14 June 1851
                        Solemnized 15 June 1851 Joseph Willis M G

Lewis Brumbelow   &   Inisey Crutcher   2 June 1851
                        Solemnized 8th June 1851 James Anderson J P

John W Martin   &   Syntha C Parker   18 June 1851
                        Solemnized June 19 1851 Thomas Martin M G

Stephen Choat   &   Rhoda Warren   6 Jany 1851
                        Solemnized 7 June 1851 R G Cole J P

Wm C Shannon   &   Martha W Baggett   23 July 1851
                        Solemnized 24 July 1851 David Henry J P

(194) Hugh Smiley   &   Martha A Harrison   19 July 1851
                        Solemnized 20 July 1851 David Henry Justice of the
                                                                    peace
Ruffin S Flowers   &   Mary C Bell   26 Feby 1851
                        Solemnized   D G Baird J P

Macon Moore   &   Bally Murphy   12 May 1851
                        Solemnized Robert Draughon J P

William L Stephen   &   Melissa A LePrade   11 Jay. 1851
                        Solemnized Tho Watts. M G 15 Jay 1851

Willie Pope   &   H A Adams   28 May 1851
                        Solemnized 29 May 1851 G B Mason J P

James M. Blackburn   &   Mary E Maddox   4 July 1851
                        Solemnized Robert Draughon J P

George W Farmer   &   Julia F Hayes   27 May 1851
                        Solemnized Thomas Farmer Justice of the peace

John Campbell   &   Anna Crunk   30 July 1851
                        Solemnized D M Wells J P

(195) Adam H Frey   &   Dorothy Quin   12 June 1832
                        Solemnized M Powell J P

William Farthing   &   Rachel C Parsons   15 July 1833
                        Solemnized M Powell J P

James L Adams   &   Louisa Gardner   23 Octo. 1834
                        Solemnized M Powell J P

Darby Ryan   &   Milly Farmer   5 June 1834
                        Solemnized M Powell J P

Miles Draughon Jun.   &   Caroline Ann Clark 2 Oct. 1834
                        Solemnized M Powell J P

Henry Dunn   &   Elizabeth Farless   12 Decr. 1830
                        Solemnized M Powell J P

(196) Clement (Noel)Brown & Mary Smith   9 March 1933
                        Solemnized 13 March 1833 M Powell J P

       Joseph W Watts   &   Sally C Green   6 Nov. 1851
                        Solemnized A B Sowyars J P

       Joel Harris   &   Dicy J Walker   20 October 1851
                        Solemnized   A B Sowyars J P

       Wm R Huddleston &   Barbary A Stanley 25 November
                        Solemnized M C Banks J P

       C A Binkley   &   M E Binkley   1 January 1851
                        Solemnized   M C Banks   J P

       J C Holman   &   L A Baggett   30 Nov. 1851
                        Solemnized   David Henry J P

(197) James H Murphy   &   Mary Ann Binkley   4 Dec 1851
                        Solemnized Ro Draughon J P

       J M Suter   &   Mary A Wall   29 Sept 1851
                        Solemnized   Thomas Farmer Justice of the pease
                                           for Robertson Con Tenn.

       Edward Carter   &   Penelope Condway   21 March 1851
                        Solemnized F C Plaster

Wm. Repetoe	&	Nancy Chewning	2 November 1851
		Solemnized J M Henry J P	
R C Lawrence	&	Sarah Head	9 Oct. 1851
		Solemnized J Lorence J P	
Marcus L Jones	&	Mary L Simmons	9 October 1851
		Solemnized WCH Rife J P	
(198) Zaack H Dell	&	Elisa J Powoll	11 Nov 1851
		Solemnized J M Gunn J P	
J H Long	&	Sally Farmer	14 Oct 1851
		Solemnized J Batts J P	
S C Durrett	&	Malinda Gingo (?)	29 Oct 1851
		Solemnized H M Pill J P	
David M Lucas	&	L J Surpt (?)	27 October 1851
		Solemnized H W Pill J P	
A. J. Hunt	&	Elizabeth Sanders	22 October 1849
		Solemnized John Forbes J P	
(199) G. W. Moake	&	H Jackson	15 January 1858
		Solemnized John Forbes J P	
F. M. Thaxton	&	E Everett	14 Sept. 1848
L Richerson	&	R (M) Binkley	
		Solemnized Dec 16 1846 John Forbes J P	
James Winn	&	Dosha Hooper	14 July 1847
		Solemnized John Forbes J P	
(200) Wm. C Sanders	&	Rhoda Hunt	21 Dec 1843
		Solemnized John Forbes J P	
Jonathan Edwards	&	M Lucas (Smith)	24 Dec 1848
		Solemnized John Forbes J P	
F M Grimes	&	A V Barham	5 June 1848
		Solemnized John Forbes J P	
A Martin	&	H Reener	27 Aug. 1851
		Solemnized Thomas Farmer J P	
(201) J Stewart	&	N Harris	6 Dec 1849
		Solemnized John Forbes J P	
W J Gossett	&	E Ayres	8 March 1849
		Solemnized R B Dorris	
John P Dorris	&	E Willson	1 January 1850
		Solemnized R B Dorris	
J P Starks	&	L Baggett	
		Solemnized October 29 1851 T Farmer Justice P	

J W Dickerson   &   E W Richerson   21 Nov 1849
                             Solemnized John Forbes   J P

(202) Carter Roberts   &   V Martin   13 Oct. 1851
                             Solemnized I Steele

       C Conway   &   M Sayle   14 Nov. 1850
                             Solemnized I Steele

       Samuel Campbell   &   V L Barker   3 June 1851
                             Solemnized Isaac Steele

       R I Samuel   &   M J McDonals   15 March 1850
                             Solemnized Isaac Steele

       W. Hawkins   &   M Caudle   15 April 1832
                             Solemnized M Powell J P

       A Mathers   &   B G Murphy   13 October 1831
                             Solemnized M Powell J P

(203) A Gowing   &   M E Huddleston   4 January 1852
                             Solemnized M C Banks

       L C Clayton   &   M A Dorris   26 October 1851
                             Solemnized D G Baird J P

       W P Mathers   &   Harriet Rice   11 January 1852
                             Solemnized B Rawls M G

       R Swan   &   N J Smith   11 April 1851
                             Solemnized Joseph Willis M G

       Wm. R Shepherd   &   E J Grayon   25 Sept 1851
                             Solemnized   D G Baird J P

       T Hughlett   &   L. M. Murrey   17 Dec 1851
                             Solemnized T West, minister

       Henry Newton   &   Nancy Adams   11 Nov. 1851
                             Solemnized W H Adams M G

(204) E Eubank   &   M A White   16 Oct. 1850
                             Solemnized O. H. Morrow Esq. Minister

       L Dunn   &   M L Barnes   8 Jan. 1852
                             Solemnized Robert Draughon J P

       William Powell   &   Mary Price   25 Dec. 1851
                             Solemnized Joseph Willis M G

       J Payne   &   C A Sharp   15 Jan. 1852
                             Solemnized T B Mathews J P

       W. C. Draughon   &   E H Frey   28 Aug. 1851
                             Solemnized T B Mathews J P

H L Ragsdale   &   M A Ragsdale   19 Oct. 1851
                        Solemnized G. B. Mason J P

Wm. Braswell   &   N M Mason   27 Nov 1851
                        Solemnized G B Mason J P

(205)   Isaiah Morris   &   L Frey   23 Dec 1851
                        Solemnized J Sprouse J P

John Ayres   &   M R Willis   10 Dec 1851
                        Solemnized Tho. W felts

R E James   &   M A Williams   21 Jan. 1852
                        Solemnized T W Ruffin J P C

J. B. Harrison   &   M. E. Barham   19 Jan. 1852
                        Solemnized Tho. W Ruffin J P

J. G. Barham   &   M F Rust   20 July 1851
                        Solemnized T W Ruffin J P C

(206)   H Maxy   &   E Walker   29 Jan 1852
                        Solemnized W W Williams J P

J M Eatherly   &   Will L Pitt   27 Jan 1852
                        Solemnized B Randolph J P

C Prine   &   E Smith   15 Jan 1852
                        Solemnized F R Gooch M G

R R Redford   &   E A Traughber   4 Nov. 1851
                        Solemnized D G Baird J P

T M Henry   &   Harriett Gunn   21 Oct. 1851
                        Solemnized Jo Willis M G

J E Morrow   &   An Rosson   5 Feb. 1852
                        Solemnized R. Williams Gospel Minister

Tho. A. Holmes   &   L J Parker   21 Jan. 1851
                        Solemnized Benjamin Rawls M G

(207)   Q R Miles   &   V. A. Darden   26 Nov. 1851
                        Solemnized P. H. Fraser Baptist Minister

C E Peacher   &   I H Darden   10 Feb. 1852
                        Solemnized Robert Williams Gospel Minister

A Farthing   &   W A Jones   20 Nov 1851
                        Solemnized E W Gunn M G

C. A. Hudgins   &   M A C Fortune   29 Oct. 1851
                        Solemnized   P M Frasier Elder Baptist Ch

John R Solomon   &   E Price   1 Feb 1852
                        Solemnized Joseph Willis M G

W W Hopkins   &   M Brasier   29 Nov 1847
                           Solemnized David Henry J P Rob Count

William Fletcher   &   Franses J Dates   10 Jan. 1848
                           Solemnized David Henry Justice of the Peace for
                                             Robertson County

(208) WL Granger   &   S V Jones   10 March 1848
                           Solemnized David Henry J P For Robertson Con

Wm Woodard   &   L Savage   12 Oct. 1848
                           Solemnized D Hering J P Rob County

B Porter   &   Malind Roe   6 Nov. 1848
                           Solemnized David Henry J P R C

T Krisle   &   E Woodard   19 Jan 1850
                           Solemnized Da Henry J P R C

H Cohea   &   M Pitt   19 Nov 1851
                           Solemnized David Hering J P R C

Perry Cohea   &   Mary Benton   23 Dec 1850
                           Solemnized D Hering J P R C

William A Larence   &   O E Helsom(?)
                           Solemnized 28 April 1851 David Hanry J P R C

(209) R O Mantlo   &   H E Roe   22 Aug. 1851
                           Solemnized David Henry J.P.R.C.

E Benton   &   Nancy Powell   31 Aug 1851
                           Solemnized D Hering J P Rob Coun.

J. B. Tarpley   &   J Steel   21 Jan. 1852
                           Solemnized W B Browning

R. D. Richard   &   L L Binkay   11 Feb. 1852
                           Solemnized Isaac Steel

Larnice Fillart   &   Elizabeth Watson   3 Dec 1851
                           Solemnized B. A. Rose M. G.

John Colbren   &   E. A. Conn   30 Oct. 1851
                           Solemnized A. Rose M. G

W.G. Glover   &   P E Wilson   15 June 1852
                           Solemnized A B. Soryers J P

(210) L. F. Felts   &   M Harris   16 Oct 1851
                           Solemnized A B Soyrew J P

J. R. Jones   &   Eliza Baggett   2 Dec. 1851
                           Solemnized R B Dorris

E. P. Grubbs   &   M Dorris   13 Dec 1849
                           Solemnized R B Dorris

C. I. Williams   &   C Warren   2 Dec. 1850
                          Solemnized R B Dorris

Wm B Murry   &   L H Strickland   20 April 1851
                          Solemnized R. B. Dorris

Wm T Sawyers   &   Martha Ewing   11 Sept 1851
                          Solemnized R. B. Dorris

(211) L. M Tucker   &   M Bennett   11 Feb 1851
                          Solemnized R. B. Dorris

G. W. Davis   &   E. J. Connel   24 Feb. 1852
                          Solemnized Joseph Willis M. G

William S Shaw   &   F. A. Cattle   24th. Dec. 1849
                          Solemnized 25th. Dec. 1849 Thomas W Felts, Esqr.

John D Reeves   &   Frances V. Kave   22nd. Octr. 1857
                          Solemnized 23rd. Oct. 1857 J. W. Hunt J P

Ge. Brack   &   Rebecca Bobbett   28th May 1851
                          Solemnized June 1st 1851 W. W. Williams J P

Boliver Payne   &   Lydia Woodall   28 Decr 1846
                          Solemnized 31 Decr. 1846 W. L Payne J P

William Stringer   &   Rachel K West   Decr. 27 1851
                          Solemnized Decr. 30 1851 John M Billingsley
                                                  Gospel Minister
(212) General Jackson Gorham & Jamima Ray   Sept. 11 1851
                          Solwmnized Jas. Woodard

Joseph I Freeman   &   Elizabeth Vilott   May 21, 1851
                          Solemnized Jas. Woodard

Ephriam Benton   & Scina Moore   Jany 18th 1851
                          Solemnized Jas. Woodard

Jonathan J Reeves   &   Mary A. E. Moore   May 27th 1851
                          Solemnized J. W. Hunt J P

J. W. Head   &   R A R Harris   9th March 1852
                          Solemnized March 11 1852 J. W. Hunt J P

William Anderson   &   Lutilda Chesser   Decr. 13 1852
                          Solemnized 14 Decr. 1852 J S Hollis J P

John W Williams   &   Margaret A Hackney Jany 1st. 1852
                          Solemnized J Crafford J P

(213) And. J. Frey   &   Julia A Bernard   13th Feby. 1852
                          Solemnized 15 Feby. 1852 P. H. Fraser B. E.

B. F. Reed   &   Mary A Miles   March 2 1852
No return

Joseph I Sherron   &   Mary Maxey   Feby 25th 1852
Solemnized 27 February 1852 W. W. Williams

Wm. W. Payne   &   Emily Steele   28th April 1852
Solemnized James Sprouse J P

I. S. Rosson   &   Sarah V Peck   5th April 1852
Solemnized 7 April 1852 Robert Williams G M

William C Porter   &   Susan O Wilks   4th May 1852
Solemnized 6 May 1852 David Henry J P

J. T. Parson   &   Mary E Bell   1st May 1852
Solemnized 6 May 1852 Joseph Willis M G

(214) M. W. Draughon   &   P B Watson   5th May 1852
Solemnized Robert Draughon J P

A. H. Walker   &   M. A. Johnson   May 9 1852
Solemnized J. W. Hunt J P

Abraham Moudy   &   Priscilla Brazier   2 June 1852
Solemnized Herring J P

James C Craig   &   Elizabeth Redding   30th June 1852
Solemnized 1 July 1852 A. B. Soyars J P

W. H. Couts   &   Lydia A Moore   22 June 1852
Solemnized 23 June 1852 David Herring J P

Samel Osburn   &   Susan I Knight   21 June 1852
Solemnized 4th July 1852 J. S. Hollis J P

L. T. Fiser   &   Martha Stoltz   24th June 1852
Solemnized 27th June 1852 J. Batys J P

Thomas Nipper   &   Mary Mathews   19th June 1852
22 June 1852 L. B. Mathews J P

(215) Geo. B Redding   &   Flora Jane Chadion   28th June 1852
Solemnized Benjamin Rawls

James W Kirtly   &   Martha E Vaughon   1st June 1852
Solemnized James Woodard

Isaac N Luster   &   Annis W Hart   24th July 1852
Solemnized G. B. Mason J P

James Webster   &   Martha Ann Ayrew   July 11 1852
Solemnized J Crafford J P

Grandison McMurry   &   Elvin Clark   12th July 1852
Solemnized James Sprouse J P

Robert M Villines   & Julia Halcomb   July 12 1852
                           Solemnized 13 July 1852 Green Berry Kelly M. G.

John W. Adams   &   Sarah C Crawford   15th july 1822
                           Solemnized 18 July 1852 J. M. Gunn J P

Harris Simmonds   &   Martha I. Felts   9th Aug 1852
                           Solemnized 15th August B. F. Binkley M G.

(216) Frank Duncan   &   Agusta Mantlo   21st Aug 1852
                           Solemnized David Herring J P

James E Pitman   &   Margaret Morrison   17th Aug 1852
                           Solemnized 18 Aug. 1852 J Lawrence J P

William H Long   &   Nancy Biggs   24th Aug 1852
                           Solemnized 25 Aug. 1852 Thos. West Minister

Sol Williams   &   Mary Ann Smith   7th Aug. 1852
                           Solemnized 8th Aug. 1852 T. D. Mathews J P

Richd. Porter   &   Martha J Wilks   17th Aug 1852
                           Solemnized David Henry J P

William Johnson   &   Nancy Vance   11th Aug 1852
                           Solemnized D. M. Wells J P

William Morris   &   Eliza Ann Felts   2 August 1852
                           Solemnized 5 Aug 1852 J W Hunt J P

Baxter Powell   &   Manervis Porter   15th September 1852
                           Solemnized David Herring J P

(217)   James Sherrick   &   Wilmouth Sellers   30th September 1852
                           Solemnized G. B. Mason J P

William Powell   &   Sarah Powell   25 Septemder 1852
                           Solemnized 26th Sept 1852 William Thomas Chowing

Geo. W Pitt   &   Caroline Bagbee   11th Sept 1852
                           Solemnized 12 September 1852 J. C. Barbee J P

Jesse Glisson   &   Martha May   1st September 1852
                           Solemnized 2 Sept. 1852 J. M. Wells J P

Henry Barham   &   Lucy Ann Rust   8th Sept 1852
                           Solemnized 14 Sept 1852 Thos. W Ruffin J P

John Mequair   &   Elizabeth Pond   27th Sept. 1852
                           Solemnized 28 Sept. 1852 Isaac Steel M. G

M. V. Dowlan   &   E. R. H. Williams   6th Sept. 1852
                           Solemnized Benj. Rawls M. G

Frances Boyd   &   Margaret Atkins   13th Sept 1852
                           Solemnized 2 3 Sept. 1852 Robert Williams M. G.

(218)   Joseph L Akin   &   Emaline Smelser   4 Sept 1852
                               Solemnized James Woodard

        James K Polk   &   Maranda A Bell   Oct. 4 1852
                               Solemnized Oct. 6th 1852 L H Gardner H P

        John H Dunn   &   Mary F Gunn   21 Oct 1852
                               Solemnized F. R. Gooch M. G.

        Saml. Byram   &   Ellen Jane Yates   19th Oct 1852
                               Solemnized 20 Oct. 1852 W. H. Rife J P

        W. L.Kemnraugh   &   B. E. P. Terry   18th Oct. 1852
                               Solemnized 20 Oct. 1852 R. F. Ferguson

        Eli McMurry   &   Octovia True   22 Oct. 1852
                               Solemnized 23 Oct. 1852 John Crafford

        Geo. 1 Harris   &   Charlott Eubank   2 Oct 1852
                               Solemnized 7 Oct 1852   _____

        Aaron T Bagby   &   Mary E Connell   19th Oct 1852
                               Solemnized 20 Oct. 1852 J. M. Stemmons

(219)   Joseph Fuqua   &   Susan Binkley   Oct. 14th 1852
                               Solemnized B Rawls M G

        Washington Mathews   &   Martha G Draughon   Oct 20, 1852
                               Solemnized Benj. Rawls M. G.

        George Jenkins   &   Samantha Chandler   Oct. 29 1852
                               Solemnized James Woodard

        Jas. L. McGan   &   M J Warford   Nov 29 1852
                               Solemnized L. R. Dennis M. G.

        Henry J Watta   &   Sarah A Muller   1st Nov 1852
                               Solemnized W vS Baldry JM G

        J. H. Harris   &   Sarah C Parker   5th Nov. 1852
                               Solemnized David Henry J P

        L. B.Brewer   &   Sarah West   29th Nov 1852
                               Solemnized 1st Dec. 1852 Thomas West, Minister

        Henry J Bell   &   Sarah J Mayes   11th Nov. 1852
                               Solemnized 12th Nov. 1852 John Crafford J P

(220)   Thomas Stroder   &   A. E. Desoiberry   4th Nov. 1852
                               Solemnized James Woodard J P

        James H Elliott   &   Martha C Butts   14th Decr. 1852
                               Solemnized D Herring J P

        N. W. Holland   &   E. P. Evans   1st Decr. 1852
                               Solemnized Dec. 2 1852 J.C Barbee J P

John H Rawls   &   Mary J Hinkle   22 Decr. 1852
                                Solemnized H. L. Burney M. G.

David Chandler   &   S. S. Simmons   20th Decr 1852
                                Solemnized Wm. Thomas Chowning J P

George H Garret   &   Nancy L Johnson   16th Decr. 1852
                                Solemnized Thos. N Langford M.G.

E. H. Gardner   &   Catherine Head   20th Decr 1852
                                Solemnized 22 Dec 1852 I Lawrance J P

John Ayres   &   F. O. A. Fry   22 Decr 1852
                                Solemnized F. R. Gooch M. G.

(221)   William Solomon   &   Elizabeth Morris   22 Decr. 1852
                                Solemnized 23 Dec. 1852 Robt. Draughon J P

Elvis Benson   &   Sarah Bigbee   25th Decr. 1852
                                Solemnized 26 Decr 1852 J. C. Barbee J P

William F. Whiteside   &   M.D Hammond   20th Decr 1852
                                Solemnized L. R. Dennis M. G.

Robert Pince   &   Susan Noe   30th Dec. 1852
                                Solemnized J. C. Barbee J P

George W Maxey   &   Martha A Nicholson   7th Decr 1852
                                Solemnized Dec. 9 1852 W. W. Williams J P

F. M. Newton   &   A. P. Chance   25th Decr. 1852
                                No return

R. N. Drake   &   Elizabeth G Ross   8th Decr 1852
                                Solemnized J. M. Noels M. G

William Ward   &   Permila Allen   6th Dec. 1852
                                Solemnized   James Woodard

(222)   Obediah Chandler   &   Rebecca A Crabtree   Jany 6th 1853
                                 Solemnized Wm. Thomas Chowning J P

William S Simmons   &   Milly Doss   Jany 8 1853
                                Solemnized Isaac Steel

John W. Ferguson   &   Martha W Persise   9th Jany. 1853
                                Solemnized L. R Dennis

Joseph Cobb   &   Eliza A Jernigan   13th Jany. 1853
                                Solemnized   D. M. Wells J P

D. S. W. Minns   &   Elizabeth Rose   13th Jany. 1853
                                Solemnized J. W. Mimms

George G Carter   &   M. A. Martin   18th Jany 1853
                         Solemnized Thos. Martin M. G.

James W. Sherros   &   Lucy Barnes   20th Jany. 1853
                         Solemnized J. W. Featherston

Rich. Benton   &   Nancy Binkley   20th Jany 1853
                         Solemnized Robert Draughon J P

(223) R. P. Dozier   &   · Martha Holland   26th Jany 1853
                         Solemnized 27th Jan. 1853 John Gammon M G

John F Mansker   &   Martha P Kiger   27 Jany 1853
                         Solemnized Benj. Rawls M. G.

Reubin C Wrights   &   Mary West   31st January 1853
                         Solemnized 1 Feb. 1853 Thomas West, Minister

Harvey Troughber   &   Martha Ann Davis   7 Feby. 1853
                         Solemnized Jas. Woodard J P

William A Cook   &   Susan M Gorham   2 Feby 1853
                         Solemnized 3 Feby. 1853 David Henry J P

William T Peck   &   Mary E Ellis   7th Feby 1853
                          Solemnized Feby. 10. 1853 Milton Ramey M G

James H Crafford   &   Martha I Wallace   8th Feby. 1853
                         Solemnized J Sprouse J P

R. G. Glover   & Martha E Fountain   9th Feby 1853
                         Solemnized 10 Feby. 1853 Benjamin Rawls

(224) William H Rose   &   Susan Roberts   10th Feby 1853
                         Solemnized J. M. Gunn J P

Danl. Kiger   &   Jane Cannon   15th Feby. 1853
                         Solemnized J. S. Hollis J P

W. H. Nightt   &   Mary Benton   16th Feby 1853
                         Solemnized Benjamin Rawls M. G.

James A House   &   Polly Moore   16th July 1853
                         Solemnized Feby.17 1853 T. W. Felts

James S Williams   &   Maria L Northington   21st Feby 1853
                         Solemnized 23 Feby 1853 Robert Williams G. M.

Reubin Farthing   &   Lucy A Adams   2 March 1853
                         Solemnized 3 March 1853 E. W. Gunn

John F Adames   &   Mary Baggett   2 March 1853
                         Solemnized, James Sprouse J P

Norfleet Pool   &   Tempty Clark   11 March 1853
                         Solemnized March 16 1853 L. R. Dennis M. G

(225) D. L. Johnston   &   Elizabeth C Long   March 12th 1853
                               Solemnized 17th March 1853 L. H. Gardner J P

       Chest. Halloway   &   Elizabeth Ann Adams   March 21, 1853
                               Solemnized 22 March 1853   E. W. Gunn M G

       John W Starke   &   Margaret Powell   March 24 1853
                               Solemnized David Herring J P

       William W Gordon   &   Mary Ann Chapman   March 24th 1853
                               Solemnized 31 March 1853 J. C. Barbee J P

       Milton Green   &   Mariah T Davis   March 27 1853
                               Solemnized W. W. Pepper Judge of the 7th.
                                                          Circuit of Tennessee

       Alsey Babb   &   Susan McIntosh   31st March 1853
                               Solemnized Isaac Steele

       Thomas H Warren   &   Eliza E Rigsbee   Apr. 2 1853
                               Solemnized April 10 1853 Daniel Mullory J P

       Alexander Norris   &   Clirinda Chambers   April 5th 1853
                               Solemnized Robert Williams J P

(226) John F England   &   Susan I Tucker   April 7 1853
                               Solemnized James Sprouse J P

       James Vaughon   &   Matilda Broderick   April 9th 1853
                               Solemnized J Lawrence   J P

       Spencer H Page   &   Mary Jane Pince   April 9 1853
                               Solemnized 12 April 1853 J C Barbee J P

       W. A. Pinson   &   Charity E Wallace   April (1853
                               Solemnized 10 April 1853 John Crafford J P

       Thomas Woodard   &   Eliza I Ryan   April 13 1853
                               Solemnized David Henry J P

       Franklin Stark   &   Martha Pitt   April 14 1853
                               Solemnized David Henry J P

       Benjamin Suddoth   &   Nancy Starks   April 24 1853
                               Solemnized Jas. Wppdard J P

(227) Thomas Crowder   &   Martha Brandon   April 28th 1853
                               Solemnized _____

       Robert T Farley   &   Zelica V Gossett   April 30 1853
                               Solemnized May 3 1853 L.R Dennis M. G.

       William F Benton   &   Nancy E Willson   May 13, 1853
                               Solemnized 15 May 1853 W. D. Baldwin V. D. M.

       John Webb   &   Amanda Ervin   May ;6 1853
                               Solemnized May 18 1853 James Sprouse J P

Isiah Glover   &   Mary A. E. Douglass   May 23 1853
                      Solemnized 26 May 1853   Robert Williams J P

James W Villines   &   Lydia K Strother   May 27 1853
                      Solemnized 29 May 1853   W. H. Rife J P

Jackson Phipps   &   Angeline Holmes   May 30
                      Solemnized May 31 1853   John Crafford J P

(228) John F Lawrence   &   Harriet Dunn   June 14 1853
                      Solemnized June 5 1853 T. H. Gardner J P

Asa Harper   &   Lydia M Zeck   June 10th 1853
                      Solemnized 11 June 1853 John Crafford J P

Josiah Turner   &   Eliza Godard   June 13 1853
                      Solemnized I Lawrence J P

M B Pitman   &   Mary K Morrison   June 15tj 1853
                      Solemnized I Lawrence J P

W. H. Willis   &   Martha W Simmons   June 30th 1853
                      Solemnized Isaac Steel

Elisha Hollins   &   Susan E Villines   July 8 1853
                      Solemnized July 13 1853   W. F. Hickman M. G.

Hiram Bell   &   Julia Graffprd   Julu 11 1853
                      Solemnized W. B. Baldwin V. D. M.

David F Sharp   &   Nancy A Dunn   July 11 1853
                      Solemnized Robert Draughon J P

(229) John W Woodard   &   Mary J Dycus   Feby. 14 1853
                      Solemnized J. W. Featherston M. G

Joseph Broderick   &   Amanda Escue   July 16 1853
                      Solemnized 17 July 1853 David Henry J P

Robert H Murphy   &   Ann E Braden   18 July 1853
                      Solemnized L. R. Dennis M. G.

Francis C Criswell   &   George Ann Thomas   26th July 1853
                      Solemnized   J. M. Gunn J P

Benjamin H Anderson   &   Sarah J Porter   July 28 1853
                      Solemnized July 30 1853   Benjamin Rawls M. G.

G. W. Dorris   &   Nancy Clayton   July 28 1853
                      Solemnized   _____

John H Benton   &   Martha Ann Willson   Aug 2 1953
                      Solemnized Aug. 4 1853 Peter Hinkle Esq.

William Escue   &   Susan Warren   Aug. 5 1853
                      Solemnized 7 August 1853 David Henry J P

(230)   John E. Phelps   &   Lucinda Ury   Aug 7 1853
                                 Solemnized   Isaac Steele

        William W Felts   &   Martha J Hunt   Aug 9 1853
                                 Solemnized Aug. 11 1853 Robert Williams J P

        P. E. Herndon   &   S. I. Venable   Aug. 15 1853
                                 Solemnized W. W. Pepper, Judge

        D. C. Herndon   &   Bettie A Butler   Aug 15 1853
                                 Solemnized W. W. Pepper, Judge

        Richard VanHook   &   Cynthia Payne   Aug. 18 1853
                                 Solemnized 19 Aug. 1853 T. H. Gardner J P

        William R Vick   &   Margaret A Grayson   Aug 19, 1953
                                 Solemnized 21 Aug. 1853 J. C. Barbee J P

        John Holland   &   Pricilla Jackson   Aug 20 1853
                                 Solemnized 23 Aug 1853 W. L. Baldry M. G.

        D. C. Blackburn*   &   Emily C Jackson   Aug. 31, 1953
                                 Solemnized F. C. Plaster, Paster of Red River
                                                              church
(231)   James M. Rawls   &   A. A. Parker   Sept. 4 1853
                                 Solemnized Thomas Martin

        James Ryan   &   Martha Stone   Sept. 15 1853
                                 Solemnized 11 Sept. 1853 W. L. Chowning J P

        Burrel Featherston   &   Sophia Hart   Sept. 10 1853
                                 Solemnized 11 Sept. 1853 James Woodard J P

        Thomas R Wright   &   Susan Ham   Sept. 12 1853
                                 Solemnized 13 Sept. 1853 John H Gammon M. G
        E. W. Hammond   &   Susan Clark   Sept 17 1853
                                 Solemnized David Henry J P

        Alfred Winset   &   Louisa Farmer   Sept. 22 1853
                                 Solemnized J Lawrence J P

        Robert G Cook   &   Mary J England   Sept 23 1853
                                 Solemnized W L Chowning J P

        R. A. Poor   &   E. A. Barbee   Sept. 26 1853
                                 Solemnized 27th September 1853 E. W. Gunn M. G

(232)   J. H. Huglett   &   Susan Payne   1st Oct 1853
                                 Solemnized 4 Oct. 1853 Thos. West M. G

        R. L. Mathews   &   Tennessee White   1st. Oct. 1853
                                 Solemnized 2nd. Nov.1853 Robert Draughon J P

        Saml. Page   &   Louisa Pankey   4th Oct. 1853
                                 Solemnized J. H. Gammon M. G.

Henry Nimoue   &   Sarah Long   9th Oct. 1853
                                Solemnized   John M Billingsly Gospel Minister

Joseph J Edwards   &   Sarah Frances Morgan   Oct. 7 1853
                                Solemnized Jo Lawrence J P

E. P. Warren   &   C Ann White   13th Oct. 1853
                                Solemnized   John K Woodson M. G.

William E. Willis   &   Emaline Keller   13th Oct 1853
                                Solemnized Jas. Woodard J P

(233) Geor. R. Head   &   J. F. Moore   21 Oct 1853
                                Solemnized   Jo Lawrence J P

G. N. Baugh   &   M. V. Booker   21st. Oct 1853
                                Solemnized James Woodard J. P.

James Cooper   &   W. E. Touman   22 Oct. 1853
                                Solemnized Oct. 24 1853 G. B. Mason J P

Saml. J Lett   &   Eliza Traughber   26th Oct 1853
                                Solemnized 28th Oct 1853 James Woodard J P

W. W. Maguire   &   Mary A Chisum   Oct. 26 1853
                                Solemnized 27th Oct. 1853 M. Hodge M. G.

W. L. Smith   &   R. E. Ruffin   29th Oct 1853
                                Solemnized 30th. Oct. 1853 Robt. Draughon J P

D. Ashabranah   &   E. R. Williams   27 Oct 1853
                                Solemni zed 28th Oct. 1853 Jas. Woodard J P

David Fisher   &   Mary Flood   2 Nov. 1853
                                Solemnized 3 Nov. 1853 J. C. Barbee J P

(234) Joel Adcock   &   Fanny Shoecraft   9th Nov. 1853
                                Solemnized James Anderson J P

W. B. Langston   &   S. C. Donaldson   Nov 10th 1853
                                Solemnized 15th Nov. 1853 Thos. J Fort. J.P.

William Night   &   Mary Shelton   Nov 10th 1853
                                Solemnized Peter Hinkle J P

Isaac W Rust   &   Elizabeth Dillard   Nov. 10th 1853
                                Solemnized H. C. Plaster Minister of Gospel

R. M. C. Holland   &   Martha A Wells   Nov 14th 1853
                                Solemnized 17 Nov. 1853 John H Gammon M G

E. B. Eidson   &   Susan Browning   Nov. 22 1853
                                Solemnized B. Rawls M G

Jesse J Rawls   &   Lucinda E Gooch   Nov 23 1853
                                Solemnized B. Rawls M. G

A. W. Kiser   &   M. A. E. Duke   Nov. 23 1853
                                Solemnized 27 Nov. 1853 J. B. Walton

(235) Thomas Woodard   &   Mineva J Perry   Nov. 23 1853
                               Solemnized 24 Nov 1853 R. Green J P

       William R. Dorris   &   W. M. Blackburn   Nov 26, 1853
                               Solemnized 27 Nov 1853 J. C. Barbee J P

       John Garrett   &   Mary Jane Crafton   Nov 29 1853
                               Solemnized Francis Johnston

       W. W. Garrett   &   Margaret H Johnson   Nov. 29 1853
                               Solemnized B. M. Stephens

       Jeremiah Pitt   &   Peruissa Holman   Mov 29 1853
                               1 Dec. 1853 David Henry J P

       William L Mathews   &   S. A. M.Murphy   Nov 30 1853
                               Solemnized 1 Dec. 1853 L. B. Mathews J P

       Thomas B. Harris   &   Sarah A Woodruff   5th Dec. 1853
                               Solemnized B. Rawls M. G.

       Robert P Wilson   &   H. P. Sprouse   7th. Decr. 1853
                               Solemnized David Henry J P

(236) William Ledbetter   &M. W. Elliott   Decr 12, 1853
                               Solemnized 14 Dec. 1853 Robert Williams J P

       James J Dorris   &   Sarah Watson   Decr. 12 1853
                               Solemnized 13 Dec. 1853 W. D. Baldwin V.D.M.

       B. N. Swan   &   N. M. Brewer   Decr. 15th 1853
                               Solemnized W. H. Rife J. P.

       W. H. Ashbrand   &   Amanda Traughber   18 Decr. 1853
                               Solemnized Jas. Woodard J P

       John G Benton   &   Martha Murphy   18 Decr 1853
                               Solemnized F. R. Gooch M. G.

       James W. Harris   &   Martha Follis   18 Decr. 1853
                               Solemnized A Ros M. G.

       Richd. L Smith   &   Lucy Ann Young   19 Decr. 1853
                               Solemnized Thos. Bottomley M. G.

       James B. Babb   &   Caroline Wilson   19 Decr. 1853
                               Solemnized W. H. Rife J P

(237) W. H. Wilson   &   Susan P Wilson   21st Decr 1853
                               Solemnized B. W. Bradley J P

       James B Smelser   &   Elizabeth P Holman   21 Decr 1853
                               Solemnized 22 Decr. 1853 Robert Green J P

       William J Chandler   &   Nancy J Pepper   22 Decr 1853
                               Solemnized David Henry J P

Robert F. Warren   &   H. A. A. Tennison   22 Decr 1853
                          Solemnized Solemnized G Tanison M. G.

W. A. Smith   &   Mary J Wilkerson   23 Decr 1853
                          Solemnized David Herring J P

John K Johnson   &   Martha Johnson   24th Decr 1853
                          Solemnized L. B Marhews J P

F. M. Woodard   &   Catherine Woodard   · 24th Devr. 1853
                          Solemnized 25 Decr. 1853 David Henry J P

Richd. Powell   &   Susan Benton   24 Decr 1853
                          Solemnized* John Crafford J P

(238) William Traughber   &   Elizabeth Cook   26 Decr. 1853
                          Solemnized Jas. Woodard J P

       Isaac Barr   &   Elvina Cook   27 Decr. 1853
                          Solemnized 29 Decr. 1853 O.H.Morrow M. G.

       John G. Harrison   &   E. S. Freland   30th. Decr. 1853
                          Solemnized F. L. Plaster Gospel Minister

       G. B. Clayton   &   Olive Smith   31 Decr. 1853
                          Solemnized 1 Jan. 1854 J. C. Barbee J P

       J. C. Winters   &   Susan P Hawkins   2 Jany 1854
                          Solemnized 18 Jan. 1854 P. H. Fraser B. E.

       James C Holmes   &   Elizabeth Bradley   2 Jany 1854
                          Solemnized 4 January 1854 Robert Williams J P

       S Wilson   &   A. MCMurry   · 5th Jany. 1854
                          Solemnized 6 Jany. 1854 W. D. Baldwin V. D. M.

       William Duncan   &   D. Powell   7th Jany 1854
                          Solemnized 8 Jan. 1854 David Herring J P

(239) J. E. Pride   &   Gracy J Moore   7 Jany 1854
                          Solemnized J Lawrence J P

       James Vantress   &   Julia Glover   9 Jany 1854
                          Solemnized 10 Jany. 1954 Robert Williams J P

       R. A. Mart   &   F. S. Atkinson   11 Jany 1854
                          Solemnized 12th 1854 _____

       W. F. Cunningham   &   Mary A Baldry   12 Jany 1854
                          Solemnized W. L. Baldry M. G.

       David Featherston &   Susan Crafford   13th Jany 1854
                          Solemnized David Herring J P

       Morgan Shephard   &   Eliza Dillard   14th Jany 1854
                          Solemnized J Lawrence J P

T. W. Honeycut   &   Emily W Edison   16th Jany 1854
                          Solemnized   John Crafford J P

Saml. Slack   &   Sally Shurron   17th Jany 1854
                          Solemnized 19th Jan. 1854 G. B. Walton

(240) J. W. Crockeyy   &   Harriet Rawls   21 Jany 1854
                          Solemnized 22 Jany. 1854 Robert Draughon J P

Geo. Murphy   &   Susan Portor   31 Jany 1054
                          Solemnized 22 Jany 1854 Robt. Draughon J P

John Ledbetter   &   Nancy Powell   30 Jany 1854
                          Solemnized 31 Jany. 1854 Robert Williams J P

Quincy Adams Ely   &   M. A. Douglas   28th Feby 1854
                          Solemnized James Anderson J P

W. A. Watson   &   Lourina Stovall   1st Feby 1854
                          Solemnized G. B. Mason J P

Joseph J Forbes   &   Martha Gent   7 Feby 1854
                          Solemnized 9th Feby. 1854 B.F.Bihkley M. G.

R. G. Bell   &   E. M. Gunn   7th. Feby 1854
                          Solemnized Feby 8th 1854 F. R. Gooch M. G.

James H Long   &   Mary Ann Darden   9th Feby 1854
                          Solemnized 8th February 1854 F. R. Gooch M.G.

(241) W. W. Fry   &   Martha Ann Morris   11th Feby 1854
                          Solemnized J. B. Walton

Charles Reasons   &   Sarah E. F. Pitman   28th Feby 1854
                          Solemnized   J Lawrence J P

James Crafton   &   Mary Caudle   24th Feby 1854
                          Solemnized 28th Feby. 1854 W. M. C. Barr J P

John B Herndon, Sr.   &   Eliza Q Atkison   21st Feby 1854
                          Solemnized F. C. Paster

David Hyde   &   Genetta Ray   20th. Feby 1854
                          Solemnized 21th Feby. 1854 B. F. Binkley M.G.

R. S. Demunbro   &   Sarah L Binkley   20th Feby 1854
                          Solemnized 25th Feby. 1854 B. F. Bibkley M. G.

Jackson V Holland   &   Olevia Robertson   28th. Feby 1854
                          Solemnized Feby. 23 1854 Jesse H. Gammon M. G.

John R. Ridges   &   Sally A David   14th Feby. 1854
                          Solemnized 16th Feby. 1854 B. M. Stephens M. G.

(242) Marion Magee   &   Nancy A Woodard   2 March 1854
                             Solemnized F. R. Gooch M. G.

       John L Felts   &   Elizabeth Reed   3 March 1854
                             Solemnized 9th March 1854 F. R. Gooch M. G.

       Jos. Haynes   &   Mary Ann Murphy   11th March 1854
                             Solemnized 12 March 1854 F. R. Gooch M. G.

       Kelly Shannon   &   Luiosa Lucas   13 March 1854
                             Solemnized M. T. Chowning J. P.

       John Graves   &   Mar____ Harris   24th March 1854
                             Solemnized 25th March 1854 M. D. Baldwin V. .D.M.

       Alex Robertson   &   Elizabeth H Johess   23 March 1854
                             Solemnized 28th March 1854 F. R. Gooch M. G.

       Joshua I Jones   &   A. P. Newton   16th March 1854
                             Solemnized F. R. Gooch M.G.

       John Elmore   &   Elizabeth Johes   23 March 1854
                             Solemnized James Sprouse J P

(243) John A Bough   &   M.I. Blanchard   2 April 1854
                             Solemnized James Woodard J P

       Henry Kiger   &   Alineda E Rawls   4th April 1854
                             Solemnized April 5th 1854 J. D. Hollis J P

       Robt. B Murrah   &   Mary Morgan   11th April 1854
                             Solemnized Jas Woodard J P

       Hartwell Allen   &   Eliza Payne   29th April 1854
                             Solemnized J. H. Gammon

       Saml. B. Brown   &   Ann I Baird   11th April 1854
                             Solemnized Isaac Steel

       Lemuel Pepper   &   E. W. Glover   25th April 1854
                             Solemnized W. D. Baldwin M.V.D.

       W. P. Adkins   &   Rebecca M Morrison   21st April 1854
                             Solemnized April 23 1854 W. R. Saddler J P

       W. F. Pride   &   B. I. Mason   12th April 1854
                             Solemnized 13 April 1854 F. R. Gooch M. G.

(244) James W Parkinson   &   Catherine Spayne   15th April 1854
                             Solemnized Jesse B White J P

       James Moon   &   Elizabeth Bennett   8th May 1854
                             Solemnized May May 11th 1854 F. C. Blaster

       Levi Smith   &   M. A. Polk   15th May
                             Solemnized 17th May 1854 Robt. Williams G.M.

Saml. Riley	& Elizabeth Smiley	15th May 1854

Solemnized   John Crafford

Arch. Blackburn	& Martha Jordan	17th May 1854

Solemnized   Jas. Woodard J P

Jasper N Clark	& Clara E Baggett	17th May 1854

Solemnized May 18th 1854 James Cook J P

Thomas E Morris	& Elizabeth Mathews	17th May 1854

Solemnized 18th May 1854 F. R. Gooch M. G.

Harry Westen	& Jane Sams	21st May 1854

No return

(245) | Thomas Walker | & Delila Harris | 24th May 1854 |
|---|---|---|

Solemnized 25th May 1854 W. W. Williams J P

Ramsey Wrights	& Mary House	31st May 1854

Solemnized 2 June 1854 W. M. C. Barr J P

Willie L Draughon	& C. L. Clark	11th June 1854

Solemnized B. Rawls M. G.

Isaac L Winters	& Martha M Clark	12th. June 1854

Solemnized 22 June 1854 B. W. Bradley J P

George Rigsbee	& Elemore Phibbs	3 July 1854

Solemnized 4 July 1854 A. Rose J P

Thomas Nipper	& Martha A N Mathews	4th July 1854

Solemnized T. B. Mathews J P

Allen Jones	& Adaline Porter	5th July 1854

Solemnized 6 July 1854 A. Rose J P

Isaac C Dorris	& Pricilla Choat	15th July

Solemnized 16 July 1854 J. R. Gunn J P

(246) | S. S. Covington | & Eveline E McMillon | 15th July 1854 |
|---|---|---|

Solemnized 16 July 1854 W. T. Chowning J P

James R. Davis	& Eliza Hughlett	17th July 1854

Solemnized 20 July 1854 Benjamin Gambell J P

James N Winters	& Julia M Crutcher	17th July 1854

Solemnized 30 July 1854 Jesse B White J P

Richard Murphy	& Mary A. E. Elliott	27th July 1854

Solemnized Robert Williams J P

James C Stone	& Susan McCarley	2 August 1854

Solemnized 3 August 1854 J W.T. Chowning J.P.

John Sellers	& Elizabeth Newton	10th August 1854

Solemnized F. R. Gooch M. G.

Silvester F Webb   &   Judian I. Boiswell   15th August 1854
                        Solemnized 17 August 1854 Robert Ferguson M.G.

Z. A. Bradford   &   Mary Harris   17th August 1854
                        Solemnized Aug. 20 1854 A. I. Brights J O

(247) Eli Jones   &   Arena C Gorham   23 Aug. 1854
                        Solemnized 24 August 1854   David Henry J P

Henry P Murrah   &   Mary Ann Felts   25th Aug. 1854
                        Solemnized 30th August 1854 Robert Williams J P

C.W. Crawford   &   Elvira R. Anglin   26th Aug 1854
                        Solemnized 27 Aug. 1854 John K Woodard M. G.

Green B Wrights   &   Ellen C Berry   26th Aug. 1854
                        Solemnized 29th August 1854 W. M. C. Barr J P

Miles T Barughon   &   Loretts Solomon   26th Aug. 1854
                        Solemnized 27th Aug. 1854 G Benton J P

James H Nimmo   &   Frances Huglett   4th Sept. 1854
                        Solemnized 6th Sept. 1854 Benjamin Gambill J P

Toliver Hughlett   &   Milly Murry   4th Sept 1854
                        Solemnized 6 Sept 1854 Benjamin Gambill J P

Robert G. Wilson   &   Nancy A. H. Adams   8th. Sept 1854
                        Solemnized   Jas. Woodard J P

(248) Andrew J Cook   &   Eva J Burchett   9th Sept. 1854
                        Solemnized 10th Sept. 1854 David Henry J P

William Gatewood   &   Elizabeth S Hunt   9th Sept 1854
                        Solemnized Sept. 13 1854 L. C. Bryan M. G.

William Holt   &   E.A.Marshall   11th Sept. 1854
                        Solemnized Sept 14, 1854 Elisha Luter M. G.

Kinchen Woodard   &   America N Fry   14th Sept 1854
                        Solemnized J. B. White J P

R. P.Aull   &   Sarah E Atkinson   15th Septr. 1854
                        No return

Wesley M Jernigan   &   Harriet Berry   20th Sept 1854
                        Solemnized 21st Sept. 1854 Thomas West, Minister

William Watson   &   Jane Stratton   29th Sept 1854
                        Solemnized Octr. 1 1854 G. B. Masom J P

J. E. Ruffin   &   Sarah R. E. Batts   30th Sept. 1854
                        Solemnized Oct. 7th 1854 W. S. Adams J O

****

(249) George R Link   &   Amanda Williams   6th Oct 1854
                               Solemnized Daniel Mulloy J P

       James Traughber   &   Caroline Drane   6th Octr. 1854
                               Solemnized Isaac Steel

       D. A. Archey   &   Louisa S Allen   10th Octr. 1854
                               Solemnized 16 Oct. 1854 Robert Williams G. M.

       John MacKafee   &   Mary Anderson   16th Octr. 1854
                               Solemnized 17th Octr. 1854 John Crafford J P

       Henry Heysmight   &   Nancy Adams   17th Octr. 1854
                               Solemnized October 19 1854 G. B. Mason J P

       James W Glover   &   Angeline Bracy   21st Octr 1854
                               Solemnized 27 Octr. 1854 Robert Williams J P

       C. H. Browning   &   Amanda Porter   30th Octr 1854
                                Solemnized David Henry J P

       Coleman Boyd   &   Eliza Ann Sayles   30th Octr. 1854
                               Solemnized 31 October k854 G. B. Mason J P

(250) James Mayes   &   Margaret Adams   1 Novr. 1854
                               Solemnized John Crafford J P

       Charles Campbell   &   Janes Edwards   4th Nov. 1854
                               Solemnized 5 Nov 1854 Jesse B. White J P

       Samuel Durham   &   Nancy M. Winters   6th Nov 1854
                               Solemnized 9 Nov. 1854 B. W. Bradley J P

       James Spain   &   Mary Ann Reeder   14th Nov 1854
                               Nov. 16 1854 J. T. Craig J P

       Stokley Cook   &   Amanda Lucas   17 Nov 1854
                               Solemnized 19 Nov 1854 David Henry J P

       James L Davis   &   Lettia M Thomas   25th Nov. 1854
                               Solemnized 26 Nov. 1854 W. W. Pepper Judge & c

       James M Newland   &   Mary Ann Dickerson   28th Nov 1854
                               Solemnized 30 Decr. 1854 Robert Williams J P

       Albert Rogers   &   Andeline Blackburn   30th Nov 1854
                               Solemnized 1 Dec. 1854 Benjamin Gambell J P

(251) J. I. Clark   &   Frances Winters   30th Nov 1854
                               Solemnized 5 Decr. 1854 B. W. Bradley J P

       Saml. P. Markham   &   Susan R Hardaway   2 Decr 1854
                               Solemnized 21 Decr. 1854 Saml. D Ogburn

       James R Mason   &   Clemantine Danks   4th Decr 1854
                               Solemnized James Woodard

James W Pike   &   Meriah A Parker   7th Decr 1854
                       Solwmnized J. S. Hollis J P

Robert F. P. Trimble   &   Nancy B Ashuranah   8th Decr. 1854
                        Solemnized Benjamin Gambill J P

J. M. Slack   &   Lucretia Basford   11th Decr. 1854
                       Solemnized 14 Decr. 1854 J. B. Walton

D.C. Hockersmith   &   Virginia L.Darden   13th Decr. 1854
                       Solemnized 14 Dedr. 1854 Samuel D. Ogburn M.G

Isaac Fraser   &   Mary I Fraser   15th Decr. 1854
                       Solemnized 21 Dec. 1854 William L Baldry G.M.

(252) P.A.Williams   &   M artha Williams   15th Decr. 1854
                       Solemnized B. W. Bradley J P

Richard Shannon   &   Ann E. Chamberlain   16th Decr. 1854
                       Solemnized John F.Hughes

Andrew D. Walton   &   Mary E Norfleet   18th Decr 1854
                       Solemnized Decr. 19 1854 L.H Gardner J P

Paterick Moore   &   Mary Ann Bennett   18th Decr. 1854
                       Solemnized 20 Decr 1854 F. C. Plaster

James H Mallory   &   E. A. Wimberly   19th Decr 1854
                       Solemnized 20 Decr 1854 F. C. Plaster

Elijah Warren   &   Frances England   20th Decr. 1854
                       Solemnized 21 Decr. 1854 James Cook J P

Saml. Conway   &   Rachel C Green   21st Decr 1854
                       Solemnized Samuel D Ogburn

William H Edwards   &   Manervia Ann Frey   22 Decr 1854
                       Solemnized Decr. 24 1854 G. B. Mason J P

(253) James B Pitt   &   Mary Ann Cook   23rd. Decr 1854
                       Solemnized. 25 Decr. 1854 Benjamin Gambill J P

Alexander Robertson   &   Zerilda E Frey   26th Decr 1854
                       Solemnized 27th Decr. 1854 F. R. Gooch G. M.

Simeon Clinard   &   Julia Parker   26th Decr. 1854
                       Solemnized B Rawls M. G.

William D Rust   &   Synthia A Hysmith   27th Decr 1854
                       Solemnized Jan. 4 1855 G. R. Mason

Thomas W Taylor   &   Sarah West   28th Decr. 1854
                       Solemnized Thomas West M. G.

E. L. Durrett   &   Medora Clark   29th Decr 1854
                       Solemnized 31 Decr. 1854 C. B. Davis M. G.

Washington Walton   &   Mary Pitt   29th Decr 1854
                     Solemnized 31 Dec. 1854   David Henry J P

Christopher Manlove   &   Sarah A. I. Haraway   30th Decr 1854
                     Solemnized   G. Benton J P

(254)   John Phipps   &   Elizabeth Williams   Jany 1st. 1855
                     Solemnized 7 Jany 1855   John Crafford J P

William H Hensle   &   Sarah E Fisher   Jay. 1st 1855
                     Solemnized 4 Jan/ 1855   David Hanry J P

R. S. Henry   &   Sarah E Purtle   1st January 1855
                     Solemnized   S. D. Ogburn

James E Worsham   &   Louisa Cobb   1st January 1855
                     Solemnized W. H. Hynnes

Chesterfield G Rust   &   Mary E. M. Smith   1st, January 1855
                     Solemnized   C. Farthing J P

William P Wynn   &   Sarah I Fry   1st January 1855
                     Solemnized F. R. Gooch M. G.

James Robertson   &   Evaline Burrus   5th January 1855
                     Solemnized Hobert Williams   J P

W. I. Walker   &   Virginia F. Williams   6th January 1855
                     Solemnized 18th Jan. 1855   W. I. Cooleu M.G.

(255)   William H Riggan   &   Martha I Jernigan   9th January 1855
                     Solemnized 10th Jan. C. B. Davis M. G.

John K Brinkley   &   Lucy E Ellison   10th January 1855
                     Solemnized 18 Jan. 1855   C. F. Lucas   J P

Wm. I Grigsby   &   Nancy L Gooch   11th Jany. 1855
                     Solemnized F. R. Gooch M. G.

Thos. Jefferson McMurry &   Louisa Frey   11th January **1855**
                     Solemnized   W. H. Chowning J P

Dempsey House   &   Margert Edwards   13th January 1855
                     Solemnized 14 Jan. 1855 G. W. Featherston,   pel
                           a regular ordained Minister of the Gos-

G. H. M. Gampton   &   Susan C Jones   17th January 1855
                     Solemnized 18 Jan. 1855   David Henry J P

W. C. Cmith   &   Fannie E Howard   22 January 1855
                     Solemnized 23 Jan. 1855   G. R. Gunn J P

L. S. Randolph   &   Lucretia Nicholson   23 January 1855
                     Solemnized 1 Feby. 1855 W. W. Williams J P

(256) A. I. Wynn   &   Martha A Wynn   31st Jany. 1855
                                 Solemnized 1 Feby. 1855   W. S. Baldry M. G.

       Joseph Rawls   &   Margaret Fuqua   5th Feby 1855
                                 Solemnized Benjamin Rawls M. G.

       James S Dunn   &   Sophia G Couts   5th. Feby. 1855
                                 Solemnized 7th Feby. 1855 F. C. Plaster

       William Durham   &   Pricilla Murphy   6th Feby 1855
                                 Solemnized 9 Feby. 1855   B. W. Bradley J P

       Walter I Price   &   Adeline Henderson   8th Feby. 1855
                                 Solemnized F. R. Gooch M. G.

       J. A. Eckles   &   G. P. Hockersmith   9th Feby. 1855
                                 Solemnized 11th Feb. 1855 Saml. D. Ogburn M. G

       W. B. Jones   &   Hulda A Binkley   10th Feby 1855
                                 Solemnized Thos. Martin M. G.

       Henry Maxey   &   Mary Ann Wilson   10th Deby 1855
                                 Solemnized 15 Feby 1855   W. W. Williams J P

(257) William D White   &   Mary R Briggs   12th February 1855
                                 Solemnized 12 Feb. 1855   J. M. Copeland J P

       W. H. C. Murphy   &   Martha A Morgan   13th Feby 1855
                                 Solemnized 14 Feb. 1855 Robert Williams J P

       James M Conner   &   Ellen F Crawfprd   13th February 1855
                                 Solemnized 15 Feby. 1855 F. C. Plaster Minister
                                                          of Baptist Church

       John C Murphy   &   Mary England   14th February 1855
                                 Solemnized 15 Feb. 1855   James Cook J P

       Frederick A Mayes   &   Mary Ward   17th February 1855
                                 Solemnized 18th. Feby. F. R. Gooch M. G.

       Andrew F Price   &   Mary E Page   24th Feby. 1855
                                 Solemnized G. B. Mason J. P

       W. I. Benton   &   Angeline Binkley   28th Feby 1855
                                  Solemnized G. Benton J P

       James C Vick   &   Dorcus P Dunn   2 March 1855
                                 Solemnized Sam. D Ogburn M. G.

(258) M. T. Robertson   &   Martha Stone   3 March 1855
                                 Solemnized 10 March 1855 F. R. Gooch M. G.

       W. T. Smith   &   Caroline Sherrod   3 March 1855
                                 Solemnized 4 March 1855 B. B. Batts J P

       Thos. I Jones   &   Emily F Huskey   3 March 1855
                                 Solemnized 6 March 1855 A. M. Greer J P

Byram Boakfield   &   Martha Harris   5th March 1855
                         Solemnized 6 March 1855 W. S. Baldry M. G.

B. W. Edwards   &   Narcissa Edwards   9th March 1855
                         Solemnized 10 March 1855   G. R. Gunn J P

William Thompson   &   Caroline Dorris   9th March 1855
                         Solemnized A. Rose J P

W. I. Dunn   &   Louisa Stolts   17th March 1855
                         Solemnized 18 March 1855   J Byrns J P

M. L Kellebrew   &   M. E. Laprade   2 April 1855
                         Solemnized 27 April 1855 F. C. Plaster

(259) William Armstrong &   Rebecca Chapman   3 April 1855
                         Solemnized 6 April 1855 Benjamin Gambell J P

E. R. Mosley   &   Mary E Weldon   5th April 1855
                         Solemnized S. D. Ogburn M. G.

William Swift   &   Susan Robins   11th April 1855
                         Solemnized 12 April 1855 Jno. Crafford J P

Orville Harrison   &   Mary Stainback   16th April 1855
                         Solemnized 17th April 1855   John Crafford JP

John Davidson   &   Martha Barnett   28th April 1855
                         Solemnized   Jas. Woodard

Samuel S Freland   &   Emily I Barham   25th May 1855
                         Solemnized May 27 1855 W. R. Saddler J P

George W Adams   &   Ann Holland   19th May 1855
                         Solemnized May 20th 1855   T. H. Gardner J P

Levi Wells   &   Amanda Page   7th May 1855
                         Solemnized May 8th 1855   G.B.Mason J P

(260) I. N. Brewer   &   Priscilla E George   9th June 1855
                         Solemnized Benj. Gambill   J P

Barnet Guill   &   Mahala D Crothran   18th June 1855
                         Solemnized 21 June 1855   G. F. Lucas J P

William Stratton   &   Mary J Burchett   18th June 1855
                         Solemnized June 19 1855   G. B. Mason J P

Benjamin Gambill   &   Catherine M George   18th June 1855
                         Solemnized   G. B. Mason

George B Randolph   &   Leah A Moore   21st June 1855

                         Solemnized 24 June 1855 I. M. Copeland J P

John W Stark   &   Mary Ann Powell   30th June 1855
Solemnized 1st July 1855 I. B. White J P

John Morris   &   Amanda Krisle   30th June 1855
Solemnized July 1st 1855 John Woodard J P

John M Frey   &   Mary H Bradley   2 July 1855
Solemnized 4 July 1855 Robert Williams J P

M. D. W.Batts   &   Arrena Dunn   7th July 1855
Solemnized 15th July 1855 W.S.Adams J P

(261) Benjamin Bagby   &   Martha Woodson   12th July 1855
Solemnized July 1855 W. R. Sadler J P

W. S. Barnes   &   Nancy Douglas   17 July 1855
Solemnized W. S. Adams J P

Jesse Warner   &   Nancy E Bennett   24th July 1855
Solemnized August 2 1855 F. C. Plaster M. G.

W. A. Dorris   &   Airy Phipps   28th July 1855
Solemniaed 29 July 1855 John Crafford J P

C. N. England   &   Mahaley E Payne   31st July 1855
Solemnized James Cook J P

Silas K Stanfield   &   Amelia F Nuckolds   2 August 1855
Solemnized Benjamin Rawls M. G.

Benjamin F Reek   &   Emily C Cook   2 August 1855
Solemnized Benjamin Rawls M. G.

John L.C.Adams   &   Mary A. E. Binkley   3 August 1855
Solemnized 6 August 1855 A Rose M. G.

Francis M Page   &   Roberta H Bagley   4 August 1855
Solemnized 5 August 1855 Jno. Gammon

(262) G. A. Gambill   &   Milley C Brewer   August 6 1855
Solemnized Thomas W Felts

W. H. Menees   &   Sallie K Menees   August 9th 1855
Solemnized F. R. Gooch M. G.

Daniel Campbell   &   Harriet L Doyle   16 August 1855
Solemnized A. Rose J P

Elijah Willis   &   Mary Simmons   22 August 1855
Solemnized 23 August 1855 G. W. Featherstone
                                                 V. D. M

W.I. Felts   &   Louisa Herrington   August 24 1855
Solemnized August 26 1855 I. T. Craig J P

John Reed   &   Martha E James   August 29th 1855
Solemnized F. R. Gooch M. G.

William L King   &   Harriet E Waggoner   August 29 1855
                        Solemnized Jesse B White J P

George A King   &   Mary E Krisle   1st. Sept. 1855
                        Solemnized Sept 2 1855 Isaac Steel M. G

John A Porter   &   Malvine C Wolf   Sept. 4 1855
                        Solemnized Saml. D Ogburn M. H.

(263) Jesse Shuman   &   Burchet Maxey   Sept. 4th 1855
                        Solemnized 6 Sept. 1855 W. W. Williams

A.F. Barry   &   Mary E Jones   Sept. 5 1855
                        Solemnized 6 Sept 1855 G. M. Featherstone V.D.M.

Williams C Binkley   &   Nancy Ann Pool   Sept 8th 1855
                        Solemnized Sept. 9 1855 J. T. Craig J P

George W Magee   &   Bedy A Mangrund   Sept. 8th 1855
                        Solemnized Sept 9 1855 G. B. Mason J P

W. L. Mason   &   Lareny Batts   Sept. 14 1855
                        Solemnized Sept 16 1855 G. R. Gunn J P

L. H Huffman   &   Alice J Strickland   Sept 27 1855
                        Solemnized   G. R. Gunn J P

Robert V Draughon   &   Nancy Ann Cohea   29th Sept 1855
                        Solemnized 30 Sept. 1855 Jesse B White J P

W. J. Cooley   &   Martha W Batts   3 Oct 1855
                        Solemnized 4 Oct 1855 F.R. Gooch M. G.

Robert Bagby   &   Mary E Mimms   9th Octr. 1855
                        Solemnized   John H Gammon Minister Gospel

(264) Leroy Henry   &   Rebecca Moon   15th Octr. 1855
                        Solemnized 18th Octr. 1855 W. S. Baldry M. G.

W. K. Berry   &   Sophia Payne   15th Octr. 1855
                        Solemnized 17 Octr. 1855 G. W. Featherston M.G.

Barnet D. Husley   &   Matilda Crassline   19th Octr 1855
                        Solemnized Octr. 20 1855 J. Crawford J P

Thomas W. Murphy   &   Louisa P Adams   21st. Oct 1855
                        Solemnized T. B. Mathews J P

James M. Sale   &   Catherine D Fort   30th Octr. 1855
                        Solemnized 31st Octr. 1855 F. C. Plaster

William Cummings   &   Mary Powell   1st Nov 1855
                        Solemnized J. Batts J P

William Clinard   &   Catherine A Parker   1st Nov. 1855
                        Solemnized J. S. Hollis J P

Jacob Harcrider   &   Rachel Maxey   1st Nov. 1855
                        Solemnized J. W. Cullum M. G.

William E Felts   &   Huldy Homes   5th Nov. 1855
                         Solemnized 11th Nov. 1855 A. Rose M. G.

(265) Meredith P Yates   &   Elizabeth Cannon   11th November 1855
                         Solemnize Nov. 12 1855 J. M. Copeland J P

Martin Frey   &   Urcilla Dowlen   21st. Nov 1855
                         Solemnized 22 Nov. 1855 Robt. Williams J P

Zachariah W Winters   &   Mary V Whitehead   25th Nov 1855
                         Solemnized Robert Williams J P

Hyram Jones   &   Sarah Seat   27th Nov 1855
                         Solemnized W. S. Adams J P

W. B. Farmer   &   Eliza S Justice   27th Decr. 1855
                         Solemnized T J Craig J P

A. H. Nicholson   &   Lucy Ann Walker   3 Decr. 1855
                         Solemnized Decr. 7 1855 W. W. Williams J P

Roland Warren   &   Susan Porter   6th Decr 1855
                         Solemnized H. G. Lucas

Willie T Farmer   &   Jane Dillard   7th Decr. 1855
                         Solemnized F. R. Gooch M. G

L. Lewis   &   Mary F Murrah   8th Decr 1855
                         Solemnized Decr. 12 1855 Jas. Woodard

(244) Thos. D Woldrom   &   Louisa Megaire   10th Decr. 1855
                         Solemnized Isaac Steel

Larkin Vaught   &   Mary Ann Darham   10th Decr 1855
                         Solemnized 11 Decr 1855 Benjamin Gambill

Amos B Marshall   &   Eliza Jane Shreeve   19th Decr. 1855
                         Solemnized 23 December 1855 F. R. Gooch M. G.

Richard D Taylor   &   Rachel Bozworth   19th Decr 1855
                         Solemnized W. W. Pepper, Judge &C

W. J. Winn   &   Elizabeth Mason   20th Decr 1855
                         Solemnized 23 Decr 1855 W. S. Baldry M. G.

A. J. Akin   &   Martha J Bagby   21st Decr 1855
                         Solemnized 23 Decr. 1855 G. B. Mason J P

Washington Yates   &   Matilda Link   22 Decr 1855
                         Solemnized G. B. Kelly M. G.

Thomas Holland   &   Elizabeth W Stark   24 Decr 1855
                         Solemnized 26 Decr. 1855 G. B. Mason J P

(267) G. R. Shepherd   &   Mary E Crunk   25th Decr. 1855
                             Solemnized Decr. 27 1855 J. W. Cullum M. G.

       Frederick Moulton   &   Caroline Jackson   27th Decr. 1855
                             Solemnized John Burns, J P

       W. H. Balthrop   &   M. J. Harris   28th Decr 1855
                             Solemnized 1 Jan. 1856 Robert Williams J P

       James J Luton   &   Madora Armstrong   29th Decr. 1855

                             Solemnized Decr. 30, 1855 W. T. Chowning J P

       Joseph Traughber   &   Harriet Brakfield   29th Decr 1855
                             Solemnized Jno. W. Smith J P

       Thos. W Sory   & Pricilla Batts   29th Decr. 1855
                             Solemnized W. S. Adams J P

       Joseph Brakfield   &   Mary K Chapman   31st Decr 1855
                             Solemnized Jan. 1 1856 John W Smith J P

       C. D. Jamison   &   Sophrina Roberts   1st. Jany 1856
                             Solemnized L. J. Neely M. G.

(268) Jerome Danley   &   Susan Edwards   3 Jany. 1856
                             Solemnized G. Benton J P

       Henry Shoemaker   &   Elizabeth Lawrason   8th Jany. 1856
                             Solemnized 10th January 1856 Jno. H Gammon M. G.

       F. B. Epps   &   E. B. Persise   9th Jany 1856
                             Solemnized J. W. Cullum M. G.

       Meredith Powell   &   Nancy H. Fiser   10th Jany 1856
                             Solemnized J. W. Cullum M. G.

       John A Gunn   &   M. A. E. Bigbee   22 Jany 1856
                             Solemnized Jas. Woodard J P

       John Coffman   &   Moody Ann Sullivan   11th Jan 1856
                             Solemnized G. B. Mason J P

       Isaac Barry   &   Susan Allen   28th Jany 1856
                             Solemnized 24 March 1856 R. H. Harrison J P

       John Sayles   &   Mary Campbell   30th Jany 1856
                             Solemnized Isaac Steel

(269) Richard B Rose   &   Catherine A Frey   4th Feby 1856
                             Solemnized Feby. 5 1856 G. Benton J P

       James M Henkle   &   Catherine W Swift   5th Deby 1856
                             Solemnized 7th Feby 1856 John Crawford J P

       Ephriam M Dannington &   Rebecca E Wrights   15th Feby 1856
                             Solemnized 19th Feby. 1856 Thomas West M. G

George J Rigsbee   &   Elizabeth F Riddle   16th Feby 1856
Solemnized 18th February 1856 R. H. Harrison J P

James C Moss   &   Nancy Fisher   19th Feby 1856
Solemnized Feby. 20 1856 W. T. Chowning J P

James M Johnson   &   Missouri Barry   23rd Feby 1856
Solemnized 26th Feb. 1856 W. T. Chowning J P

John McDonald   &   Elizabeth Faullin   27th Feby 1856
Solemnized 28 Feb. 1856 Geo. W. Featherston M.G.

Carroll Poor   &   Sarah H Barbee   3 March 1856
Solemnized 4 March 1856 W. S. Baldry M. G.

(270) Knight Curd   &   Mary Couts   11th March 1856
Solemnized J. W. Cullum M. G.

James Grass   &   Milley Whitner   12th March 1856
Solemnized J. W. Cullum M. G.

Jackson Gossett   &   Mary Blackburn   13th March 1856
Solemnized W. M. C. Barr J P

Alexander G Adams   &   Mary Hollis   19th March 1856
Solemnized J. W. Smith J P

Jacob B Winger   &   Catherine Abbott   19 March 1856
Solemnized 20th March 1856 J. W. Cullum M. G.

Philander D Bradley   &   Margaret E Wright   22 March 1856
Solemnized 24th March 1856 R. H. Harrison J P

J. L. Tounsend   &   Florence Farmer   26th March 1856
Solemnized Benjamin Gambill J P

John B Yates   &   Virginia Cannon   6th April 1856
Solemnized 7th April 1856 J. M. Copland J P

(271) E. P. Benton   &   Lucy Ann Porter   7th April 1856
Solemnized April 8th 1856 J. W. Cullum M. G.

William P Simmons   &   Elizabeth D. I Lucas   16th April 1856
Solemnized April 21 1856 James Cook J P

Lewis O White   &   Martha Swift   21st. Apr. 1856
Splemnized 23 April 1856 John Crawdorf J P

Joseph Gunn   &   Elizabeth F Barnes   21st April 1856
Solemnized 21 April 1856 J. W. Featherston

George A Smith   &   Elvira Pitt   21st April 1856
Solemnized 22 April 1856 E. W. Gunn M. G.

William Biggs   &   Rebecca Ann Crafton   22 April 1856
Solemnized 23 April 1856 W. M. C. Barr J P

Wesley S Dorris   &   Eliza Jane Freeland   22 April 1856
                         Solemnized April 24 1856 H. L. Covington J P

William P Traughber   &   Susan Brannon   1st May 1856
                         Solemnized Benj. Gambill J P

(272) J.D.Cole   & Jennetta Corner   3rd May 1856
                         Solemnized May 4 1856 E. W. Gunn M. G. J P

Hiram G Grainger   &   Rosa Ann Anderson   7 May 1856
                         Solemnized L. J. Fort J P

John L Williams   &   Margaret I Luter   5th May 1856
                         Solemnized May 8 1856 H. L. Covington J P

Saml D Fryer   &   Mary Binkley   7th may 1856
                         Solemnized May 8 1856 J. S. Hollis J P

Joseph W Barham   &   Harriet N Gatewood   24 May 1856
                         Solemnized May 25 1856 W. R. Sadler J P

Simeon Rippy   &   Elizabeth Philips   7th June 1856
                         Solemnized 8 June 1856 R. H. Harrison J P

William Moore   &   Martha A Lowe   12th June 1856
                         Solemnized J W Cullum M. G.

J. W. Huddleston   &   Mary F Cannon   18th June 1856
                         Solemnized Jesse B White J P

(273) J. M. Pinson   & Mary A Powell   19th June 1856
                         Solemnized A Rose J P

William P Warren   &   Nancy A. C. Redding   21st June 1856
                         Solemnized 22 June 1856 J. F. England M. G.

William Choat   &   Elizabeth Doyal   24th June 1856
                         Solemnized 26 June 1856 A Rose J P

James Head   &   Amanda Murphy   24 June 1856
                         Solemnized 25 1856 Isaac Carter M. G.

William Latimer   &   Mary A. E. Moss   28th June 1856
                         Solemnized July 3 1856 Wm. Thomas Chowning J P

Carroll Haly   &   Martha Rose   3 July 1856
                         Solemnized Jas. Woodard

Obadiah Ethridge   &   Marsha Leake   4th July 1856
                         Solemnized 5 July 1856 R. H. Harrison J P

James F Hurt   &   Nancy W Jones   9th July 1856
                         Solemnized 10th July 1856 G.W. Featherston M. G.

(274) W. H. Riggins   &   Phebe Summerville   15th July 1856
                         Solemnized R. H. Harrison J P

James Swift   &   Amanda E Hampton   23 July 1856
                       Solemnized 24 July 1856 John Crawford J P

Calvin Jones   &   Martha J Davidson   25th July 1856
                       Solemnized 27 1856 James Cook J P

Stephen T Jones   &   Nancy J Warren   26th July 1856
                       Solemnized July 27 1856 John Crawfors J P

William Whiten   &   Emaline J Thompson   26th July 1856
                       Solemnized 27 July 1856 A. Rose J P

William T Ferguson   &   Mary E Gish   5th August 1856
                       Solemnized J. W. Cullum M. G.

G. W. Philps   &   Catherine m McFarland   5th August 1856
                       Solemnized Aug 6th 1856 Isaac Steel M. G.

Thomas Barry   &   Harriet Allen   8th August 1856
                       Solemnized 10 Aug. 1856 Thomas West M. G.

(275) N. J. Hardy   &   Elizabeth Holland   9th August 1856
                       Solemnized 10 August 1856 G. R. Gunn J P

Martin G Benson   &   Nancy Williamson   16th August 1856
                       Solemnized 17th Aug. 1856 J. W. Cullum M. G.

Geo. W Randolph   &   Parile Walton   27th August 1856
                       Solemnized 28th August 1856 G.R. Gunn J P

Robert W Thompson   &   Rhoda Ann Lowry   30th August 1856
                       Solemnized Aug. 31st. 1856 G. E. Mason J P

Richard Leonard   &   Elizabeth Vaught   1st September 1856
                       Solemnized 2 Sept. 1856 Benjamin Gambill J P

Saml. Osburn   &   Sarah Clinard   6th Sept. 1856
                       Solemnized 7 Sept. 1856 J. S. Hollis J P

Calvin J Mehaffy   &   Julia A Pike   6th Septr. 1856
                       Solemnized 11 Sept. 1856 A. Rose J P

Hardy W Glisson   &   Susan Huddleston   10th Sept. 1856
                       Solemnized C Farthing J P

(276) Byard B Murphy &   Mary F. E. Mayes   11th Sept 1856
                       Solemnized J. W. Cullum M. G.

Josiah Toler   &   Maranda W Toler   13th Sept 1856
                       Solemnized 14 Sept. 1856 G. Benton

Wesley W Watts   &   Martha E Felts   15th Sept 1856
                       Solemnized 18 Sept. 1856 Robert Williams J P

J. B Pitman   &   Elizabeth G Glisson   15th Sept 1856
                       Solemnized Sept 16, 1856 F. R. Gooch M. G.

Robertson Co., TN - Marriage Records - Volume 1 - 1839 - 1861   109

****

R. C. Nipper   &   Amanda Solomon   15th Sept. 1856
Solemnized Sept. 16 1856 G. Benton J P

H. V. Harrison   &   Virginia C Batts   16th Sept 1856
Solemnized J. W. Cullum M. G.

Saml. Gray   &   Martha McFarland   17th Sept. 1856
Solemnized H. H. Orndoff J P

David S Rawls   &   Nancy Anderson   18th Sept 1856
Solemnized J. T. Craig J P

E. R. Owen   &   Rosabelle Q Warren   18 Sept. 1856
Solemnized J. W. Cullum M. G.

(277)   Thos. Husky   &   Mary Adams   20th Sept 1856
Solemnized 21 Sept 1856 John Burns J P

Alexander Cohea   &   Adeline Draughon   20th/ Septr1856
Solemnized G. Benton J P

James A Clinard   &   Sarah Street   22 Sept. 1856
Solemnized J. T. Craig J P

R. H. Izer   &   Sarah F. Mathews   24 Sept 1856
Solemnized Sept. 24 1856 H. L. Burney M. G.

James M Ramsey   &   Deliha A Arnold   25th Sept. 1856
Solemnized Thomas West M. G.

W. L. Bracy   &   Elizabeth J Felts   27th Septr. 1856
Solemnized George W Martin M. G.

Charles E Rawls   &   Sarah E Hunkle   29th Sept 1856
Solemnized Sept 30 1856 L. J. Craig J P

William Mastin   &   Dicy A. Smith   1st Novem. 1856
Solemnized G. Benton J P

M. W. Hemington   &   Susan D Felts   3 Octr 1856
Solemnized 4 Oct 1856 Benjamin Rawls M. G.

(278)   Thos. L. West   &   Maranda R. Vanhook   4th Octr. 1856
Solemnized 5 Octr. 1856 A. M. Greer J P

William Cole   &   Angeline Irvin   8th Octr. 1856
Solemnized 9 Octr. 1856 John Crawford J P

William Grow   &   Amanda E Trimble   9th Octr. 1856
Solemnized 12 Oct. 1856 Benjamin Gambill J P

W. W. Connell   &   M. C. Goodman   13th Octr. 1856
Solemnized Oct. 19 1856 W. R. Sadler J P

James H Chamberlain   &   Abiah Hawkins   13th Octr. 1856
Solemnized Jesse B White J P

B. W. Dickerson   &   Ann E Russell   15 Octr. 1856
                         Solemnized   John W Smith J P

R. S. Smith   &   Mary J Lett   15 Oct. 1856
                         Solemnized John W Smith J. P

Pleasant Cook   &   Lucy Ann Tate   21 Oct 1856
                         Solemnized G. M. Featherston M. G.

James Culbeetton   &   S. J. Fryer   22 Oct 1856
                         Solemnized J. B. White J P

(279) Henry Traughber   &   Roena Elliott   23 Octr. 1856
                         Solemnized 25 Oct 1856 J. W. Smith J P

Noah Walker   &   Elizabeth S Williams   23 Octr. 1856
                         Solemnized G. W. Martin M. G.

James P Murphy   &   Martha M King   28th Octr. 1856
                         Solemnized B. Rawls M. G.

Henderson H Conway   &   Rebecca E Neil   4th Nov 1856
                         Solemnized F. C. Plaster M. G.

Josphua W Tune   &   Martha M Bell   Nov 4 1856
                         Solemnized Nov 6th L856 L.B. Davidson M. G.

Lemuel I Winfield   &   F. E. Chowning   5th Nov 1856
                         Solemnized   James Cook J P

David W Cirbitt   &   Louisa A Withers   6 Nov 1856
                         Solemnized J. W. Cullum M. G.

William J Jacobs   &   Mary J Rawls   14 Nov 1856
                         Solemnized 13 Nov. 1856 Benjamin Rawls M. G.

Edward Wilks   &   Josephine Merritt   12th Nov. 1856
                         Solemnized Nov 15 1856 H. L. Covington J P

(280) William Stark   &   Winnery Covington   12th Nov 1856
                         Solemnized 13 Nov 1856 H. L. Covington J P

John V Walker   &   Catherine Woodard   13th Nov 1856
                         Solemnized H. H. Orndorf J P

George S Rogers   &   Sarah S. E. Bowls   ;3th Nov 1856
                         Solemnized Thomas West M. G.

Leroy Roe   &   Edmy F Rogers   13th Nov 1856
                         Solemnized H. H. Orndorf J P

J. S. Atkins   &   Lucy Stout   16th Nov 1856
                         Solemnized 17 Dec. 1856 T. H. Gardner J P

W. J. Holt   &   L. C. Watsom   19th. Nov 1856
                         Solemnized J.W. Cullum M. G.

Wm Williams	&	Nancy E Capps	19th Nov 1856
	Solemnized 20th Nov 1856 H. L. Covington J P		
John Bonley	&	E. A. Johnson	22nd Nov 1856
	Solemnized 23 Nov. 1856 R. H. Harrison J P		
(281) John Halpin	&	Mary Bain	22 Nov 1856
	Solemnized H. H. Orndorff J P		
Larkin Bradford	&	Narcissa Foot	24th Nov 1856
	Solemnized 25 Nov 1856 G. R. Gunn J P		
L. W. Love	&	Sarah Taylor	28th Nov 1856
	Solemnized J. W. Cullum M. G.		
Robert A Smith	&	Margaret M Homes	24thDecr 1856
	Solemnized 25th Decr. 1856 George H Smith M.G.		
Jonathan Loyd	&	Mary Wilson	1st Decr 1856
	Solemnized 2 Decr. 1856 J. B. Sandford J P		
J.A. W. Jackson	&	Susan W Ellis	1st Decr. 1856
	Solemnized 2 Decr. 1856 J. W. Cullum M. G.		
J. R. Dunn	&	Emma E Menees	1st Decr 1856
	Solemnized Decr. 4 1856 John A Jones		
George B Sory	&	Mary Farmer	3 Decr 1856
	Solemnized 4 Decr 1856 W. S. Adams J P		
(282) George B Benton	&	Ann Pope	4th Decr 1856
	Solemnized 14 Decr. 1856 J. W. Cullum M. G.		
James H Whitfield	&	Sallie I Boune	8th Decr 1856
	Solemnized 10 Decr 1856		
J. T Mathews	&	Catherine Black	11th Decr 1856
	Solemnized F.R. Gooch M. G.		
George W Murphy	&	Martha F Elliott	15th Decr 1856
	Solemnized 17th Decr 1856 T. H. Gardner J P		
Wesley Cavitt	&	Sarah Horton	17thDecr. 1856
	Solemnized 18th Decr. 1856 R. H. Harrison		
F. M. Luter	&	Margaret Jane Ellis	18th Decr 1856
	Solemnized J. W. Cullum M. G.		
B. N. Hale	&	Joanah Binkley	18th Decr 1856
	Solemnized H. H. Orndorff J P		
Jacob A Crabtree	&	Mary Jane Briley	20th Decr 1856
	Solemnized Decr. 21 1856 James Cook J P		
(283) Smith McCormick	&	Rose Ann Traughber	20th Decr 1856
	Solemnized Benjamin Gambill J P		

William L Tounsend   &   Mary A Chaatine   22 Decr. 1856
Solemnized 23 Decr. 1856 J. C. Plaster M. G.

William J Stanley   &   Nancy Fryer   23 Docr 1856
Solemnized J. A. Jones

James Maguire   &   Sallie M Couts   23rd Decr 1856
Solemnized Isaac Steel M. G.

David Payne   &   Mary Ann Wright   29th Decr 1856
Solemnized 1 Jan. 1857 Thomas West M.G.

Richard Traughber   &   Elizabeth Campbell   29th Decr 1856
Solemnized 30 Decr 1856 Benjamin Gambill J P

Silas C Sharp   &   Amanda E Troughber   29th Decr 1856
Solemnized 30 December 1856 Benjamin Gambill J P

James Crabtree   &   Mary A Chandler   30th Decr 1856
Solemnized James Cook J P

(284) Alfred Traughber   &   Lucinda J. Smelser   31st Decr1856
Solemnized Jany 1, 1857 Jas. Woodard

James M Morris   &   Ann Eliza King   3 Jany 1857
Solemnized 4 Jany 1857 A Rose J P

G. R. Millekin   &   Martha A. M. Cockran   5th Jany 1857
Solemnized Jan 6th 1857 J. T. Craig J P

James C Dotson   &   Mary F Grimes   5th Jany 1857
Solemnized 5 Feby 1857 H. H. Orndorff J P

S. W. Dalton   &   Sarah J Mason   6th Jany 1857
Solemnized 7 Jan. 1857 John W Smith J P

John W Chilton   &   Martha L Burgess   10th Jan. 1857
Solemnized B. B. Batts J P

Albert Burgess   &   Eliza Chilton   12th Jany 1857
Solemnized Jany 11 1857 B. B. Batts J P

L. R. Border   &   Mary Edwards   12 Jany 1857
Solemnized 2o Jany 1857 F. C. Plaster

(285) William Chandler   &   Matilda J Crabtree   13th Jany 1857
Solemnized James Cook J P

John L Tomberlin   &   Martha J Tomerlin   14th Jany 1857
Solemnized _____

Pleasant B Roberts   &   Artimissa McIntosh   15 Jany 1857
Solemnized J. W. Cullum M. G.

T. W. Jernigan   &   Josephine Roney   17th Jany 1857
Solemnized 22 Jan. 1857 H. L. Covington J P

Wm. E Jernigan   &   Mary E Baird   20th Jany 1857
Solemnized Jan. 22 1857 W. T. Chowning J P

John W Gambill   &   Amanda E Brewer   23 Jan. 1757
Solemnized Jan. 29 1857 G. W. Featherston

Alexander W Byram   &   Melissa Williams   24th Jan. 1857
Solemnized 25 Jan. 1857 Isaac Steel M. G.

John L Almon   &   Nancy Appleton   26th Jany 1857
Solemnized John H Gammon M. G.

(286) Burrell W Baggett   &   Martha S Shannon   27 Jany 1857
Solemnized Jany. 28 1857 James Cook J. P.

W. W. Gill   &   M.E.Bailey   28th Kany 1857
Solemnized 29th Jany. 1857 F. C. Plaster M. G.

John W Fuqua   &   Nancy E Parker   31 Jany 1857
Solemnized Feby 1st 1857 J. T. Craig J P

C. S. Covington   &   Nancy M Carr   2 Feby 1857
Solemnized 3 March 185p W. T. Chowning J P

William D Murphy   &   Martha J Chandler   2 Feby 1857
Solemnized Jas. Cook J P

Samuel Eddy   &   Susan C Grayson   7th Febb 1857
Solemnized Jany. 8 1857 Benjamin Gambill J P

Joseph Pitt   &   Drucilla J Jones   7th Feby 1857
Solemnized Feby. 12 1857 W. T. Chowning J P

John Stanfield   &   Tempe Nuckolds   11 Feby 1857
Solemnized B. Rawls M. G.

(287) D. W. Travathan   &   Nancy Porter   11th Feby 1857
Solemnized Feby 12 1857 G. Benton J P

James S Dunn   &   Victoria A Laprade   13th Feby 1857
Solemnized 15 Feby 1857 F. C. Plaster M. G.

Daniel J Fraser   &   Sallie A Polk   16th Feby 1857
Solemnized 17 Feby 1857 J. B. Walton

John W Choat   &   Cine Simmons   18th Feby 1857
Solemnized James Cook J P

William White   &   Nancy Martin   25th Feby 1857
Solemnized 26 Feby 1857 R. H. Harrison J P

James M Mays   &   Moresty E Redding   1st March 1857
Solemnized 22 March 1857 John F England M. G.

John Baldwin   &   Nancy A Cannon   5th March 1857
Solemnized Solemnized Jesse B White J P

William Foreman   &   Eliza M Porter   7th March 1857
                         Solemnized 8th March 1857 J. M.Copeland

(288)   Nathaniel Magaire   &   Eliza F Cordle   14th March 1857
                         Solemnized 19 March 1857 Isaac Steel M.G.

L. W. McLeland   &   Meldred V Watson   15th March 1857
                         Solemnized H. H. Orndorff J P

James S Wilson   &   Martha J Berry   21st March 1857
                         Solemnized Benjamin Gambill J P

L. F. Dillard   &   Sarah S Anderson   23 March 1857
                         Solemnized March 29 1857 Benjamin Gambill J P

Sampson Davis   &   Saraphine Warren   2 April 1857
                         Solemnized C Farthing J P

Henry Trice   &   Elizabeth Thompson   4th April 1857
                         Solemnized 5th April 1857 G. B. Mason J P

Erastus Payne   &   Louisa Groves   7th April 1857
                         Solemnized Thomas West M. G.

William Phipps   &   Alice Payne   12th. April 1857
                         Solemnized James Cook J P

(289)   J. B Sugg   &   Eugenie Wimberly   21st April 1857
                         Solemnized April 23 1857 F. C. Plaster M. G.

Joseph Chapman   &   Martha V Gorham   25th April 1857
                         Solemnized 26 April 1857 John W Smith J P

A Jackson Lipscomb   &   Nancy J Cobb   5th May 1857
                         Solemnized 7th May 1857 Geo. W Martin

William B Young   &   Frances Gunn   5th May 1857
                         Solemnized May 6th 1857 L.B. Davidson M. G.

Saml. F Redding   &   Nancy A Holemes   21 May 1857
                         Solemnized Geo W. Martin M. G.

George L Ryan   &   Martha A. W. Burr   21st May 1857
                         Solemnized G.B. Mason J P

Jacob F Covington   &   Evaline M Luter   30 May 1857
                         No return

Rufus E Farmer   &   Lucy L Vaughn   2 June 1857
                         Solemnized 5 June 1857 F. C. Plaster

(290)   P E Mayhiegh   &   Sarah Jane Baldridge   2 June 1857
                         Solemnized 3 June 1857 H. T. Crighton J P

John W Grubbs   &   Malvine P Ford   4 June 1857
                         Solemnized J W Cullum M. G.

B. W. L. Vaughon   &   Harriet P Browder   6th June 1857
                          Solemnized 7th June 1857 E. W. Gunn M. G.

Peter Hinkle   &   Nancy Cochran   9th June 1857
                          Solemnized J. S. Hollis J P

A. J. Allensworth   &   Ellen E Hughes   24th June 1857
                           Solemnized 25 June 1857 J. W. Cullum M. G.

Thomas D Goodrum   &   Elizabeth E Turner   6th July 1857
                          Solemnized July 7 1857 L. B. Davis M. G.

David Jones   &   Luantha E Moulton   11th July 1857
                          Solemnized 12th July 1857 G. W. Featherston M. G.

David Woodson   &   Mary A Cherer   16th July 1857
                          Solemnized J. K. Woodson G. M.

(291) William Johnson   &   Sarah Henson   23 July 1857
                          Solemnized H. H. Orndorff J P

J Y Hicks   &   Mary E Braden   28th July 1857
                          Solemnized July 29th N. F. Gill

Joseph C Baker   &   Semantha J Whitmore   1st Aug 1857
                          Solemnized 2 Aug. 1857 A. Rose J P

Marshal D Wellhelm   &   Sarah C Williams   2 Aug. 1857
                          Solemnized J. W. Cullum M. G.

Eli Orndorff   &   Elizabeth A Ryan   6th Aug. 1857
                          Solemnized J. W. Cullum M. G.

Lewis Keith   &   Elizabeth Cummings   10th Aug. 1857
                          Solemnized 12 Aug 1857 W. M. C. Barr J P

G. L. Bartlett   &   Mary A Glover   12th Aug 1857
                           Solemnized 14 Aug. 1857 H. H. Orndorff J P

John H Binkley   &   Sarah A Martin   17th Aug. 1857
                          Solemnized C. T. Craig J P

(292) Robert Yates   &   Sarah Pope   19th Aug. 1857
                          Solemnized 20 Aug. 1857 Greenberry Kelly M.G.

R. L. A. Bardry   &   Mary Ann Fuqua   27th Aug 1857
                          Solemnized W. S. Baldry M. G.

Gideon J Morris   &   Martha E Bartlett   29th Aug. 1857
                          Solemnized 30 Aug. 1857 F. R. Gooch M. G.

Jasper England   &   Amanda Savage   30 August 1857
                          Solemnized James Cook J P

Cheatham Dozier   &   Virginia F Starke   1st Sept. 1857
                          Solemnized H. H. Orndorff J P

116   **Robertson Co., TN - Marriage Records - Volume 1 - 1839 - 1861**

****

Thomas C Edison   &   Nancy Powell   2 Sept 1857
             Solemnized 3 Sept. 1857   A. Rose   J P

Jesse Hinkle   &   Icevilla Choaty   3 Sept. 1857
             Solemnized A Rose J P

Marcus Briley   &   Nancy A Toliver   5th Sept. 1857
             Solemnized 6 Sept 1857 M. L. Covington J P

(293) M. F. Marberry   &   Mary E Gorham   7th Sept 1857
             Solemnized J •W.Cullum M. G.

William W Taylor   &   M. P. Holman   8th Sept 1857
             Solemnized Sept 10th 1857 G. ᴰ• Mason J P

Sanford G. M. Jackson &   Mary A. P. Barnes   10 Sept 1857
             Solemnized J. W. Featherston

William Logan   &   Mary T Connell   15th Sptr. 1857
             Solemnized J W• Cullum M. G.

J. M. Winn   &   P. S. Farmer   16th Octr. 1857
             Solemnized 29 Oct. 1857   G. B. Mason J P

Harston Shelton   &   Margaret Prince   17th Sept 1857
             Solemnized John W Smith J P

John C Moore   &   Mary E Wilks   21st Sept 1857
             Solemnized 22 Septr. 1857 J. M. Copland

David Cross   &   Rebecca Wilkins   24 Sept. 1857
             Solemnized G. B. Mason J P

(294) J. W. Parker   &   Mary C Fuqua   24 Sept 1857
             Solemnized J. T. Craig   J P

A. W. Burd   &   Nancy A Doty   2 Octr. 1857
             Solemnized H. H. Orndorff J P

F. R. Mason   &   V. I. Taylor   5th Pct 1857
             Solemnized 8 Oct. 1857 John W Smith J P

Leroy Wright   &   Joice Ponds   7th Octr. 1857
             Solemnized 8 Octr. 1857 W. M. C. Barr J P

Azariah Doss   &   Rebecca Chapman   7th Oct. 1857
             Solemnized 8th Oct. 1857 G. B• Kellt M. G.

W. H. Tompson   &   M. F. Gordon   8th Oct 1857
             Solemnized G. B. Mason   J. P.

James B. Fentress   &   P.I.Herrington   8th Octr. 1857
             Solemnized T. I. Craig J P

Benjamin F Gambill   &   Molley C Brewer   10th Octr. 1857
             Solemnized   G. R. Gunn J P

(295) J. D. Reeks   &   S. L. Luter   10th Oct 1857
                            Solemnized 13th Oct 1857 Jno. M. Nolen M. G.

       Joseph Payne   &   Matrisa Cole   10th Octr. 1857
                            Solemnized 11 Oct 1857 H. L. Covington

       A. B. Couts   &   Susan C Green   10th Oct 1857
                            Solemnized 11 Oct. 1857 Benjamin Rawls M. G.

       James H Jones   &   Susan D Hysmith   12th Octr. 1857
                            Solemnized Oct. 15 1857 G. B. Mason J P

       J. A. Shannon   &   J. A. Baggett   13th Octr. 1857
                            Solemnized W. T. Chowning J P

       R. H. Allen   &   M. E. Ogg   13th Oct 1857
                            Solemnized 15th Oct. 1857 Robert Williams M. G.

       A. W. West   &   Emily Ormand   14th Octr. 1857
                            Solemnized 15th Oct. 1857 Thomas West M. G.

       J. A. Covington   &   Mary Grimes   15th Octr. 1857
                            Solemnized 18 Octr. 1857 R. Elmore J P

(296) Jno. W Hall   &   Susan Powell   20th Octr. 1857
                            Solemnized 22 Oct. 1857 A. Rose J P

       H. W. McIntosh   &   Rachel E Keller   21st Octr 1857
                            Solemnized Oct 22 1857 G. B. Mason J P

       Robt. F Glover   &   Levina Parker   22 Oct. 1857
                            Solemnized J. T. Craig J P

       Daniel W Benton   &   Susan E Fryar   27 Oct 1857
                            Solemnized Nov Lst 1857 J. T. Craig J P

       Chas. A Simmons   &   Celia Holland   2 Nov 1857
                            Solemnized 12 Nov 1857 Benjamin Gambill J P

       Richard Qualls   &   Sarah E Ogg   2 Nov 1857
                            Solemnized 10 Nov 1857 W. S. Adams J P

       J. W. Sneed   &   Amanda E Farthing   5th Nov 1857
                            Solemnized G. B. Mason J P

       G.S.Keese   &   Martha C Murphy   6th Nov 1857
                            Solemnized 10th Nov 1857 J. B. Walton

(297) James A Soyars   &   Martha V Dowlin   7th Nov 1857
                            Solemnized Nov 12 1857 Geo. W Martin

       B. F. Porter   &   Agnes L Benson   12th Nov 1857
                            Solemnized 13 Nov. 1857 Rheuben Elmore J P

       M. W. Edawrds   &   Artimissa Jones   17th Nov 1857
                            Solemnized F. R. Gooch M. G.

	Geo. E Jones	& Mary A Bladwin	19th Nov
		Solemnized G. W. Featherston M. G.	
	Sugg Fort	& Virginia C Sugg	21st Nov 1857
		Solemnized 1st Decr. 1857 F. C. Plaster	
	L. F. Felts	& S. L. Craig	21st Nov 1857
		Solemnized Geo. W. Martin M. G.	
	R. C. Anderson	& Josaphine Holland	21st Nov 1857
		Solemnized H. H. Orndorff J P	
	B. B. Roach	& Sarah S Sherod	5 Decr. 1857
		Solemnized F. R. Gooch M. G.	
(298)	James A Hysmith	& N. S. A. Brakfield	12 Decr 1857
		Solemnized 13 Decr. 1857 G. B. Mason J P	
	Newton L Turner	& Martha A Burton	14th Decr. 1857
		Solemnized 17 Decr. 1857 L. B. Davidson M. G.	
	Jesse Shannon	& Martha Mathews	19th Decr 1857
		Solemnized 20 Decr. 1857 James Cook J P	
	Danl C Hines	& Martha J Young	9th Decr. 1857
		Solemnized Decr. 10 1857 L.B. Davidson M. G.	
	William Crickmore	& Nancy Hickman	19th Decr. 1857
		Solemnized 20th Decr 1857 Benjamin Gambill J P	
	Henry P Rogers	& Mary A Gibson	22d Decr 1857
		Solemnized 24th Decr. 1857 A. Rose J P	
	John G Adams	& Penine Rose	24th Decr. 1857
		Solemnized G. B. Mason J O	
	John H Sherod	& Frances T Roach	24th Decb 1857
		Solemnized F. R. Gooch M. G.	
(299)	Lewis H Chambless	& Malinda C Hollis	24th Decr 1857
		Solemnized J. T. Craig J P	
	Perry Hannum	& Lucinda Dunn	24th Decr. 1857
		Solemnized W. C. Haslip M.G.	
	John Mills	& Eliza A Hardaway	26th Decr 1857
		Solemnized Decr. 29 1857 J. W. Smith J P	
	John T Owen	& Lucinda F Baggett	3oth Decr 1857
		Solemnized Decr 31st 1857 James Cook J P	
	Sebert Holman	& J. A. E. Murphy	31st Decr 1857
		Solemnized H. H. Brndorff J P	
	William Powell	& Louisa Patton	4th Jany. 1858
		Solemnized January 5th 1858 H. T. Covington J P	
	Wilson Krisle	& Lucy C Wallace	5th Jany 1858
		Solemnized 6 Jan. 1858 Reuben Elmore J P	

William Hudson   &   Nancy Gilbert   7th Jany 1858
Solemnized 8th Jan. 1858 R. H. Harrison J P

(300) Robert Sanford   &   Susan E Davis   9th Jany 1858
Solemnized 10th Jan. 1858 John Crawford J P

James E Eidson   &   N Randolph   10 July 1858
Solemnized 11 July 1858 R. H. Harrison

Saml M Wade   &   Mary T.E.Sherrod   13th Jany 1858
Solemnized 14th Jany 1858 F. R. Gooch M. G.

Robert S Shannon   &   Argail Durrett   Jany 15th 1858
Solemnized W. T. Chowning J P

George E Short   &   Virginia M Boisseau   13th Jany 1858
Solemnized 14 Jan. 1858 E. W. Coleman M. G.

Saml Fairfield   &   Ellen Anderson   13th Jany 1858
Solemnized A. Rose J P

Walton Lanson   &   Nancy A Warren   19th Jany 1858
Solemnized Jno. H. Gammon M. G.

Nathan Usry   &   Dicy J Doyle   19th Jany 1858
Solemnized 20th Jan. 1858 Reubin Elmore J P

(301) George B Levell   &   Elizabeth Cheatham   19th Jany 1858
Solemnized B Rawls M. G.

John T Wilkerson   &   Melissa J Draughon   27th Jany 1858
Solemnized 28 Jany 1858 W. W. Pepper Judge & C

Richard B Madole   &   Martha A Conner   1st Feby 1858
Solemnized Isaac Steel M. G.

John W Woodson   &   Parilee Binkley   1st Feby 1858
Solemnized 4th Frb. 1858 Geo. W. Martin M. G.

William Wood   &   Manervia J Baldry   1st Feby 1858
Solemnized 4th Feby 1858 Jas Woodard

William Phipps   &   Margaret Heath   2 Feby 1858
Solemnized 4th Feb. 1858 John F England M. G.

W. D. Read   &   Mary C Stoltz   5th Feby 1858
Solemnized F. R. Gooch M. G.

William B Woodruff   &   Lucy A Harris   8th Feby 1858
Solemnized 11 Feb. 1858 M. W. Winters J P

(302) F. M. Welch   &   Jane Rogers   8th Feby 1858
Solemnized 14th Day Feb. 1858 W. M. C. Barr J P

John R Moore   &   Susan C Miller   10th Feby 1858
Solemnized 11 Feb. 1858 Geo W Martin M. G.

Fielden L Warren   &   Jane Cole   11th Feby 1858
Solemnized Hiram Warren J P

J. C. Bell	&	Mary Mileken	11th Feby 1858
	Solemnized W. C. Haislip M. G.		
Daniel H Simmons	&	Eliza H Holland	12th Feby 1858
	Solemnized 14th Feby 1858 John H Gammon M. G.		
David McMurry	&	Mary A Frey	24th Feby 1858
	Solemnized W. T. Chowning J P		
A. W. Sandford	&	M. F. Gressam	9th March 1858
	Solemnized W. R. Sadler J P		
John W Mason	&	Terresa B Patterson	13th March 1858
	Solemnized 23 March 1858 H. Warren J P		
(303) James Lipscomb	&	Virginia Irey	15th March 1858
	Solemnized March 16th 1858 G. B. Mason J P		
Jacob House	&	Elizabeth Jones	15th March 1858
	Solemnized 16th March 1858 G. W. Featherston		
John Robins	&	Margaret Kiger	3rd April 1858
	Solemnized 6th April 1858 John Crawford J P		
Paterick Ford	&	Mary Scruder	5th April 1858
	Solemnized 6th April 1858 R. H. Harrison J P		
Saml H Robins	&	Martha J Tucker	5th April 1858
	Solemnized 15th April 1858 Jno. Crawford J P		
John A Lamb	&	Sarah McCance	6th April 1858
	Solemnized April 8th 1858 W. R. Sadler J P		
Richard Gorham	&	Winney Farharty	9th April 1858
	No return		
Alvis Evans	&	Lucy Ellmore	15th April 1858
	Solemnized 18th April 1858 Benjamin Gambill J P		
(304) James Y Freeman	&	Nancy C Miller	19th April 1858
	Solemnized Geo. W. Martin M. G.		
P. N. Pollock	&	Mary F Bugg	21st April 1858
	Solemnized Jas. Woodard		
William C Murry	&	Mary Ford	21 April 1858
	Solemnized 25th April 1858 John F England M.G.		
William Ward	&	Sarah Davis	26th April 1858
	Solemnized John H Gammon V. D. M.		
James Travis	&	Amanda Winsett	2 May 1858
	Solemnized W. S. Adams		
William Kiger	&	Sarah Swift	19th May 1858
	Solemnized 23 May 1858 John Crawford J P		

	B. S. Chance	&	Nancy Dycus	26th May 1858
		Solemnized May 31st. 1858 F. R. Gooch M. G.		

	C. B. Russell	&	M. D. Fort	27th May 1858
		Solemnized 28th May 1858 F. C. Plaster M. G.		

(305)   James Mahaffy   &   Elizabeth Benton   4th May 1858
        Solemnized 5th May 1859 Reubin Elmore J P

        John I Wynn   &   Elizabeth O Donnott   3d June 1858
        Solemnized 3 June 1858 M. B. Parson M. G.

        James Webster   &   Nancy Thompson   6th June 1858
        Solemnized 8th June 1858 John Crawford J P

        Lafayette Traughber   &   S. F. Slack   8th June 1858
        Solemnized 10th June 1858 Jno. W. Smith J P

        Richd. C Williams   &   Martha E Bracy   20th June 1858
        Solemnized 22 June 1858 John Dowlin J P

        John McDearman   &   Mary Smith   22 June 1858
        Solemnized 23 June 1858 F. C. Plaster M. G.

        Thos. I. Wilks   &   Sarah Ponds   June 30th 1858
        Solemnized July 2 1858 R. H. Harrison J P

        Thos. Considine   &   Hanora Davet   3d July 1858
        Solemnized 5th July 1858 L Haste Catholis Priest

(306)   David L S Sutton   &   Julia A Jenkins   5th July 1855
        Solemnized Jas Woodard

        James Lovell   &   Mary A Barker   5th July 1858
        Solemnized 6th July 1858 G. W. Featherston

        Anderson Jones   &   Catherine Crossline   15th July 1857
        Solemnized Jno. Crawford J P

        William A Langston   &   M. E. Fletcher   14th July 1858
        Sept 15th 1858 F. R. Gooch M. G. Solemnized

        Jackson E Williams   &   Sarah McCarley   19th July 1858
        Solemnized July 20th 1858 G. B. Mason J P

        N. I. Akin   &   A. M. Shackelford   21st July 1858
        Solemnized July 22 1858 James Woodard

        D. Darden   &   Sarah Culbertson   22 July 1858
        Solemnized Jesse B White J P

        Mathew W Cheser   &   Amanda W Franklin   22 July 1858
        Solemnized F. R. Gooch Minister of the Gospel

(307)   John Wilson   &   Eliza F Brown   29th July 1858
        Solemnized Jas. Woodard

Thomas Mayes	&	Rose Ann Ford	2d. August 1858
	Solemnized 6th Aug. 1858. John F England M.G.		
Stephen A Jones	&	Mary K Hendley	6th August 1858
	Solemnized 8th Aug. 1858 Benjamin Gambill J P		
William Elmore	&	Nancy J Jones	10th August 1858
	Solemnized A Rose J P		
John N Coffman	&	Rebecca A Stark	12th August 1858
	Solemnized J. Hardaway J P		
Thomas Ragsdale	&	Angeline N Fisher	13th August 1858
	Solemnized August 29th 1858 G. W. Featherston		
John L Soward	&	Amanda L Petty	16th August 1858
	Solemnized Elder, G. W. Featherston		
Benjamin Stark	&	Z. D. Horton	17th Aug 1858
	Solemnized 18th August H. L. Covington J P		
	For Robertson County District No 11th.		

(308) James A Howard   & Martha E Drane   1st Sept 1858
Solemnized 4th Sept. 1858 Benjamin Gambill J P

H. C. Draughon	&	Susan M Ogg	5th Sept 1857
	Solemnized 6th Sept. 1857 Jeremiah Batts J P		
Dewitt W Powell	&	A J Scott	8th Sept 1858
	Solemnized A. B. Coke M. G.		
Benjamin Majors	&	K. I. Garland	17th Sept 1858
	Solemnized 18 Sept. 1858 R. H. Harrison J P		
A. Y. Donelson	&	M.E.Parker	24th Sept 1858
	Solemnized 28th Sept. 1858 W. L. Caskey M. G.		
John H McFaran	&	Adaline Odle	26th Sept 1858
	Solemnized 27th Sept 1858 Isaac Steel		
H. D. Hacker	&	H.E.Coleman	1st Oct. 1858
	Solemnized John P Campbell M. G.		
James Standley	&	Mary E Standley	11th Oct 1858
	Solemnized 12th. Oct. 1858 John F England M. G.		

(309) G. L. Baggett   & Amanda M Dozier   12th Oct 1858
Solemnized Oct. 14 1858 G. B. Mason J P

Meredith Stratton	&	Sarah A Page	12th Oct 1858
	Solemnized 14th Oct. 1858 H. Warren J P		
John R Long	&	Adaline Batts	13th Oct. 1858
	Solemnized 14th Oct. 1858 John Byrnes J P		
S. B. Preston	&	Rhoda M Jernigan	14th Oct 1858
	Solemnized T. B. Mathews J P		

O.C.Brooks   &   Elizabeth L Allen   16th Oct. 1858
                      Solemnized   Jas. Woodard

W. W. Doss   &   L. A. Murrah   20th Oct 1857
                      Solemnized Oct. 23 1857 Jas. Woodard

Phillip Sneed   &   Mary Ann Elizabeth Taylor 25th Oct. 1858
                      Solemnized G. B. Mason J P

Thomasn M Darden   &   Susan F Davis   26th Oct 1858
                      Solemnized 27th Oct 1858 J. P. Campbell M. G.

(310) Richard C Nipper   &   Susan Jones   27th Octr. 1858
                      Solemnized 28th Octr. 1858 F. R. Gooch M. G.

W. R. Barham   &   N. C. Watts   22 Oct. 1858
                      Solemnized Oct. 24 1858 W. R. Sadler J P

James M Hiett   &   Roxana Dunnington   24th Oct. 1858
                      Solemnized 25th Oct. 1858 R. H. Harrison J P

Clinton M Barnes   &   Lucretia Mantello   28th Oct. 1858
                      Solemnized A. Rose J P

William J Pope   &   Matilda Thomas   28th Oct 1858
                      Solemnized 30th Octr. 1858 H. Warren J P

Charles C Bell   &   Menerva Henry   1st Nov. 1858
                      Solemnized 4th Nov 1858 W. W. Pepper Judge &C

John W Culbertspn   &   Marthy P Frey   6th Nov 1858
                      Solemnized 7th Nov. 1858 John Crawford J P

James A Stark   &   Narcissa Wrights   12th Nov 1858
                      Solemnized 14th Nov. 1858 Thomas West M. G.

(311) James W Pope   &   E. Z. Colthrop   15th Nov 1858
                      Solemnized Jo Hardaway J P

James D Shepherd   &   Elizabeth E Murphy   16th Nov 1858
                      Solemnized 18th Nov. 1858 W Hurt

Jo H Farmer   &   Sarah C Adams   17th Nov 1858
                      Solemnized F. R. Gooch M. G.

Paterick Madden   &   Bridgett Murphy   17th Nov 1858
                      Solemnized Nov 18th 1858 L Host Catholic Priest

Westley Brown   &   Mary Shackelford   19th Nov 1858
                      Solemnized 21st Noc 1858 Jas Woodard

Thomas W Hughes   &   Mary A Mason   23 Nov 1858
                      Solemnized 25th Nov 1858 H. Warren J P

Jesse W Jackson   &   Eliza Jane Mason   23 Nov 1858
                      Solemnized 25th Nov 1858 H. Warren J P

A. J. King   &   L. A. Tiller   25th Nov 1858
                     Solemnized Jo Hardaway J P

(312) James P Nave &   Mary F Hall   29th Nov 1858
                     Solemnized 30th Nov. 1858 B. W. Bradley J P

James H Watts   &   Nancy A Bagbee   30th Nov 1858
                     Solemnized 1st Dec. 1858 F. C. Plaster M. G.

John Ryan   &   Amanda H Batts   30th Nov 1858
                     Solemnized 1st Dec. 1858 John Burns J P

William W Newton   &   Martha Sellers   1st Decr 1858
                     Solemnized 2 Decr 1858 F. R. Gooch M. G.

Jesse Shannon   &   Martha J Rose   3d Decr 1858
                     Solemnized 5th Decr 1858 W. T. Chowning J P

Benjamin S Morris   &   Nancy Bartlett   4th Decr 1858
                     Solemnized 5th Decr 1858 J W Featherston

William E Newton   &   Elizabeth Ruffin   6th Decr 1858
                     Solemnized 8th Decr. 1858 F.R.Gooch M. G.

Elijah T Lawrence   &   Charlotte P Lacy   30th Decr 1857
                     Solemnized 1st Jan 1858 R. H. Harris J P

(313) William P Lucas &   Eliza J Jernigan   9th Decr 1857
                     Solemnized 10 Decr 1857 H. L Covington J P

C. F. Browning   &   Mary F Gorrell   13th Decr 1857
                     Solemnized Jas Woodard

Joseph Oats   &   Polly Ann Hickman   15th Decr 1858
                     Solemnized 18th Decr 1858 B. Gambill J P

R. H. Elum   &   Nancy C Hinkle   15th Decr 1858
                     Solemnized 16th Decr 1858 T. J. Craig J P

Jacob Pitt   &   Rebecca Dozier   16th Decr 1858
                     Solemnized 19th Decr 1858 W. W. Pepper Judge &C

L. F. Edwards   &   M. W. Jackson   16th Decr 1858
                     Solemnized 19th Decr 1858 W. S. Adams

L. W. Morris   &   Elender Webb   17th. Decr 1858
                     Solemnized 23rd Decr 1858 B. W. Bradley J P

Moleys Joice   &   Margaret Flaheety   23d Decr 1858
                     Solemnized Jan. 2 1859 Lewis Host Catholic Priest

(314) John R Moore &   Amanda McNeal   25th Decr 1858
                     Solemnized Decr 26 1858 F. C. Plaster M. G.

Jas. W. Newman   &   Elizabeth Lewis   25th Decr 1858
                     Solemnized 29 Decr. 1858 F. C. Plaster M. G

Josephus Cobb   &   Mary S Crutcher   28th Decr 1858
                     Solemnized 30th Decr 1858 W. W. Wynn M. G.

Pleasant Berry   &   M. W. Wrights   28th Decr 1858
                     Solemnized Thos. West M. G.

A. F. Hilliard   &   Lorery Ragsdale   28th Decr 1858
                     Solemnized Jo Hardaway J P

W. E. Pickard   &   H. D. Dorris   29th Decr 1858
                     Solemnized 30 Decr 1858 G. W. Featherston M. G.

B. F. Gossett   &   Matilda McMunn   29th Decr 1858
                     Solemnized 30 Decr 1858 Geo. L Staley M. G.

Charles E Koepf   &   Rachell P Garratt   30th Decr 1857
                     Solemnized 3d Jany 1858 A. Rose J P

(315) Warren Gladwell   &   Lucretia Jernigan   3d Jany 1859
                     Solemnized 6th Jan 1859   _____

Wilson T Morris   &   Ellen Guinn   4th Jany 1857
                     Solemnized A. Rose J P

William Gravel   &   America Ratcliff   9th Juny 1859
                     Solemnized Paul L H Walker J P

J. H. Boyles   &   D. M. White   13th Jany 1859
                     Solemnized 16th Jan. 1859 H. L. Covington J P

George Sanford   &   Mary F Browning   15th Jany 1859
                     Solemnized 16th Jan. 1859 A. Rose

Elisha Briley   &   Mary O Crabtree   17th Jany 1859
                     Solemnized James Cook J P

Robert F Kays   &   Sarah J Bpthick   17th Jany 1859
                     Solemnized Isaac Steel

Daniel W Benton   &   Amanda E Fryor   19th Jany 1859
                     Solemnized Jany 20th 1859 Jesse B White J P

(316) Lewis Pool   &   Sallie H Thomas   24th Jany1859
                     Solemnized 25th Jany 1859 T. J. Craig J O

T. J. Wilson   &   Missouri C Gossett   28th Jany 1859
                     Solemnized 29th Jany 1859 Thos West M. G.

D. D. Hanley   &   A. C. Cook   2 Feby 1859
                     Solemnized 3 Feby 1859 G. W. Featherston M. G.

AAron Evans   &   O.E.Pettie   5th Feby 1859
                     Solemnized Isaac Steel

William Stanley   &   Martha Ayers   5th Feby 1859
                     Solemnized 6th Feb. 1859 J. F. England M. G

Robert Heffman   &   Harriet Fletcher   7th Feby 1859
                        Solemnized 8th Feby 1859   J. W. Featherston

Cyrus W Washburn   &   Eliza F. A. Fleppen   12th Feby 1859
                        Solemnized 13 February 1859 B. W. Bradley   J P

G. W. Walker   &   Sarah Wilson   21st Feby 1859
                        Solemnized B. W. Bradley J P

(317) S. D. Ogburn   &   Mary Ann Hutcherson   24th Feby 1859
                        Solemnized Jno. R Ellis M. G.

Paterick Hanan   &   Mary Mullory   24th Feby 1859
                        Solemnized 6 March 1859 L Host Catholic Priest

Willice McCort   &   Adeline Woodson   8th March 1859
                        Solemnized 10th March 1859 G. R. Gunn J P

W. H. Villines   &   Nancy Yates   9th March 1859
                        Solemnized 31st March 1859 J. M. Copeland J P

John Smith   &   N.A.Murrey   12th March 1859
                        Solemnized James Cook J P

Benjamin F Webster   &   Matilda Swift   27th March 1859
                        Solemnized 28th March 1859 John F England M G

John P Tollison   &   Lucinda Rosson   11th April 1859
                        Solemnized 12th April 1859 A. M. Greer J P

Green Benton   &   Emily S Bell   5th April 1859
                        Solemnized Jno. A Ellis M. G.

(318) William H Stark &   V. I. Benton   12th April 1859
                        Solemnized J. B. Anderson M. G.

Thomas Alsbrook   &   V. I. Benton   12th April 1859
                        Solemnized A. Rose J P

L. D. Empsom   &   N. A. Jernigan   15th April 1859
                        Solemnized _____

William M Pollock   &   Olivia Solomon   16th April 1859
                        Solemnized 21st April 1859 Jas Woodard

J. A. Ramer   &   N. A. Fowler   19th April 1859
                        Solemnized 21st April 1859 W. B. Fenary

Robert Watson   &   Harriet Redman   21st April 1859
                        Solemnized 2 May 1859 L Host Catholic Priest

B. O Mitchell   &   Jane R. Collins   24th April 1859
                        Solemnized Jo Hardaway J P

G. W. Pence   &   N. A. Thompsom   25th April 1859
                        Solemnized James Woodard

(319)   M. F. Jones   &   Frances Spain   27th April 1859
                             Solemnized 28 April 1859 Jno. A. Ellis M. G.

        Preston Honeycutt   &   Elender Dorris   1st May 1859
                             Solemnized 19th May 1859 Reubin Elmore J P

        W. P. Voloy   &   Mary Glisson   4th May 1859
                             Solemnized 22 May 1859 J. W. Featherston M.G.

        Austin Mayes   &   Caroline Harper   10th May 1859
                             Solemnized 12th May 1859 John F England M. G.

        Brown Clinard   &   Eliza Parker   12th May 1859
                             Solemnized Benj. Rawls M. G.

        L. J. Bell   &   Laura V Henry   16th May 1859
                             Solemnized 19th May 1859 A. B. Coke M. G.

        William W Dorris   &   Lucy Ann Jones   16th May 1859
                             Solemnized 19th May 1859 G. W. Featherston M. G.

        J. H. Hardin   &   Mary E Drake   17th May 1859
                             Solemnized 18th May 1859 E. T. Hart M. G.

(320)   William Rodgers   &   Martha A Edison   18th May 1859
                             Solemnized 19th May 1859 A. Rose J P

        S. G. Hindman   &   Nancy Woodard   21st May 1859
                             Solemnized 22 Lay 1859 G. B. Mason J P

        William Derrett   &   Martha Jones   23 May 1859
                             Solemnized 24 May 1859 H. L. Covington J P

        Andrew J Demumbre   &   Mary E Glover   25th May 1859
                             Solemnized 26th May 1859 B. W. Bradley J P

        J. A. Warren   &   Mary J Warren   1st June 1859
                             Solemnized   James Cook J P

        James W Gordon   &   Rebecca J Shannon   10th June 1859
                             Solemnized H. L. Covington J P

        David H Parker   &   Nancy Clinard   25th June 1859
                             Solemnized Benj. Rawls M. G.

        B. M. Jordan   &   C. F. Adams   28th June 1859
                             Solemnized A. M. Greer J P

(321)   W. J. Bowers   &   S. A. Glisson   8th July 1859
                             Solemnized 9th July 1859 F. R. Gooch M. G.

        Joseph Rinehart   &   Catherine White   8th July 1859
                             Solemnized 9th July 1859 R. H. Harrison J P

        M. P. Jones   &   Virginia H. Williamson 13th July 1859
                             Solemnized E. W. Coleman M. G.

C. M. Mitchell   &   Mary Head   16th July 1859
                      Solemnized 21st July 1859   M. W.Winters J P

J H Page   &   Columbia Chard   16th July 1859
                      Solemnized 19th July 1859 Jno. W. Smith J P

Archer Thomas   &   Mary Jane Egmond   2oth July 1859
                      Solemnized 21st July 1859   W. F. Smith

James M England   &   Elizabeth Jane Warren   22 July 1859
                      Solemnized 23 July 1859   John Crawford J P

William S Hardnall   &   Finula Simmons   23rd July 1859
                      No return

(322) John B Malloy   &   Nancy A Hutcheson   24th July 1859
                      Solemnized 28 July 1859   W. T. Chowning J P

H. D. Drane   &   Harriett Traughber   27th July 1859
                      Solemnized 2 August 1859 E. T. Hart

William A Robertson   &   Rebecca J Jackson   28th July 1859
                      Solemnized H Warren J P

M. R. Willis   &   M. J. Dorris   2 August 1859
                      Solemnized 4th August 1859 G. R. Gunn J P

A. J. Bartholomu   &   Amanda Gainus   6th August 1859
                      Solemnized 7 August 1859 A Rose J P

Meredith Long   &   Sarah A Woodard   8th August 1859
                      Solemnized 9th Aug. 1859   G. B. Mason J.PG.

Thomas L Green   &   Rosanna A Lowe   9th August 1859
                      Solemnized 10th August 1859 Jno A. Ellis M. G.

William McPherson   &   Mary E Rogers   15th August 1859
                      Solemnized 18th Aug. 1859 B. Gambill J P

(323) Mathew Maddrix   &   A Mackey   16th August 1859
                      Solemnized 17th Aug. 1859 John W Smith J P

J. B Richmond   &   Emily V Hutcheson   17th August 1859
                      Solemnized 18 Aug. 1859 R. H. Harrison J P

F. F. Solomon   &   Martha Dorris   17th Aug 1859
                      Solemnized 18th Aug. 1859 G. W. Featherston M. G.

Joel Bell   &   Pernecia F Woodard   25th August 1859
                      Solemnized 1 Sept. 1859   John W Smith J P

James H Blackburn   &   Catherine Swift   27th August 1859
                      Solemnized 28th Aug 1859 J. F. England M. G.

Presley McDole   &   Emily Horton   3d Septr. 1859
                      Solemnized Wm. M. C. Barr J P

	Wesley Simmons	& Charlotte Covington	5th Septr 1859
		Solemnized 6th Septr. 1859 W. T. Chowning J P	
	George Barkfield	& Tennessee Mansker	8th Septr. 1859
		Solemnized 8th Septr. 1859 J. B. Anderson M G	
(324)	J. N. Frey	& Mary Morris	26th Septr. 1859
		Solemnized 27 Sept. 1859 G. B. Mason J. P.	
	William Crasslin	& Sarah George	27th Septr. 1859
		Solemnized 29th Sept. 1859 Benjamin Gambill J P	
	Hugh A Morrison	& Margaret J Gill	28th Sept 1859
		Solemnized 29 Sept. 1859 A. M. Greer J P	
	Thomas F Sadler	& Edney Powell	29th Sept 1859
		Solemnized A Rose J P	
	Parson Woodard	& Virginia A Draughon	29th Aept 1859
		Solemnized John W Smith J P	
	Thomas W Thaxton	& Lucinda Stark	30th Sept 1859
		Solemnized 2 Oct. 1859 Benjamin Gambill J P	
	Jo Anderson	& Sarah A Dickerson	1st Octr. 1859
		Solemnized 2 Oct. 1859 W. W. Wunn M. G.	
	Richard Lyles	& Mary E Jones	3d Octr. 1859
		Solemnized Joel W. Whitten M. G.	
(325)	Hyram Lacy	& Sarah Horton	8th Octr 1859
		Solemnized 9 Octr. 1859 Wm. C. M. Barr J P	
	Samnes Stark	& Mary Shannon	10th Octr/ 1859
		Solemnized 16 Octr. 1859 W. T. Chowning J O	
	J. J. Chadowin	& Harriet E Roe	10th Octr. 1859
		Solemnized Ruebin Elmore J P.	
	Monroe Willard	& Elizabeth Reeder	10th Octr. 1859
		Solemnized 16 October 1859 W. B. Fordsn	
	W. T. Gunn	& Martha J Pride	19th Octr 1859
		Solemnized 20 Oct. 1859 W. Gunn M. G.	
	M. V. Frey	& Lucy S Rust	21st Oct. 1859
		Solemnized 23 Oct. 1859 G.B.Mason J P	
	John B Page	& Almira Robertson	26th Oct 1859
		Solemnized 27 Oct. 1859 H. Warren J P	
	H. E. Canover	& S. E. Trainnum	28th Oct. 1859
		Solemnized 29 Oct. 1859 F. C. Plaster M. G.	
(326)	J. M. Cannon	& Martha A White	31st Octr. 1859
		Solemnized Jesse B White J P	

W. F. Jernigan   &   Martha A White   4th Nov 1859
                        Solemnized 6 Nov 1859 H. L. Covington J P

Eli Cook   &   Sarah J Swift   7th Nov 1859
                        Solemnized 8 Nov. 1859 John Crawford J P

W. A. Williams   &   Mary E Vaughon   9th Nov 1859
                        Solemnized C. H. Cross M. G.

J. L. Harris   &   Mary D Wynn   12 Nov 1859
                        Solemnized 13 Nov 1859 J. T. W. Davis M. G.

R. H. Alley   &   Sarah J Keller   14th Nov 1859
                        Solemnized 15 Nov. 1859 Jerome B Anderson M.G.

Paterick Husley   &   Elizabeth Wolf   21st Nov 1859
                        Solemnized 24 Nov 1859 J. T. Craig J P

Robert Green   &   Martha A Sprouse   27th Nov 1859
                        Solemnized W. W. Pepper Judge & C

(327) B. F. Pace   &   Mary C Hawkins   5th Decr 1859
                        Solemnized 8th Decr. 1859 M. W. Winters J P

James W Burnett   &   Lucy Ann Lipford   10th Decr 1859
                        Solemnized 12 Decr. 1859 F. C. Plaster M. G.

W. M. Jackson   &   Susan J Winfield   14th Decr 1859
                        Solemnized 15th Dec. 1859 H. L. Covington J P

James Darden   &   Susan C Frey   17th Decr 1859
                        Solemnized 18th Dec 1859 J. T. W. Davis M. G.

James M Summerville   &   Victoria Bigbee   20th Decr 1859
                        Solemnized 21 Dec. 1859 R. H. Harrison J P

John C McGoldrick   &   Amelia Murrah   21st Decr. 1859
                        Solemnized 22 Decr. 1859 J. W. Smith J P

W. W. Adams   &   Mary S Woods   23 Decr 1859
                        Solemnized 25th Decr 1859 John W Smith J P

James Appleton   &   Sarah J Traughber   24th Decr 1859
                        Solemnized 27 Dec 1859 Benjamin Gambill J P

(328) A. L. Parks   &   Susan A Pepper   25th Decr 1859
                        Solemnized Jo Hardaway J P

Meredith Powell   &   Mary M Cobb   20th Decr 1859
                        Solemnized 28 Decr 1859 J. T. W. Davis M. G.

Milton Dame   &   Sarah E Elliott   29 Decr 1859
                        Solemnized   J. B. Anderson M. G.

M. W. Draughon   &   Olive Petsway   12th May 1855
                        Solemnized May 13 1855 Jas Woodard

J. C. Bowen   &   M. A Fountain   21st July 1858
                        Solemnized Benj Rawls M. G.

R. C. Blair   &   Lydia A Rawls   13th Sept 1858
     Solemnized 14 Oct. 1858 Benj. Rawls M. G.

John J Underwood   &   Mary J Thomas   17 Sept 1859
     Solemnized 22 Sept 1859 John Crawford J P

J. T. Fort   &   E L Fort   31st May L860
     Solemnized 2 June 1860 F. C. Plaster M. G.

(329)   W. B. Beach   &   J A McNeil   19th Decr 1859
     Solemnized 22 Decr 1859   F. C. Plasters M. G.

John R Turner   &   Mary F Dammon   5th May 1860
     Solemnized Jas. H Mallory J P for Robertson Co.

Charles D Cannon   &   Martha Warmath   16th April 1860
     Solemnized   17 April 1860 W C Rawls J P

G. W. Draughon   &   Piety Pittman   15th June 1860
     Solemnized 16th June 1860   J. M. Speer J P

George Adams   &   Mary M Clark   13th June 1860
     Solemnized 14 June 1861 Wm Draughon J P

John M Gibbs   &   Nancy M Pike   16th June 1860
     Solemnized Jo Hardaway   J P

Benjd. Ponds   &   Sophrona Cook   22 Decr 1859
     Solemnized 25th Decr 1859 G. W. Featherston M G

Larkin Payne   &   Susan Arnold   2nd Jay 1860
     Solemnized 11 Jay 1860 G. W. Featherstpn M.G.

(330)   J. L. Jones   &   Virginia Boyd   17th Jany 1860
     Solemnized   19 Jany 1860   G. W. Featherston   M.G.

Thos. N Brooks   &   Mary R Greer   10 Oct 1855
     Solemnized   S. D. Ogburn M. G.

James Goerge   &   Jane Brown   1st May 1860
     Solemnized 3 May 1860 W M. C. Barr J P

Robert Moore   &   Martha F Bracy   30th April 1860
     Solemnized   Williw H Head M. G.

M. B. Ford   &   L. B. Cooksey   28th May 1860
     Solemnized W. W. Pepper Judge of 10th Circuit of
                                          Tennessee

B. D. Hollin   &   M. E. Cromwell   4th June 1860
     Solemnized 5th June 1860 A. B. Moore M. G.

E. L. Aingell   &   L. J. May   25th May 1860
     Solemnized 26 May 1860 E Burr J P

R. M. Covington   &   Mary E Freeland   2nd June 1860
     Solemnized _____

(331)   W. J. Mantle   &   Mary A Hart   14th April 1860
                              Solemnized Francis Barnes

        R. L. Adams   &   Martha A Ogg   7th May 1860
                              Solemnized 15 May J.A. Bell J P

        James H Frizzell   &   Sarah J Farmer   30th May 1860
                              Solemnized 31st May 1860 Jas H Mallory J P

        F. M. Brown   &   M J Easley   10th May 1860
                              Solemnized W R Saddler J P

        Meredith T Robertson &   Lucy Jane Winn   8th May 1860
                              Solemnized 10 May 1860 J M Speer J P

        Isaac G Coles   &   Mary E Gillum   17th May 1860
                              Solemnized W W Pepper, Judge 10th Circuit of Tenn.

        W. R. Pope   &   Mary A Pike   16th May 1860
                              Solemnized W W Pepper Judge 10th District of Tenn.

        J.A.Darden   &   A M Fiser   15th March 1860
                              Solemnized J T W Davis M G

(332)   John W Briely   &   Lucinda Murphy   16th Jany 1860
                              Solemnized   James Cook J P

        William Winfield   &   Frances E Owen   17th April 1860
                              Solemnized   —————————

        T H W Parrish   &   Tabitha Fowler   28th March 1860
                              Solemnized 8 April 1860 J S Hollis J P

        Jesse B Draughon   &   Miss B A Batts   10th April 1860
                              Solemnized 16 April 1860   J W Smith J P

        W. A. Bennett   &   M A Ireland   2nd April 1860
                              Solemnized 3 April 1860 H Warren J P

        Jackson Fort   &   Sarah Head   7th Jany 1860
                              Solemnized 15 Spril 1860 W M Winters

        Tazwell Hyde   &   Ellen Green   3oth April 1860
                              Solemnized W W Pepper Judge 10th Circuit of Tenn.

        Drewery Warren   &   Almarinda Parker   5th Decr 1859
                              Solemnized 6 Decr 1859 John F England M G

(334)   James F Dunn   &   Nancy J Menees   8th March 1860
                              Solemnized F R Gooch M G

        James M Shelton   &   Letta Y Heddleston   11th April 1860
                              Solemnized 12 April 1860 Jesse B White J P

        George McMurry   &   Lucinda Elizabeth Stone 25th Jany 1860
                              Solemnized 26 Jan. 1860 James Cook J P

Carroll Huey	&	Miss M M Holland	23rd Feby 1860
	Solemnized 24 Feby 1860 G R Gunn J P		
Henry Carlisle	&	Mary Ann Fletcher	15th Feby 1860
	Solemnized 16th Feby 1860 J W Featherston		
William Fletcher	&	Carina Hall	22nd March 1860
	Solemnized Jo Hardaway J P		
John W Smith	&	Adeline Lett	16th March 1860
	Solemnized John W Smith J P for Robertson County		
E G Strange	&	Mary E Braswell	5th March 1860
	Solemnized 6th March 1860 John Bryns J P		
(335) Wm W Naive	&	Sarah J Tally	28th Jany 1860
	Solemnized Feby. 8 1860 W R Saddler J P		
Charles Palmer	&	Jennatta Elizabeth Greer 8th March 1860	
	Solemnized J T W Davis M G		
Thos. Holland	&	Mary Ann Griffin	2nd March 1860
	Solemnized 8th March 1860 John W Smith J P		
W. F. Willis	&	Mary Ann Hooper	1st March 1860
	Solemnized H L Covington J P		
Jacob Peck	&	Lettitia Balthrop	24 Feby 1860
	Solemnized 1st March 1860 M W Winters J P		
R H Bradshan	&	Susan Barler*	20th Feby 1860
	Solemnized M. W. Winters J P		
W E Maurey	&	Sue D Percise	18th Feby 1860
	Solemnized 19th Feby 1860 J W Cullum Minister		
M D Cobb	&	Sarah C T Binkley	15th Feby 1860
	Solemnized 16th Feby 1860 J T W Davis Minister		
(336) William M Toliver	&	Mary M Freeman	14th Feby 1860
	Solemnized 17th Feby 1860 Benjamin Gambill J P		
M. V. Ingram	&	Anna Lurie Farmer	8th Feby 1860
	Solemnized John W Duncan M G		
William H Elliott	&	Virginia T Naive	28th Jany 1860
	Solemnized 9th Feby 1860 M. W. Winters J P		
William H Cannon	&	Dorotha Payne	30th Jany 1860
	Solemnized J B White J P		
C J Owen	&	Cordelia Winfield	30th Jany 1860
	Solemnized 2 Feby 1860 W T Chowning J O		
Connell O Donnell	&	Bridget O Donnell	16th Jay 1860
	Solemnized T B Mathews J P		
James B Holman	&	Martha J Barbee	11th Jany 1860
	Solemnized 12 Jany 1860 John W Smith J O		

Xenophpn Simmons   &   Sarah P Knight   8th Jany 1860
                          Solemnized 9 Jany 1860 Jo Hardaway J P

(337)   W. J. Anderson   &   Ginory Grise   7th Jany 1860
                          Solemnized 8th Jan. 1860 John W Smith J P

        Samuel P Baldwin &   Nancy Catherine Borrew 5th Jany. 1860
                          Solemnized Jesse B White   J P

        John F Smith   &   Elizabeth Woodard   5th Jany 1860
                          Solemnized Jo Hardaway J P

        Hiram W Pentecost &   Martha J Farmer   2nd Jany 1860
                          Solemnized 19Jany 1860 'M. W. Winters J P

        O C Morrison   &   Minerva A Fletcher   7th Nov 1859
                          Solemnized Decr 11 1859 W. W. Adams

        Wm H whitehead   &   Miss Harriet E Gill 2nd Jany 1860
                          Solemnized 5 July 1860 A. M. Greer J P

        James Lipscomb   &   Eliza J Traughber   21st Aug. 1860
                          Solemnized E. Burr J P

        William T Anderson &   M. A Rawls   26th Aug 1860
                          Solemnized 27 Aug 1860 J B Anderson M G

(338)   J. W. Babb   &   M. J. Roney   3rd Jany 1859
                          Solemnized 7 Aug 1859 _____

        Sycurgua Randolph &   Martha A Gunn   6th July 1859
                          Solemnized   _____

        John T Bains   &   Susan Hope   3rd Aug. 1859
                          Solemnized   _____

        G W Briggs   &   A. W. Jackson   29th June 1860
                          Solemnized 3 July 1860 J B Anderson M G

        J N McCrary   &   Mary Lewis   22 July 1860
                          Solemnized W W Pepper Judge 10th Circuit Tenn

        W A Pike   &   M J Bridges   14th July 1860
                          Solemnized 15th July 1860 W W Pepper Judge

        W A Prince   &   Mary E Edwards   12th July 1860
                          Solemnized John W Smith J P for Robertson CO.

        Jesse McFarland   &   Louisa Odle   18th June 1860
                          Solemnized 18th June 1860 Isaac Steel

(339)   E. M. Markham   &   Virginia C Williams   3rd Decr 1860
                          Solemnized G W Featherston

        J M Smart   &   Mary J Summerville   6th Jany 1860
                          Solemnized 8th Jany 1860 J M Copeland J P

****

Josephus Williams   &   Mary J Strickland   31st Decr 1860
                       Solemnized 3 Jany. 1861 Reubin Elmore J P

Thos J Eidson   &   Elizabeth Shy   7th May 1860
                       Solemnized 10 May 1860 J N Thornhill J P

T J Babb   &   Sarah E Brewer   25th June 1860
                       Solemnized 28th June 1860 G W Featherston M G

John Swann   &   Mary F Webb   10th Aug. 1860
                        Solemnized 13 Aug 1860 Thos. West Minister

Hugh Henry   &   Louisa Cole   10th March 1860
                       Solemnized 12 March 1860 H L Covington J P

William A Cole   &   Elanor L Moss   7th July 1860
                       Jas N Thornhill J P Solemnized 9th. July. 1860

(340) Jas. F Cole   &   Harriet Stark   7th July 1860
                       Solemnized 8 July 1860 E Burr J O

Benj F King   &   Margaret Blackburn   7th July 1860
                       Solemnized 8 July 1860 Francis Barnes J P

Cyrus E Butt   &   Milley Traughber   4th July 1860
                       Solemnized 8 July 1860 E Burr J P

James Fisher   &   Armetta Willis   21st July 1860
                       Solemnized 23 July 1860 T O Tarpley J P

George McMillin   &   Tabitha J West   27th July 1860
                       Solemnized 2 Aug 1860 T O Tarpley J P

Charles Ellison   &   Harriet Pepper   1st Aug 1860
                       Solemnized 2 Aug 1860 Jas Cook J P

Robert Gory   &   L F Edwards   13th Aug 1860
                       Solemnized 15 Aug 1860 W S Adams

J C Carver   &   Eliza F Ford   4th Aug 1860
                       Solemnized 5 Aug 1860 J M Speer J P

(341) J Q A Simmons   &   Mary Jane Porter   28th Aug 1860
                       Solemnized Jo Hardaway J P

R B Daniels   &   E A Tollison   14thAug 1860
                       Solemnized 16 Aug 1860 D K Moreland Pastor
                                        Harmony Church Rob. Co. Tenn

Shelby Barsley   &   John Ellen Pence   29th Spet 1860
                       Solemnized Isaac Steel

W A Campbell   &   Josephine Wells   26th Sept 1860
                       Solemnized 27 Sept 1860 John W Smith J P

James Fletcher   &   Ellen Oran   25th Sept 1860
                       Solemnized W F Pride J P

J H Johnson   &   Martha E Reed   3rd Sept 1860
                       Solemnized 6 Sept 1860 J A Bell J P

P H Bowling   & Elizabeth A Shannon 21st Sept. 1860
        Solemnized _____

James Osburn   & Mary A Kiger 27th Sept. 1860
        Solemnized W C Rawls J P

(342) Charles Dickinson & Mary Matilda Pentecost 3rd Sept 1860
        Solemnized 6 Sept 1860 W M Winters J P

J R Highsmith & N G Tayler 3rd Sept 1860
        Solemnized 6th Sept 1860 W F Pride J P

William Fuqua & Mary A Clinard 29th Sept 1860
        Solemnized 30 Sept 1860 W C Rawls J P

William Clinard & Thirsey Fuqua 18th Sept 1860
        Solemnized 23 Sept 1860 W C Rawls J P

Thomas Doyle & F V Williams 6th Sept 1860
        Solemnized J M Speer J P

Phillip Athony Polly Hill 15th Sept 1860
        Solemnized 18 Sept 1860 G W Martin M G

J R Anderson & E F Batts 23 Oct 1860
        Solemnized J T W Davis Minister Gospel

Jas. W Chambers & Lucy W Bell 18th Sept 1860
        Solemnized 2 Oct 1860 J B Anderson Minister of
               the Gospel

(343) W J Bruce & Lucy Pepper 19th Oct. 1860
        Solemnized Jo Hardaway J P

Malichi Benton & Roxane Benton 4th Oct. 1860
        Solemnized W W Pepper Judge of Circuit Court Tenn.

John W Warren & Mary F McMurry 25th Oct 1860
        Solemnized _____

W W Glover & W V Bidwell 1st Oct 1860
        Solemnized 3 Oct. 1860 Geo. W Martin M. G.

Obadiah Chandler & Nancy A Crabtree 26 Nov 1860
        Solemnized 28 Nov 1860 W B Kelly M G

J T W Davis & Mary E Batts 31st Oct 1860
        Solemnized 1 Nov 1860 Jerome B Anderson M G

L A Tatum & Allice N Taylor 14th Nov 1860
        Solemnized W H Bugg J P Robertson County

(344) M L Fisher & E J Babb 6th Nov 1860
        Solemnized 8th Nov 1860 J M Copeland J P

L W WL Wiles & Mary E Gallaher 17th Nov L860
        Solemnized 18 Nov 1860 G Benton J P

W H James   &   Susan A Stolts   24th Oct 1860
                       Solemnized 1 Nov 1860 J J Bradley J P

William R Radford   &   Piety H Fort   24th Nov 1860
                       Solemnized 26 Nov 1860 F C Plaster M G

Josiah Clinard   &   Harriet A Parker   1st Oct 1860
                       Solemnized 4th Nov 1860 J L Hollis J P

J W Burchett   &   W E Lipford   16th Nov 1860
                       Solemnized F C Plaster M G

W A Huffman   &   M C Higgs   5th Nov 1860
                       Solemnized 14th Nov 1860 J S Hollis J P

(345) G C Elmore   &   Sarah Thurman   20 Decr 1860
                       Solemnized _____

James Berry   &   Melissa A Webb   22 Decr 1860
                       Solemnized 23 Decr 1860 J W Featherston M G

David Nimo   &   Sarah Chism   21st Decr 1860
                       Solemnized 23 Decr 1860 J W Featherston M G

Wm H Head   &   Mary W Murphy   28th Nov 1860
                       Solemnized 6 Decr 1860 W. M. Winters J P

George W Williams   &   Mildred V Watson   10th Decr 1860
                       Solemnized 17th Decr 1860 John W Smith J P

M D Taylor   &   M. E. Stark   17th Decr 1860
                       Solemnized 20th Decr 1860 John W Smith J P

H W Warreh   &   Fanny B Burch   3rd Decr 1860
(346)   Solemnized   W F Pride J P

M O Mason   &   Melissa D Taylor   17th Decr 1860
                       Solemnized 20 Decr 1860 W H Pride

D L Holland   &   Mary J Powell   3rdDecr 1860
                       Solemnized 4 Decr 1860 J W Smith J P

J L Townsend   &   E M Graves   17 Decr 1860
                       Solemnized 25 Decr 1860 E Burr J P

J W R McIntosh   &   Sarah Jane Fuqua   14th Decr 1860
                       Solemnized on 16th Decr 1860 E Burr J P

Thos. M Rust   &   Sarah M Highsmith   3rd Decr 1860
                       Solemnized 12 Decr 1860 F C Plaater M G

Wesley Bransford   &   Chissie Thomas   5th Decr 1860
                       Solemnized 6 Decr 1860 A P McFerrin Minister

Samuel Keller   &   Minie F England   1st Jany 1862
                       Solemnized James Cook J P

(347)   A J Gee   &   Mary Boatnight   24 Oct 1861
                                Solemnized E W Gunn M G

         M M Lurie   &   Catherine Warner   21st Feby 1861
                                Solemnized W R Sadler   J P

         H E Hyde   &   Susan M Justice   19th Nov 1861
                                Solemnized J J Bradley J P

         Perry C annon   &   Elizabeth Baldwin   19th Nov 1861
                                Solemnized Wm Draughon J P

         W W Roby   F A Sumner   25th May 1861
                                Solemnized J M Copeland J P

         S J Yates   &   Louisa Carr   10th June 1861
                                Solemnized J M Copeland J P

         John B Strother   &   Martha M Boyles   29th June 1861
                                Solemnized J M Copeland J P

(348)   James P Frey   &   Amelia Simmons   10th June 1861
                                Solemnized   J M Copeland J P

         G W Harper   &   N M Barker   21st Nov 1861
                                Solemnized E Burr J P

         James B Harper   &   L J Ragsdale   21st Nov 1861
                                Solemnized E Burr J P

         E C Mason   &   Mary F Winn   25 Jany 1861
                                Solemnized H Warren J P

         J M Evans   &   Sarah C Nevell   30th July 1861
                                Solemnized J L Durrett J P

         G Kennedy   &   Ellen Howard   20th Aug 1861
                                Sqlemnized Isaac Steel

         O W Smith   &   C M Page   29th Aug 1861
                                Solemnized W F Pride J P

(349)   Meredith Traughber   &   Nancy C Henderson   29th Decr 1861
                                Solemnized J W Smith J P

         B F King   &   Frances Todd   27th Decr 1861
                                Solemnized Jas H Mallory J P

         Wm H Todd   &   Jane Farmer   13th Nov 1858
                                Solemnized B B Batts J P

         Alonzo Ryan   &   N I Boyd   24 Decr 1861
                                Solemnized E Burr J P

         Samuel Violett   &   Elizabeth Copeland   11 Aug 1861
                                Solemnized Isaac Steel

Mathew Morris   &   Catherine S Cobb   18 Aug 1861
Solemnized   Geo. W Martin M G

Thos. Lowell   &   Nancy A Hunter   15th Oct 1861
Solemnized   F C Plaster

(350)   Wm. Bumpass   &   Maranda Ogg   21st Feby 1861
Solemnized 27th Feby 1861 W L Adams

Henry W Williams   &   Mary G Burgess   14th April 1861
Solemnized W L Adams

W H Rust   &   Mary E Williams   _____
Solemnized 28 March 1861 W L Adams

Wm Allen   &   Virginia Shelton   22nd Jay 1861
Solemnized John W Smith J P

W J Darden   &   Mary E Gardner   14th March 1861
Solemnized A Atkins J P

J C Barry   &   M Byram   22 Aug 1861
Solemnized 22 Aug. 1861   T P Tarpley J P

Thos. Cole   &   Nellie Ellison   26th Aug 1861
Solemnized   A Cook J P

(351)   James C Shelton   &   Amanda R Barbee   19th Sept 1861
Solemnized George W Walker J P

Phillip D Summerville &   Elizabeth Ashabraner   22nd Ave 1861
Solemnized   Isaac Steel

Joshua Arnold   &   Mary F Berry   28th July 1861
Solemnized G W Featherston M G

B H Bradley   &   Nancy C Coleman   20 Nov 1861
Solemnized G W Martin M G

James Burgess   &   Mary Ayres   3rd Nov 1861
Solemnized J W Featherston

W F Stark   &   Angeline Lucas   27th Oct 1861
Solemnized Jas. Coom J P

Elizah Warren   &   Nancy England 2nd Sept 1861
Solemnized   Francis Barns J P

(352)   T J Drane   &   Nancy C Gorham   25th April 1861
Solemnized   E Burr J P

John Moudy   &   Martha Appleton   12th May 1861
Solemnized E Burr J P

C O Burr   &   Mary J Pitt   7th July 1861
Solemnized   E Burr J P

J H Newman   &   L J Hope   20th August 1861
Solemnized Jo Hardaway J P

	John E Bainbridge	& E C Hill	6th Sept 1861
		Solemnized 10th Sept. 1861 G W Martin M G	
	Thomas Watts	& M T Morris	9th Sept 1861
		Solemnized 12 ___ 1861 G W Martin M G	
	R L Ford	& Lucy Beall	24th Sept 1861
		Solemnized Jo Hardaway J P	
(353)	G W Clifton	& Louisa Bone	9th June 1861
		Solemnized Geo. W Trenary	
	W W Wautland	& Susan Neeley	26 Oct 1861
		Solemnized Jo Hardaway J P	
	David Craig	& Mrs. F C Cooley	21 Oct 1861
		Solemnized W H Bugg J P	
	L W Bowers	& H H Anderson	5 June 1861
		Solemnized W H Bugg J P	
	Alex Mackey	& Martha F Pert	9 June 1861
		Solemnized Jno. W Smith J P	
	J L Widdick	& Ophelia Doe	8 Feby 1861
		Solemnized Benj Rawls M G	
	Wm. Host	& Mary J Ivey	3 June 1861
		Solemnized J T W Davis M.G.	
(354)	J H Woodard	& A S A F Dalton	13 Feby 1861
		Solemnized 14 Feby 1861 W F Pride J P	
	Jas D Inscore	& Sarah Wilson	28 Feby 1861
		Solemnized Jo Hardaway J P	
	Avery Stark	& Mary H Newten	13 Feby 1861
		Solemnized Wm Draughon J P	
	J W Rawls	& Martha S Anderson	21 Oct 1861
		Solemnized 13 Oct 1861 J B White J P	
	T J Doss	& Susan E Ellison	20 Sept 1861
		Solemnized 22 Sept. 1861 T O Tarpley J P	
	C S Gooch	& Sarah J Bowers	25 Sept 1861
		Solemnized 29 Sept 1861 J M Speer J P	
	W A Millen	& E J Young	26 Sept 1861
		Solemnized J H Gill M.G.	
(355)	J M Drake	& Mary Wilson	11 Feby 1861
		Solemnized 14 Feby 1861 G W Trenary	
	John Southerland	& Mary E Beasley	4 Feby 1861
		Solemnized 12 Feby. 1861 G W Featherston M G	

Francis Kirby   &   Elizabeth Gainus   28 March 1861
                       Solemnized Francis Barnes J P

Jas. W Hollis   &   Madora A Clinard   16 April 1861
                       Solemnized 17 April 1861 W C Rawls J P

Jas. A West   &   Cidia E Biggs   9 Jany 1861
                       Solemnized Isaac Steel G. M.

Edward C Edwards   &   Aggelette Breeves   29 Jany 1861
                       Solemnized 30 Jany 1861 G W Featherston M G

A Doss   &   Juditha Broaderick   13 April 1861
                       Solemnized 14 April 1861 Greenberry Kelly M G

(356) Thos. H Benton & Mary Pepper   1 May 1861
                       Solemnized H Warren J P

D J Gambill   &   Margaret Brewer   8 May 1861
                       Solemnized W M Willia J. P.

G E Choat   &   Susan Woodson   14 May 1861
                       Solemnized 15 May 1861 Francis Barnes J P

W F Stone   &   N E Winfield   6 May 1861
                       Solemnized James Cook J P

W C Garth   &   Hildreth Fort   22 April 1861
                       Solemnized 10 May 1861 F C Plasters M G

Jno. W. Stark   &   Minerva Aiken   25 March 1861
                       Solemniaed 28 March 1861 R. S. Blankenship M G

Jno. Bell Jr.   &   Julia Woodard   20 April 1861
                       Solemnized 24th April 1861 A B Coke M G

(357) C H Hudwell   &   Mary E Hill   March 28 1861
                       Solemnized Jas. Woodard J P

ERRATA

(Note) The page numbers for ERRATA refer to the pages of the original volume, and are to be found on the left margin of the manuscript.

(p 5)	Should be	Herring
(p 5)	Should be	July
(p 15)	Should be	1839
(p 15)	Should be	Dec. 12, 1839
(p 15)	Should be	U. Young, J.P.
(p 20)	Should be	Lucinda
(p 24)	Should be	Nathan Morris
(p 30)	Should be	Wm. T.
(p 35)	Should be	April
(p 36)	Should be	Justin
(p 48)	Should be	Williams
(p 49)	Should be	W.W. Williams
(p 56)	Omitted Date solemnized:	June 28, 1842
(p 56)	Omitted Date solemnized:	June 28, 1842
(p 58)	Should be	Johnston
(p 59)	Omitted: 1. August 2. Solemnized	
(p 62)	Omitted: October	
(p 62)	Should be	July 13
(p 62)	Should be	July 13
(p 63)	Omitted:	Adams
(p 65)	Omitted:	J
(p 65)	Omitted:	August 2, 1842
(p 71)	Should be	Sayers
(p 76)	Omitted Date solemnized:	May 25, 1843
(p 77)	Omitted:	M
(p 79)	Should be	Harrison
(p 83)	Omitted:	Solemnized by Lewis Adams, M.G.
(p 87)	Should be	Eliz. W.
(p 90)	Omitted:	

Crumbaugh, J.B. to Nancy Bailey   28th. Mar. 1844
Solemnized   U. Young J.P.

(p 100)   Omitted:

Dresony, Warren   to   Mary A. Ford 16th Sept. 1844
Solemnized 19th. Sept. 1844 James Sprouse J.P.

(p 114)	Omitted Date solemnized:	26th Sept. 1846
(p 116)	Omitted Date solemnized:	10 March 1845
(p 118)	Omitted Date solemnized:	26 March 1846
(p 120)	Should be	Basford
(p 121)	Omitted Date solemnized:	18th. July 1846
(p 127)	Omitted Date solemnized:	28th. April 1847
(p 135)	Should be	3rd. Jan. 1847
(p 141)	Should be	12th. July
(p 141)	Omitted Date solemnized	15th. Aug. 1847
(p 144)	Omitted:	M

ERRATA

(p 148)	Should be	Jan. 23rd.
(p 150)	Should be	Lancaster
(p 150)	Should be	Michael W.
(p 151)	Should be	G.B. Mason
(p 152)	Should be	Morris
(p 152)	Should be	Carroll
(p 153)	Omitted Date solemnized:	30th. July 1848
(p 154)	Should be	Lancaster
(p 156)	Should be	Drake
(p 158)	Omitted Date solemnized:	Dec. 24, 1848
(p 159)	Omitted Date solemnized:	July 7, 1846
(p 159)	Should be	Edmond
(p 160)	Omitted Date solemnized:	Oct. 25, 1848
(p 161)	Should be	Freeman
(p 161)	Omitted Date solemnized:	Aug. 28, 1848
(p 162)	Should be Larison or Sarison ?	
(p 163)	Should be	Barker
(p 167)	Should be	July 7, 1849
(p 167)	Omitted Date solemnized:	July 10, 1849
(p 168)	Omitted Date solemnized:	Aug. 23, 1849
(p 169)	Should be	Link
(p 169)	Should be	Matilda
(p 170)	Should be	Thomas B. Matthews
(p 171)	Omitted Date solemnized:	Dec. 1, 1849
(p 173)	Omitted Date solemnized:	Feb. 25, 1850
(p 177)	Should be	A. Chambers
(p 177)	Omitted Date solemnized:	Dec. 24, 1849
(p 178)	Should be	Hamson or Harrison ?
(p 178)	Should be	T.B. Mathews J.P.
(p 178)	Should be	B. Randolph J.P.
(p 178)	Should be	Bedwell
(p 179)	Should be	Dunn
(p 181)	Should be	Lucinda
(p 181)	Should be	Harris
(p 182)	Should be	Mansfield
(p 185)	Should be	Sales or Yates ?
(p 185)	Omitted Date solemnized:	Feb. 13, 1851
(p 194)	Omitted Date solemnized:	June 12th.
(p 196)	Should be	Soyars
(p 196)	Should be	Soyars
(p 198)	Should be	April 22, 1849
(p 209)	Should be	Samiel
(p 214)	Omitted Date solemnized:	May 9, 1852
(p 216)	Omitted Date solemnized:	Aug. 22, 1852
(p 217)	Should be	Meguiar
(p 218)	Should be	Kimbrough
(p 220)	Should be	Derriberry
(p 221)	Should be	Nolen
(p 222)	Omitted Date solemnized:	March 3, 1853
(p 224)	Should be	Feb.

****

ERRATA

```
(p 226)  Omitted Date solemnized    April 10, 1853
(p 228)  Omitted Date solemnized    June 28, 1853
(p 228)  Omitted Date solemnized    June 30, 1853
(p 228)  Omitted initial L
(p 228)  Omitted Date solemnized    Aug. 11, 1853
(p 230)  Should be   Blackmore
(p 231)  Omitted Date solemnized    Sept. 18, 1853
(p 234)  Omitted Date solemnized    Nov. 20, 1853
(p 234)  Should be   John Crafford
(p 234)  Omitted Date solemnized    Nov. 25, 1853
(p 237)  Omitted Date solemnized    Dec. 25, 1853
(p 240)  Should be   Crockett
(p 240)  Should be   Jan. 18th.
(p 240)  Should be   Benj. Rawls
(p 241)  Should be   Bridges
(p 242)  Should be   W.D. Baldwin
(p 247)  Should be   Woodson
(p 254)  Omitted Date solemnized    Jan. 3, 1853
(p 254)  Omitted Date solemnized    Jan. 4, 1855
(p 254)  Omitted Date solemnized    Jan. 9, 1855
(p 260)  Omitted Date solemnized    June 14, 1855
(p 260)  Should be W. B. Kelly  M.G.
(p 261)  Should be   Draughon
(p 261)  Omitted Date solemnized    July 24, 1855
(p 261)  Should be   Clark
(p 261)  Omitted Date solemnized    Aug. 2, 1855
(p 263)  Should be   G.B. Mason J.P.
(p 269)  Should be   G.W. Featherston
(p 271)  Should be   Crawford
(p 271)  Omitted  July
(p 276)  Should be   Gilson
(p 276)  Should be   Warner
(p 277)  Should be   Ramey
(p 277)  Omitted Date solemnized    Sept. 28, 1856
(p 277)  Omitted Date solemnized    Oct. 26, 1856
(p 277)  Should be   Herrington
(p 278)  Omitted Date solemnized    Oct. 23, 1856
(p 278)  Omitted Date solemnized    Oct. 23, 1856
(p 279)  Omitted Date solemnized    Nov. 7, 1856
(p 279)  Should be   Corbitt
(p 280)  Should be   Bailey
(p 282)  Omitted   F.C. Plaster  M.G.
(p 290)  Should be   Mayhugh
(p 295)  Should be   Alley
(p 296)  Should be   Quarles
(p 297)  Should be   Kesee
(p 297)  Omitted Date solemnized    Nov. 26, 1857
(p 300)  Omitted Date solemnized    Jan. 14, 1858
```

ERRATA

(p 302)	Should be	Frey
(p 303)	Should be	Ivey
(p 303)	Should be	Fulcher
(p 314)	Should be	Ragland
(p 318)	Should be	J.A. Huddleston
(p 325)	Should be	Summer
(p 325)	Omitted Date solemnized	Oct. 15, 1859
(p 326)	Should be	Martha J. Boyles
(p 328)	Should be	Fountane
(p 331)	Omitted Date solemnized	May 18, 1831
(p 334)	Should be	Letta Z. Huddleston
(p 335)	Should be	Bradshaw
(p 335)	Should be	Susan
(p 341)	Should be	Tollerson
(p 344)	Should be	Willis
(p 346)	Should be	Chrissie
(p 347)	Should be	Boatwright
(p 351)	Should be	November
(p 353)	Should be	Colley
(p 354)	Should be	12
(p 356)	Should be	Brewer
(p 356)	Should be	1st.

146   **Robertson Co., TN - Marriage Records - Volume 1 - 1839 - 1861**

****

Marriage Records

Robertson County, Tennessee

Vol. 1
1829 - 1860

INDEX

(Note) Page numbers in this index refer to those of the
orginal book from which this copy was made. These numbers are carried
in the left hand margin of this copy. This book contains the only record
of Marriages in Robertson County prior to 1860.

A

****

Allen,Elizabeth L.	309	Appleton, James	327
Allen, Harriet	274	Appleton, Martha	185-352
Allen, Hartwell	243	Appleton, Mary	178
Allen, Louisa S.	249	Appleton, Nancy	285
Allen, Mary C	175	Archey, D. A.	249
Allen, Menervia	8	Archer, Thomas	321
Allen, Pemelia	221	Armstrong, Frances	100
Allen, Susan	268	Armstrong, Huddah	107
Allen, Wm.	350	Armstrong, Josephus	109
Allensworth, A. J.	290	Armstrong, Madora	267
Alley, Elizabeth	36	Armstrong, Nancy	124
Alley, James A.	120	Armstrong, Robert	115
Alley, Mary	84	Armstrong, William	259
Alley, R.H.	295-326	Arnold, Charity	166
Allison, Fountain S	7	Arnold, Delela A.	277
Allison, Susan J.	79	Arnold, Joshua	351
Allsbrook, A.	121	Arnold, Susan	329
Allsbrook, John	190	Arnold, T. W.	187
Ally,Alexander	585	Ashbranah, Abraham	135
Ally,Middy	112	Ashbranah, D.	233
Almon, John L.	285	Ashbranah, Nancy B.	251
Alsbrook, David L.	52	Ashbraner, Jno. W.	25
Alsbrook, Martha P.	51	Ashbrand, W. H.	236
Alsbrook, Mary E.	34	Ashbranner, Elizabeth	351
Alsbrook, N.A.	121	Ashburn, Mary A.	94
Alsbrook, Thomas	36-318	Ashworth, John	139
Alsbrook, Willie B.	108	Atkins, A	154-350
Alsbrook, Wm. R.	97	Atkins, Harriet A.	43
Amos, Ann E.	72	Atkins, J.S.	280
Amos, Jackson	39	Atkins, Margaret	217
Amos, L.I.	163	Atkins, N. J. 306	306
Anderson, Benjamin H.	229	Atkinson, Eliza C	241
Anderson, Charlotte	46	Atkinson F. C.	239
Anderson, Ellen	300	Atkinson, Sarah E	248
Anderson, H. M.	353	Auglin, E. N.	184
Anderson, J. B. 318-323-326		Auglinn, Elvira R.	247
328-337-338-342-343		Aull, R. P.	248
Anderson, James 175-193-234-240		Ayres, Caroline	58
Anderson, Jo	324	Ayres, E.	201
Anderson, Joseph	7	Ayres, Emily T.	58
Anderson,Martha S.	354	Ayres, John	205-220
Anderson,Mary	249	Ayres, L.	10-11
Anderson, M.A.M.	171	Ayres, Louisa	67
Anderson, Nancy	276	Ayres, Marinda	111
Anderson, Pleasant H.	107	Ayres, Marinda T	16
Anderson, R.C.	297	Ayres, Martha	189-316
Anderson, Rose Ann	272	Ayres, Mary	351
Anderson, Sarah S.	288	Ayres, W. W.	62
Anderson, W.J.	337	Ayres, Wm.	99
Anderson, William	212		
Anderson, William J.	337	B.	
Anderson, William T.	337	Babb, Abel O	45
Angel, Sarah A. E.	132	Babb, Alsey	225
Anglin, E. N.	184	Babb, Cinthia	12
Anglin, Elvira R.	247	Babb, E. J.	344
Anthony, Phillip	342	Babb, Elizabeth	148
Appleton, C. S.	161	Babb, James	63

Babb, James B	236		Baird, Ann I	243
Babb, John	99		Baird, D. G.	62-67-72-74-77-80
Babb, Joseph,	64		81-82-84-85-91-92-94-95-97-99-	
Babb, J. W.	338		110-111-121-125-127-130-132-135	
Babb, Nancy	50		145-148-150-151-154-158-159-161	
Babb, P.	193		174-176-177-180-194-203-207	
Babb, P.P.	111		Baird, G. W.	140
Babb, Pamelia A.	19		Baird, Mary I.	285
Babb, Sarah A.	179		Baird, Thos.	181
Babb, T. J.	339		Baker, J.H.W.	30
Babb, Young	161		Baker, James	120
Baggbee, Nancy A.	312		Baker, Joseph C	291
Bagly, Aaron	218		Baker, L.A.	163
Bagby, Benjamin	261		Baker, Robert J.	79
Bagby, Harriet	67-74		Baker, N. M.	347
Bagby, Martha J.	266		Balance, Nancy	90
Bagby, Robert	263		Balarcy, John G.	20
Baggett, Amanda	8		Baldrige, Sarah Jane	290
Baggett, Benjamin F.	117		Baldry, Amanda M.	144
Baggett, Burrell W.	286		Baldry, E. L. P.	190
Baggett, Clara E.	244		Baldry, G.L.A.	122
Baggett, E.	182		Baldry, Manervia J	301
Baggett, E. G.	165		Baldry, Mary A	239
Baggett, Eli	155-170-172-176-		Baldry, R. L. A.	292
	179-182-188		Baldry, W. L.	7-14-25-30-33-
Baggett, Eliza	210		43-45-51-64-65-71-72-77-78-81	
Baggett, G. L.	309		92-109-110-112-113-147-149-219	
Baggett, Grandberry	93		256-258-264-269-292	
Baggett, J. A.	295		Baldwin, Abram	8
Baggett, L.A.	196		Baldwin, Elizabeth	347
Baggett, L.	201		Baldwin, John	287
Baggett, Lucinda	299		Baldwin, Mary A.	297
Baggett, Mahala E.	172		Baldwin, Samuel P.	337
Baggett, Martha W.	193		Baldwin, William D.	24-36-37
Baggett, Mary	224		40-41-44-77-81-93-94-98-103-117	
Baggett, M.E.	178		126-145-227-228-236-238-242-243	
Baggett, Nancy	14		Balthrip, Letitia	335
Baggett, W. G.	188		Balthrop, W. H.	267
Bagley, Aaron L	218		Bandy, Jesse	116
Bagley, Ann	103		Bandy, Mary M.	67
Bagley, Harriet	74-67		Banfield, Asa	119
Bagley, Robert	263		Banks, M. C.	190-196-203
Bagley, Roberta H	261		Bannon, Salinia	90
Bailey, Ann	4		Barbee, Amanda R	351
Bailey, C. R.	123		Barbee, Lydia	111
Bailey, Geo. W.	151		Barbee, J.C.	4-217-220-221-225
Bailey, Mary	85		226-230-233-235-238	
Bailey, Martha A	62		Barbee, E. A.	231
Bailey, M. E.	286		Barbee, George B.	26
Bailey, Nancy	90		Barbee, Martha J.	336
Bailey, P.I.	149		Barbee, Minerva	109-130
Bailey, Samuel	56		Barbee, Sarah H.	269
Bailey, Sarah	83		Barham A.	200
Bailey, Virginia	93		Barham, Emily I	259
Bain, Mary	285		Barham, Henry	217
Bainbridge, John E.	352		Barham, J. G.	205

****

Barham, Joseph W.	272	Batts, Jermiah	9-18-30-34-42
Barham, M. E.	205	56-157-169-198-214-264-308	
Barker, A. D.	142	Batts, John T.	27
Barker, L.A.	163	Batts, Jonathan	67
Barker, Mary A	306	Batts, Leving	263
Barker, N.M.	348	Batts, M. L.	155
Barker, Susan	335	Batts, Martha W.	263
Barker, V. L.	202	Batts, Mary #	84-343
Barley, John	280	Batts, M. D. W.	260
Barnes, Clinton M.	310	Batts, Prucilla	267
Barnes, Elizabeth F	271	Batts, Sarah D. E.	248
Barnes, Frances	340	Batts, Virginia C.	276
Barnes, George	76	Baugh, G. N.	233
Barnes, H. B.	183	Baugh, John A.	243
Barnes, John T	338	Baxter, Robart	1243
Barnes, Larry S.	11	Beach, W. B.	329
Barnes, Lucy	222	Beadwell, Sarah B.	171
Barnes, M. L.	204	Beall, Lucy	352
Barnes, Mary A. P.	293	Beasley, Fanning, J.	81
Barnes, Sally A.	185	Beasley, James H.	38
Barnes, Susan E.	78	Beasley, Malinda	44
Barnes, W. J.	90	Beasley, Martha	156
Barnet, J. D.	177	Beasley, Mary E.	355
Barnet, Joseph	10	Beasley, Rebecca	20
Barnett, James W.	327	Beasley, Cyntha	23
Barns, Francis,	331-340-351-	Beaumont, Chas. M.	47
	355-356	Beckham, Creecy	10
Barns, W. S.	261	Becknell, Caroline	64
Barr, G. W.	173	Bell, Andrew	71
Barr, Isaac	238	Bell, Barbary	27
Barr, W. M. C.	156-159-172-	Bell, Charles C.	310
173-241-245-247-270-271-291-		Bell, E A.	158
	294-323-324-330	Bell, Emily	317
Barry, Isaac	268	Bell, Henry J.	219
Barry, J. C.	350	Bell, Hiram	228
Barry, Missouri	269	Bell, J. A.	331- 341
Barry, Thomas	274	Bell, J.C.	302
Barry, William L	39	Bell, J. S.	319
Barry, William P	39	Bell, James B.	192
Barsley, Shelly	341	Bell, Joel E	140-323
Bartholomew. A. J.	382	Bell, John	6- 44
Bartlett, Amy	5	Bell, Lucy W.	342
Bartlett, B.	141	Bell, Maranda	218
Bartlett, G. L.	291	Bell, Martha	119
Bartlett, Martha E.	292	Bell, Martha M.	279
Bartlett, Nancy	312	Bell, Mary C.	194
Bartlett, Robert	70	Bell, Mary E.	213
Barton, Wm.	130	Bell, Nancy	86
Basford, Kichen	120	Bell, R. G.	240
Basford, Lucretia	251	Bell, R. W.	17
Bassford, Kinchen	114	Bell, Rich. W.	58-62-70-82
Basham, W. R.	310	90-95-99-105-112-118-123-134-	
Baswell, Martha	259	140-141-143-144-145-146-150	
Batts, Adeline	309	Bell, S. J.	319
Batts, Amanda H.	312	Bell, Sarah J.	100
Batts, B. A. 33	332	Bell, Sarah W.	151
Batts, B. B.	258-284-349	Bell, Wm. H.	94
Batts, Beady M.	11	Bell Zaack	198
Batts, E. F.	342		

Bennett, Elizabeth	244	Berry, Mary F.	351
Bennett, Elizabeth C	305	Berry, Pleasant	314
Bennett, M.	211	Berry, W.K.	264
Bennett, Margaret	146	Bevens, Susan E.	78
Bennett, Mary Ann	252	Bibb, Elizabeth	148
Bennett, Nancy E	261	Bibb, Henry G.	75
Bennett, S. A.	160	Bibb, John	99
Bennett, W. A.	332	Bibb, William E.	24
Bennett, William M.	146	Bidwell, J. A.	178
Benson, Agnes L.	297	Bidwell, M. V.	343
Benson Alabama	178	Bigbee, Caroline	217
Benson, Calvin	18	Bigbee, Geo. W.	107
Benson, Elijah	122	Bigbee, John C.	66
Benson, Elvis	221	Bigbee, M. A. E.	268
Benson, E.W.	182	Bigbee, Martha	40
Benson, John C.	34	Bigbee, Mary A.	24
Benson, M.A.	113	Bigbee, Missoure	112
Benson, Martin C.		Bigbee, Pemelia	121
Benson, Martha	104	Bigbee, Sarah A	221
Benson, Mary	180	Bigbee, Victoria	327
Benson, Nancy W.	8	Biggs, Cecilia E	355
Benson, Olive	14	Biggs, Josiah	56
Benton Ann	34	Biggs, Nancy	216
Benton, C.	253	Biggs, William	271
Benton, Daniel W.	315	Bill, John	123
Benton, E.	145-209	Billingsly, John M.	211-232
Benton, E. P.	277	Binkley, Amanda	191
Benton, Elizabeth	305	Binkley, Amanda M	6
Benton, Emeline	59	Binkley, Angeline	257
Benton, Ephriam	212	Binkley, Anthony F.	115
Benton, G.	247-257-268	Binkley, B. F.	215-240-241
	269-276-277-287- 344	Binkley, C. A.	196
Benton, George C.	282	Binkley, Eliahs	48
Benton, Green	14-317	Binkley, Hulda	256
Benton, James	56	Binkley, John H.	291
Benton, John G.	236	Binkley, Joanah	282
Benton, John H.	229	Binkley, L. L.	209
Benton, Malachi	343	Binkley, M. E.	196
Benton, Mary	208-224-150	Binkley, Mariah J	151
Benton, Rhoda	139	Binkley, Mary	272
Benton, Rich.	222	Binkley, Mary A. E.	261
Benton, Roxane	343	Binkley, Mary Ann	197
Benton, Susan	237	Binkley, Nancy	222
Benton, Thos. H.	356	Binkley, Parlie	301
Benton, V.J.	317	Binkley, R.	199
Benton, W. J.	257	Binkley, Rachel	58
Benton, William F	227	Binkley, S. C.	154
Berget, Martha	27	Binkley, Sarah C,	335
Bernard, Ann	32	Binkley, Sarah L.	241
Bernard, Julia H.	213	Binkley, Sarah L.	241
Bernard, William A	74	Binkley, Susan	219
Berry A. F.	263	Binkley, William C.	263
Berry Alvin	64	Bivins, James P.	47
Berry, Ephriam	118	Black, Catherine	282
Berry, Ellen C.	247	Blachard, George	11
Berry, Harriet	248	Blackburn, Angeline	250
Berry, James	345	Blackburn, James H.	323
Berry, Martha J.	288		

Blackburn, Arch	244	Bottomley, Thos.	236
Blackburn, James M.	194	Bough, Martha Ann	95
Blackburn, Margaret	340	Bough, John A	243
Blackburn, Mary	270	Bourne, Alexander	149
Blackburn, Meredith	6	Bourne, Elizabeth	109
Blackburn, Nancy	129	Bourne, John	91
Blackburn W. M.	235	Bourne, Sally J	282
Blackburn, William	163	Bourne, Wm. A	74
Blackburn, William H	120	Bowen, J.C.	328
Blackmore, D. C.	230	Bowers, Jane	168
Blain, A. M.	107	Bowers, John	102
Blair, R. C.	328	Bowers, L.D.	151
Blanchard, M. J.	243	Bowers, L.V.	193
Blankenship, John C.	52	Bowers, L.W.	353
Blankenship, R. S.	356	Bowers, Sarah	69
Blewett, George L.	39	Bowers, Sarah J.	354
Blick, Martha L.M.	12	Bowers, W. S.	321
Blick, W. P.	47	Bowie, John	88
Boakfield, Byram	258	Bowles, J.H.	315
Boatright, Ann	42	Bowline, B	177
Boatwright, Mary	347	Bowling, D. H.	341
Bobb, Jane	85	Bowling, Susan	83
Bebbell, John	124	Bowls, Elizabeth	89
Bobett, James	174	Bowls, Sarah S. E.	280
Bobbett, Nancy	15	Box, Louisa	353
Bobbett, Rebecca	150-211	Boyd, Coleman	249
Bobbett, Sarah A.	135	Boyd, Francis	217
Bobbitt, Martha	70	Boyd, James	23
Bobo, Elizabeth	121	Boyd, Martha	149
Bobo, Frances	121	Boyd, N.J.	349
Bodine, Ider	144	Boyd, Nancy	164
Boisseau, Virginia M.	300	Boyd, Susan	91
Boiswell, Judia J	246	Boydm Virginia	330
Boleyjack E.	162	Boyd, William	27
Booker, M. V.	233	Boyder, William H.	79
Booker, Noah	137	Boyers, Frances A	79
Booker, Polly	190	Boyles, J.H.	315
Booker, Rebecca	145	Boyles, Martha M.	347
Boon, Azariah B.	28	Boyles. Mary J.	326
Boon, Eli	163	Boyles, Thomas H.	97
Borders, Elizabeth	66	Boxorth, Rachel	266
Borders, L. R.	284	Brack, Geo.	211
Boren, Bailey	16	Bracy, Angeline	249
Boren, Bazel	88	Bracey, Benj. P.	121
Boren, Eli	163	Bracy, Martha E	305
Boren, Elizabeth	18	Bracy, Martha F.	330
Boren, John	73	Bracy, Samuel	8
Boren, Kerziah	30	Bracy Samuel H. P. U3	120
Boren, Vardy	30	Bracy, Thomas W.	51
Borin, Lucinda	140	Bracy, W. L.	277
Boron, Nancy	173	Braden, Ann E.	229
Borren, Nancy Catherine	337	Braden, Mary E.	291
Borthick, John	147	Bradford, Larkin	281
Borthick, Sarah J.	315	Bradford, Z. A.	246
Bostic, M. J.	157	Bradley, B. H.	351
Bothick, John	2	Bradley, B. W. 161-167-174-177
Bottom, J. A.	162	182-237-245-250-251-252-256-312
		313-316-320

Bradley, Benj. W.	ql6		Brewer, Sally	58
Bradley, Charles	150		Brewer, Sarah E	339
Bradley, Elizabeth	238		Brewer, Sarah	55
Bradley, John G	168		Brian, Joseph	130
Bradley, J. J. 161-155-344-347			Brickles, Benard	69
Bradley, Mary H.	260		Bridges, John R.	241
Bradley, Nancy	47		Brigdes, M. J.	338
Bradley, Philander D	270		Briggs, A. H.	175
Bradshaw, R. H.	335		Briggs, David C.	73
Brady, John G.	168		Briggs, G. W.	338
Brake, James	26		Briggs, Mary R	257
Brakefield, B.	171		Brights, A. I.	247
Brakefield, Byram	34		Briley, Elisah	315
Brakefield, Elizabeth	106		Briley, John W.	332
Brakefield, George	323		Briley, Marcus	292
Brakefield, Harriet	90-267		Briley, Mary Jane	282
Brakefield, James	191		Brinain, Charlotte	173
Brakefield, Jesse	106		Brinkley, Amanda	191
Brakefield, Joseph	267		Brinkley, John K.	255
Brakefield, Katherine	93		Brinton, Elvira	131
Brakefield, Martha	180		Briton, Nancy A	138
Brakefield, N.S.A.	298		Britt, William W.	12
Brakefield, Sarah	46		Broadrick, Abraham	60
Brakefield, W.	178		Broadrick, Joseph	229
Brakefield, Wm.	12		Broadrick, Juditha	355
Brandon. Martha	227		Broadrick, Nancy	122
Brankley, Wilson	87		Broderick, Matilda	226
Brannon, Susan	271		Broke, Wm.	183
Bransford, Wesley	346		Brooks, Mary	102
Branson, Withaler	62		Brooks, Mona Louise	85
Brashear, M. R.	31		Brooks, O. C.	309
Brasier, M.	207		Brooks, Thos. N	330
Brasior, Isaac	93		Browder, David	7-74
Braswell, Mary E	334		Brownder, Harriet P.	290
Braswellm Vincent	181		Brown, Ann	130
Braswell, Wm.	204		Brown, Catherine	33
Braves, Jemima	21		Brown, Clement	196
Brazier, Priscilla	214		Brown, Eliza F	307
Breakfield, Sarah	46		Brown, F. M.	331
Brewer, Amanda E.	285		Brown, James	166
Brewer, Angelette	355		Brown, Jane	330
Brewer, Annie	35		Brown, John L	193
Brewer, Ed	112		Brown, Samuel B.	243
Brewer, Edward	109		Brown, Thomas C.	160
Brewer, Jane	34		Brown, William F.	133
Brewer, J. N.	260		Brown, Westley	311
Brewer, James	53		Browning, Charlie B	158
Brewer, Jamina	21		Browning C. F.	313
Brewer, John	49		Browning, C. H.	249
Brewer, L.	58-102		Browning, James T.	41
Brewer, L.B.	219		Browning Matilda	9
Brewer, Louisa	174		Browning, Mary Ann	43
Brewer, Margaret	356		Browning, Mary F.	315
Brewer, Milly	113		Browning, Mary J.	188
Brewer, Milly C.	262		Browning, Lucinda	3
Brewer, Molly C.	294		Browning, Susan	234
Brewer, N. M.	236		Browning, W. B.	299

Choate, Edward	126-125	Clayton, Daniel	159
Choat, Elizabeth	98	Clayton, G. B.	238
Choat, Gabriel	34	Clayton, L. C.	203
Choat, Harriet	167	Clayton, Lucy	54
Choat, Icevella	292	Clayton, Nancy	229
Choat, John	27	Clayton, Richd. L.	95
Choat, John W	287	Clayton, W. H.	166
Choat, Lucy	80	Clenton, Rebecca	99
Choat, Martha	53	Clemenger, John	73
Choat, Martha J.	91	Clifton, G. W.	353
Choat, Nancy	109-112	Cole, Matrisa	295
Choat, Polly Ann	191	Cole, N.M.	142
Choat, Priscilla	245	Cole, R. G.	114-118-123-125-
Choat, S. E.	356		126-134-139-142-145-170-173-
Choat, Stephen	193		189-191-193
Choat, Thos. J.	106	Cole, Stephen	142
Choat, William	273	Cole, Thos.	350
Chowning F. E.	279	Cole, William	278
Chowning, John	126-129	Cole, William A.	339
Chowning, Lemuel	189	Coles, Josiah	276
Chowning, M. A.	165	Coles, Isaac G.	331
Chowning, Martha	35	Coles, Maranda	276
Chowming, M. E.	173	Coleman, Edward L.	139
Chowming, Nancy	197	Coleman, E. W.	300-321
Chowning R.	113	Colemen, H.E.	308
Chowning, Richd.	34-35-53-54-	Coleman, James J.	190
	55-78-79-81-102	Coleman. M. L.	171
Chowming W. H.	255	Coleman, Nancy C.	351
Chowning, W. T.	231-242-246-267	Coleman, William L.	37
269-295-300-312-322-323-324-		Colley, F. C.	353
	336-385	Collins, Jane R	318
Chowning Wm. T.	99	Coltrap, E. A.	311
Chowming, Wm. Thomas 217-220-		Comperry, Mary	184
	222-273	Con Wm. G	89
Christmas, E.	180	Conaway, Eliza	31
Clark, Caroline A.	195	Conaway. Penelope	197
Clark, C. L.	245	Coney, Patrick	93
Clark, Edward G.	148	Conn, A	171
Clark, Elizabeth	110	Conn, E. A.	209
Clark, Elvira	215	Connell, E. J.	211
Clark, Emily C.	261	Connell, Frances W.	108
Clark, Harriet E.	66	Connell, Jacob	147
Clark, Jasper N.	244	Connell, Mary	27
Clark, Jesse	177	Connell, Mary E	218
Clark, J. I.	251	Connell, Mary S	293
Clark, John	92	Connell, Nancy	121
Clark, Katherine	107	Connell, Sarah J.	124
Clark, L.A.	188	Connell, W. W.	278
Clark, L.V.	189	Connelly L. J.	120
Clark, M. A.	159	Conner, James M.	257
Clark, Martha	95	Conner, Martha J	301
Clark, Martha M.	245	Connor, Caroline	129
Clark, Mary M.	329	Conrad, M. E.	95
Clark, Medora	253	Conrad, Minerva A	133
Clark, Sary I	183	Considine, Thos.	305
Clark Susan	231	Conway C.	202
Clark, Tempy	224	Conway, Henderson H.	279
Clark, W. A.	163	Conway Penelope	197

Conway, Samuel	252	Couts, Sallie M	283
Conwell, Mary S	293	Couts, Sophia G.	256
Cook, A.	350	Couts, Tabitha	66
Cook, A. C.	316	Couts, W. H.	214
Cook Alexander C.	50	Couts, William	139
Cook, Andrew J.	248	Covinton, Ann	86
Cook, Clarisa	162	Covington, Charlotte	323
Cook, David	104-165	Covington C.	5-286
Cook, Eli	326	Covington, Henry L.	124-128
Cook, Ellis P	21	Covington, H. L. 271-272-279-	
Cook, Eli T.	105	280-285-295-299-307-313-315-320	
Cook, Elizabeth	238	326-327-335-339	
Cook, Elisa L.	123	Covington J. A.	295
Cook, Elvira	238	Covington Jacob	289
Cook,Hannah	93	Covington, M. L.	92-292
Cook, James 66-244-252-261-271		Covington, Polly	29
274-279-282-285-286-287-288-292		Covington, R. M.	330
298-299-315-317-320-333-334-340		Covington, S. S.	246
346-351-356		Conington, Winney	280
Cook, John	55	Cow, William G	89
Cook, L.P.	165	Cowing, M. A.	165
Cook, Pleasant	278	Cox, Sebrina	20
Cook, Robert A	231	Cox, Narcissus	85
Cook, Saphrona	329	Cox, Wm.	90
Cook, Sarah M.	123	Cox. William	148
Cook, S. P.	165	Crabtree, Amand E.	139
Cook,Stokley	250	Crabtree, Benjamin	58
Cook, Thos. 8-25-53-58-110-117		Crabtree, Elizabeth J.	88
143		Crabtree, Jacob P.	282
Cook, William A.	223	Crabtree, James	283
Cookery, L.B.	330	Crabtree, Matilda J.	285
Cooley, W. J.	254-263	Crabtree, Mary J.	315
Coon, John	38	Crabtree, Nancy A	343
Cooper, James	233	Crabtree, Rebecca	16
Cooper, Malvine	71	Crabtree, Rebecca A	222
Copelland, Elizabeth	349	Crabtree, Thomas	134
Copeland, John 82-257-260-265		Crafford, Charles 29-31-34-41-4	
270-288-293-317-339-344-347-348		45-46-80-93-98-99-103-126-129-	
Cirbin, Mary	92	131-141	
Corbin, Malina	41	Crafford, Elizabeth	41
Corbitt, David W.	279	Crafford, James H.	223
Cordel, Jno. W	156-156	Crafford, James J	94
Cordle, Eliza F.	288	Crafford, John	35-180
Cornelius, Darden	152	Crafford, John 153-156-167-	
Corner, Jenetta	272	180-181-191-192-212-215-218-219	
Cort, Willie M.	317	226-227-228-237-239-244-249-250	
Cothran, Daniel	42	254-259-251	
Cothran, Rebecca L.	83	Crafford, John L	146
Cothran, Susan T.	16	Crafford, John W	120
Coursey, Chasteen	88	Crafford, Julia	228
Couts, A. B.	295	Crafford, Lucy F	122
Couts, Archer B.	130	Crafford, Martha	7
Couts, Elizabeth	15	Crafford, Martha A	81
Couts, J.A.	110	Crafford, Mary J.	93
Couts, John F.	175	Crafford, Susan	239
Couts, Martha J.	130	Crafton, James	241
Couts, Mary	270	Crafton, Mary Jane	235
Couts, S. A.	151	Craig, David	353

****

Daughorty, Kerzeah	90	Dickerson, B. W.	278
Dsughtry, Elizabeth	193	Dickerson, Charles	342
Davet, Hanora	305	Dickerson, Dicy	186
David, Sally A	241	Dickerson, Jane	184
Davidson, A. D.	149	Dickerson, John	184
Davidson, John	259	Dickerson, J. W.	201
Davidson. L.B.	279-289-298	Dickerson Martha	183
Davidson, Martha J	274	Dickerson, Mary	56
Davis, C. B.	253-255	Dickerson, Mary Anna	250
Davis, Eliz. A	175	Dickerson, Sarah A	324
Davis Eliz. Ann	55	Dickerson	
Davis, G. W.	211	Dickins, Louisa	185
Davis, J. H.	151	Dillard, Eliza	239
Davis, James J.	236	Dillard, Elizabeth	234
Davis, James L.	250	Dillard, Jane	265
Davis, James R.	246	Dillard, L. T.	288
Davis, Jesse	82	Dinning, Martha	107
Davis, Jesse M.	34	Dinning, Nancy Ann	131
Davis, J. T. W	326-327-328-	Dishman, Daniel G	97
	331-335-342-353	Dobbs, Ann Eliz.	83
Davis, John T.	42	Dobbs, Asa	5
Davis, L.B.	290	Doe, Ophelia	353
Davis, Levi	114	Dole, Presley M	323
Davis, Mariah L	225	Doll, James	119
Davis, Martha Ann	223	Dolton, Alford	66
Davis, Martha L.	181	Donelson A. Y.	308
Davis, M. E.	158	Donelson S. C.	234
Davis, R. A.	187	Dorris, A.	187
Davis, Richard A	192	Dorris, Ann	162
Davis, Sampson	288	Dorris, Archer L.	67
Davis, Sarah	304	Dorris, Caroline	258
Davis, Sarah B	20	Dorris, Cornelius	191
Davis, Sally K	241	Dorris, E. A.	187
Davis, Susan E	300	Dorris, Eldridge W.	62
Davis, Susan F	309	Dorris, Eliz.	98
Davis, William G	69	Dorris, Eliza	36
Dawson, George P	99	Dorris, Elizabeth	3-189
Dean Amanda E.	11	Dorris, Ellender	319
Dean John W	123	Dorris, G. W.	229
Dean, Julia Ann	22	Dorris, H	121
Dean, Lucinda	72	Dorris, Isaac C.	245
Debauport, Thomas	153	Dorris, H. D.	314
Deen, Elijah	76	Dorris, James	102
Deen, John M.	130-109	Dorris, James J	236
Deen, Mary J	164	Dorris, James R.	246
Deen, Wm. R	80	Dorris, James W.	189
Demumbro, R. S.	241	Dorris, John P	201
Demumbro, Andrew J	320	Dorris, Josiah M	180
Denin, George	141	Dorris, Louisa	11
Dennis, L.R.	219-221-228-224	Dorris, M.	210
Denning Grandville 71) 227-229		Dorris, M. A.	203
Denton, Eliza M	79	Dorris, Martha	177-323
Dentor, Mary E	135	Dorris, Marley	40
Derrett, Clabour F	78	Dorris, Meredith	3
Derriberry, A. E.	220	Dorris, M. J.	322
Derrett, Clabour F	78	Dorris, Nancy	88
Dick, Hiram H	90	Dorris, Phelby	65
Dick, Katherine	81		

Dorris, R. B.	201-210-211	Drake, Benj. F	171
Dorris, Robertson T	20	Drake, J. M.	355
Dorris, Sarah D.	77	Drake, Katherine	156
Dorris, Stephen A	145	Drake, Mary E	319
Dorris, Susan	84	Drake, R. N.	221
Dorris, W. A.	261	Drane, Caroline	249
Dorris, W. L.	68	Drane, H. D.	322
Dorris, Wesley S	271	Drane, Martha E.	308
Dorris, William P	8	Drane, T. I.	352
Dorris, William R	235	Draper, Noah	166
Dorris, William W	319	Draughn, E	145
Doss, A	355	Draughn, James	178
Doss, Azariah	294	Draughn, M. L.	177
Doss, Cornelius	191	Draughn, Rebecca	132
Doss, Elsunda	185	Draughn, Wm.	155
Doss, James	119	Draughon, Adeline	277
Doss, Joel R	128	Draughon, Geo. E	66
Doss, L.F.	186	Draughon, G. W.	329
Doss, Lucinda	83	Draughen, H. C.	308
Doss, Milly	222-85	Draughon, James W.	325
Doss, Saml. L	119	Draughon, Jesse B.	332
Doss, Sarah	150	Draughon, Lucinda	90
Doss, T. J.	354	Draughon, Martha G.	219
Doss, William R	29	Draughob, Mary	118
Doss, Wm.	172	Draughon, Matthew J.	189
Doss, W. W.	309	Draughon, Melissa J.	301
Dotson, James C.	284	Draughon, Miles, Jr.	195
Dotson, Lydia	5	Draughon , Miles T.	247
Doty, Nancy A	294	Draughon, M. W.	328-214
Douthett, S. E.	13	Draughon, Nancy	261
Doughtry, Bryan	5	Draughon, Prudence	162
Douglass, M. A.	240	Draughon, Robert	19-22-39-40
Douglass, Mary A. E.	227	41-46-47-54-75-82-83-84-100-118	
Dover, J. D.	57	119-122-147-164-168-169-185-186	
Dowlan, M. V.	217	194-197-204-214-221-222-228-232	
Dowlen, Rachel	141		233-240
Dowlen, Surdna	122-126	Draughon, Robert V.	263
Dowlin, L. F	171	Draughon, Virginia	324
Dowlin, John	305	Draughon, W.C.	204
Dowlin, John G	36	Draughon, William	54-329-347-
Dowlin, Martha	62		354
Dowlin, Martha V	297	Draughon, Willie L.	245
Dowlin, Ursilla	265	Draydin, Nancy	261
Doyal, C.	181	Dudley, John A	63
Doyal, Elizabeth	273	Duer, John A	24
Doyal, Manda	26	Duke, M. A. C.	234
Doyal, William R	167	Duke, John	121
Doyle, Dicy J	300	Duke, Sarah A	76
Doyle, Harriet L	262	Dumumbrane, Mariah	23
Doyle, James H	191	Duncan, Frank	216
Doyle, Thomas	342	Duncan, James A.	188
Dozier, Amanda M.	309	Duncan, John B.	336
Dozier, Cheatham	292	Duncan, William	238
Dozier, E. A.	187	Dunn, Aramiscia	170
Dozier, Rebecca	313	Dunn, Arrena	260
Dozier, R. P.	223	Dunn, Calantha V	10
Drain, Thomas H	31	Dunn, Dorcus	257
Drake, Albrittain	53	Dunn, Dorothy	6
		Dunn, George	141

160   Robertson Co., TN - Marriage Records - Volume 1 - 1839 - 1861

****

Dunn, Hannah	172
Dunn, Harriet	228
Dunn, Henry	195
Dunn, James F	334
Dunn, James S.	256-287
Dunn John H	218
Dunn, J.R.	281
Dunn, Katherine A	23
Dunn, L.	204
Dunn, L.A.	142
Dunn, Lucinda	299
Dunn, Martha J.	179
Dunn, Martha T.	184
Dunn, Nancy A	228
Dunn, Nancy J	124
Dunn, R. T.	143
Dunn, Sarah	125-127
Dunn, Susan A	142
Dunn, W. J.	258
Dunn, William J	141
Dunnington, Roxana	310
Durham, Anny	112
Durham, John Thomas	20
Durham, Mary Ann	266
Durham, Nancy D	49
Durham, Rosannah	164
Durham, Samuel	250
Durham, Willia,	256
Durham, Zachariah	182
Durrett, Abigail	300
Durrett, Clabourne	78
Durrett, E.L.	259-253
Durrett, J. S.	348
Durrett, S. C.	198
Durrett, J. T.	70
Durrett, Mary	21
Durrett, William	320
Duval, M. B.	100
Dycus, F. E.	143
Dycus, Mary J.	229
Dycus, Nancy	304
Dye, G. W.	14-22-75
E.	
Earhart, Moses F.	159
Earl, Tabitha Cumi	149
Easley, Drury	52
Easley, Frances	150
Easley. Geo. M. W.	77
Easley, M. J.	331
Easley, Martha J.	128
Easley, Mary	128
Easley, Millington	55
Easley, Wesley	129
Eatherly, J. M.	206
Eatherly, Lurinda	82
Eckles, J. A.	256
Eddings, Joseph	18
Eddings, Temperance	123
Eddings, William	189
Eddy, Samuel	286
Edison, Emily W.	239
Edmund, Sarah A	93
Edwards, Abner	32
Edwards, B. W.	161-258
Edwards, Clayton T.	187
Edwards, Ed.	21-106-107-108
Edwards, Edward G	355
Edward, Elizabeth R	131
Edwards, James	21
Edwards, Jane	250
Edwards, John W	94
Edwards, Jonathan	200
Edwards, Joseph J.	232
Edwards, L.F.	313-340
Edwards, Margaret	255
Edwards, Malone	71
Edwards, Martha	117-8
Edwards, Mary	284
Edward, Mary A	131
Edward, Mary E	338
Edwards, M. D.	13
Edwards, M. W.	297
Edwards, Meredith L.	128
Edwards, Narcissa	258
Edwards, Oliver	87
Edwards, Polly	160
Edwards, Rebecca	45
Edwards, Susan	268
Edwards, William	133
Edwards, William H	252
Egmon, Bartholemus	30
Egmond, Mary Jane	321
Edison, E. B.	234
Edison, Emily	239
Eidson, Eliza R.	127-124
Eidson, Isiah	120
Eidson, James E	300
Eidson, Martha A	320
Eidson, Thomas C	292
Eidson, Thos. J	339
Elam, R. H.	313
Elks, Noah	183
Elle, G. G.	133
Elleson, Andrew	92
Elliott, Alpheus	48
Elliott F.	176
Elliott Frances	166
Elliott, James H.	220
Elliott, John R	121
Elliott, Martha F	282
Elliott, Mary A. E.	246
Elliott, M. W.	236
Elliott, Roena	279
Elliott, Saml. H.	44
Elliott, Sarah E.	328
Elliott, William H.	336

****

****

Farmer, Thomas H	5
Farmer, W	38
Farmer, W. B.	265
Farmer, William B	36
Farmer, Willie T	265
Farmer, William H.	15
Farthing, A	207
Farthing, C.	254-275-288
Farthing, Colemen	68
Farthing, Ephraim	1
Farthing, James	179
Farthing, Jane	43
Farthing, John B	49
Farthing, Martha	49
Farthing, Milly	88
Farthing, Peter	132
Farthing, Polly	28-98
Farthing, Reuben	224-116
Farthing, Simon	102
Farthing, William	195
Faullin, Elizabeth	269
Featherstone, Adeline	35
Featherstone, Burrel	230
Featherstone, David	239
Featherston, G. W.	225-262-263
264-269-271-273-278-285-290-293	
297-303-306-307-312-314-316-318	
323-329-330-339-351-355	
Featherston, Geo. W.	58
Featherston, H. D.	158
Featherston, Henry D	118
Featherston, J. W.	316-319-
	334-345-351
Featherston, Joshua W.	83-139
158-181-182-188-192-222-229	
Featherston, Mary F	143
Featherston, Sarah C.E.	34
Felts, Amos G.	171
Felts, Eliza Ann	216
Felts, E. C.	168
Felts, Elizabeth J.	277
Felts, G. W.	90-119-149
Felts, John L	242
Felts, Joseph	136
Felts. Joseph W.	188
Felts, L.F.	210-297
Felts, Martha A.	57
Feltd, Martha E.	276
Felts, Martha J	215
Felts, Mary Ann	247
Felts, Mary C	148
Felts, Richard B	116
Felts, Robert	131
Felts, Robert D	13
Felts, Susan D.	277
Felts, Thos. W.	11-22-54-84-85
67-73-74-84-85-91-105-106-119-	
149-188-205-211-224-262	
Felts, W. E.	154

Felts, William	31-32-45-105-106
Felts, W. J.	262
Felts, William E	264
Felts,W. W.	163-151-230
Fenary, W. B.	318
Fentress, James B.	294
Feragen, Thomas	12
Ferguson, F. G.	20
Ferguson, J. W.	9-16-30- 34
Ferguson, John W	222
Ferguson, R. F.	246 -218
Ferguson, William L.	274
Ferrell, Lucenda	15
Feser, Emeline	41
Fells, William	31
Filart, Larnice	209
Finly, James M	74
Finn, John L	100
Fiser, A. M.	331
Fiser, A. W.	234
Fiser, Eliz.	61
Fiser, Emeline	41
Fiser, Geo.T.	132
Fiser, James	141
Fiser, Joseph H.	20
Fiser, L. F.	214
Fiser, Lemuel	22
Fiser, Nancy H	268
Fiser, Solomon	57-123
Fiser, Suzanne	105
Fisher,Angelina	307
Fisher, David	233
Fisher, G. E. F	132
Fisher, Hillery	174
Fisher, James	185-340
Fisher, L.A.	175
Fisher, M.K.	151
Fisher, M. L.	344
Fisher, Nancy	269
Fisher, P.M.	109
Fisher, Richard	17
Fitts, William	45
Fitzhugh, Rebecca	101
Flaherty, Margaret	313
Fleppen, Eliza F. A.	316
Fletcher, Frances	115
Fletcher, Harriet	316
Fletcher, Henderson	59
Fletcher, James	341
Fletcher, L.	105
Fletcher, Leroy	16
Fletcher, M. E.	306
Fletcher, Mary Amm	334
Fletcher, Minerva	337
Fletcher, Olive	134
Fletcher, William	334
Flood, David	175
Flood, Elizabeth	174

Flood, John	13-16	Fowler, Tabitha	332
Flood, Joseph W.	18	Franklin, Amanda W.	306
Flood, Mary	233	Franklin, J.	171
Flowers, P. J. L.	92	Franklin, Jeremiah	178
Flowers, Ruffin S.	194	Fraser, Isaac	251
Folles, Sarah D.	117	Fraser, Mary J	251
Follis, Martha	236	Fraser, P. H.	207-213-238
Foot, Narcissa	281	Frasier, Howard	105
Foote, Olive	23	Frazer, Daniel J.	287
Foote, Richard N.	79	Frazier, Leonard	117
Forbes, Joseph J	240	Frederick, John	122
Forbes, Martha F	164	Frederick, S. A.	122
Forbes, John	48-68-77-189-	Fredway, Isham	170
	199-200-201	Freland, E. S.	238
Forbs, Virginia	30	Freland, Samuel S.	259
Ford, Eliza F.	340	Freeland, Eliza Jane	271
Ford, George	57	Freeland, Mary E.	330
Ford, Malvina P.	290	Freeman, Harriet	128-186
Ford, Mary	304	Freeman, James Y.	304
Ford, Mary A	100	Freeman, Joseph J	212
Ford, M.B	330	Freeman, L.J.	65
Ford, Patrick	303	Freeman, Martha	161
Ford, Ross Ann	307	Freeman, Mary M.	336
Ford, R. L.	352	Freeman, Matthew	161
Fordson, W. B.	325	Freeman, Nancy	18
Foreman, Mathew	161	Fresh, Lucy	87
Foreman, William	287	Frey, Adam H.	195
Forister, Nancy A	49	Frey, American N	248
Fort, Catherine D	264	Frey, And. J.	213
Fort, David, J	131	Frey, Avaline	178
Fort, E. L.	328	Frey, Catherine A	269
Fort, Elisha P.	120	Frey, E. H.	204
Fort, Elizabeth	177	Frey, F. O. H.	220
Fort, Hildreth	356	Frey, Geo. W.	171
Fort, Jackson	332	Frey, James P.	348
Fort, Joseph W.	51	Frey, J. N.	324
Fort, J. T.	328	Frey, John M.	260
Fort, L. J.	272	Frey, John N.	72
Fort, Martha F	111	Frey, L.	205
Fort, M.D.	304	Frey, Louisa	255
Fort, Piety H.	344	Frey, Marthy P.	310
Fort, Sugg	297	Frey, Martin	265
Fort, Susanna C	188	Frey, Mary	71
Fort, Thos. J	224	Frey, Mary Ann	78
Forte, Olive	23	Frey, Minerva Ann	
Forte, William N	171	Frey, M. V.	325
Fortner, Moses E.	176	Frey, Nancy	53
Fortner, Priscilla	101	Frey, Sarah	99
Fortune, M. A. C.	207	Frey, Simeon	164
Foster, Moses E.	176	Frey, Susan	62
Fprtner, Priscilla	101	Frey, Susan C.	327
Foster, Emily	155	Frey, Susan K.	70
Foster, Thomas	77	Frey, Thomas	43
Foster, W. L.	42	Frey, W. L.	190
Fountain, Lucy J.	190	Frey, Zerilda E	253
Fountane, M. A.	328	Frizzell, James H.	331
Fountane, Martha E	223	Frizzle, Robert	73
Fowler, N. A.	318	Fry, Sarah I	254

Frey, Sarah A	99	Gardner, L. H.	218-225-228-230
Frey, Simeon	164		230-252-280-282
Frey, Susan	62	Gardner, L. A	82
Frey, Susan C.	327	Gardner, Louisa	195
Frey, Susan K.	70	Gardner, Martha Ann	120
Frey, Thomas	43	Gardner, Martha	170
Frey, W. L.	190	Gardner, Mary E.	350
Frey, Zerilda E	253	Gardner, Thomas H.	121
Frizzell, James H.	331	Gardner, W. M.	117
Frizzell, Robert	73	Garott, Rachall P.	314
Fry, Sarah I	254	Garland, John M 84-125- 127
Fry, W. W.	241	Garland, K.J.	308
Fryer, Amanda E.	315	Garner, John E	13
Fryer, Nancy	283	Garrett, Edward C.	43
Fryer, Samuel D	272	Garrett, George H.	220
Fryer, S. J.	278	Garrett, John	235
Fulcher, Martha J.	303	Garrett, W. W.	235
Fulton, Mary A	184	Garth W. C.	356
Fuqua, John W	286	Gatewood, Harriet N.	272
Fuqua, Joseph	219	Gatewood William	248
Fuqua, Margaret	256	Gee, A. J.	347
Fuqua, Mary Ann	292	Gent, Martha	240
Fuqua, Mary C.	294	Gentry Jane	57
Fuqua, Samuel	44	Gentry, William	37
Fuqua, Sarah Jane	346	George, Catherine M.	260
Fuqua, Thirsey	342	George, James	330
Fuqua, William	342	George, Priscille E	260
Fuquay, Jamina	95	George, Sarah	324
Fyke, James	111	Gettlebeel, Samuel	136
Fyke, Jeremiah	28	Ghurt, Charles	48
Fyke, John P.	119	Gibbs, John M.	329
Fyke, Josha	132	Gibson E. A.	153
Fyke, Mathew V.	49	Gibsob, Lucy 59-60
Fykes, Susan	81	Gibson, Mary A	298
Fykes, Syntha Mae	32	Gideon, Franklin Leonard	88
		Gilbert, James	173
		Gilbert L. J.	170
G.		Gilbert, Nancy	299
Gains, A. C.	167	Gilbert, Mary A.	104
Gains, Elizabeth	345	Gilbert, Samuel	84
Gains, Mary	145-295	Gilbert, William O.	81
Gainus, Amanda	322	Gill, George, W.	142
Gallaher, Mary E	344	Gill, Harriet E.	337
Gambill, Benj. 1-6-11-12-20-33		Gill, J.M.	354
34-38-45-50-58-246-247-250-251		Gill, Martha E.	115
253-259-260-265-270-271-278-283		Gill, Margaret J.	324
286-288-296-298-303-307-308-		Gill, N. F.	291
313-322-324-327-336		Gill, W. W.	288
Gambill, Benjamin J.	294	Gillaspy, Lucinda	91
Gambill, D. J.	356	Gillem, L. J.	177
Gambill, John	130	Gillum, E. M.	154
Gambill, John W.	285	Gillum, Mary E	331
Gambill, Mary	32	Gillum, Samuel	156
Gambill, _ J.	262	Gingo, Malinda	198
Gambill, William J.	183	Gish, Mary E	274
Gammon, John 223-231-232		Givans, Oylann	44
234-241-243-261-263-268-285-		Gladwell, Warren	315
300-302-304		Glidewell, James	107
Gardner, E. H.	220	Glisson, Elizabeth G.	276

Glisson, Hardy W.	275	Gossett, Missouri C.	316
Glisson, Jesse	217	Gossett, Sarah J.	102
Glisson, Mary	319	Gossett, W. C.	109
Glisson, S. A.	321	Gossett, W. J.	201
Glover, Delitha	97	Gossett, Zelica V	227
Glover, E. W.	243	Gothem, Daniel	42
Glover, G. W.	209	Goulding, Lucy A	99
Glover, Isiah	227	Gower, James W	67
Glover, James W.	249	Gower, Larkin	36
Glover, John	173	Gower, William E.	164
Glover, Marina O.O.	255	Gowing, E.	202
Glover, Mary A	291	Graham, Eli	101
Glover, Mary E	320	Graham, John	73
Glover, R. G.	223	Graham, William W.	45
Glover, W. W.	343	Grainger, Hiram G	272
Godard, W. W.	228	Grainger, M. E.	161
Goddard, John W	75	Granger, W. L.	208
Gooby, Susan	187	Grant, David	75
Gooch, C. S.	184- 354	Grant, Elizabeth	120
Gooch, Franklin R.	82	Grant, Joseph	43
Gooch, J. C.	184	Grason, Julian	105
Gooch, Lucinda E	234	Grass, James	270
Gooch, Nancy L.	255	Gravel, William	315
Gooch, Rebecca C.	82	Graves, Arelea D.	135
Gooche, F. R. 157-183-206-218		Graves, E. M.	346
220-236-240-242-243-244-246-		Graves, John	242
253-254-255-256-257-258-262-		Graves, Samuel A	47
263-265-276-282-292-297-298-		Graves, William D	124-127
300-301-304-306-310-311-312-		Gray, Samuel	276
321-334		Grayson, E. J.	203
Gooche, Ardra H.	67	Grayson, Julian	105
Gooche, Mary E	82	Grayson, Margaret A	230
Good, Jacob	95	Grayson, Susan C	286
Good, Noah	32	Grayson, W. H.	154
Goodman, M. C.	278	Green, Adaline A	52
Goodman, James C	148	Green, A. L .P.	59- 60
Goodwin, Green B.	135	Green, Ellen	332
Goodwin, Thomas B.	290	Green, E. W.	116
Gordon, Alexander	90	Green, Isade	117
Gordon, James W.	320	Green, John T	147
Gordon, M. F.	294	Green, Julina	172
Gordon, L.A.	189	Green, Martha	106
Gordon, William W.	225	Green, Mary A. M.	57
Gorham, Arena C	247	Green, Mary J.	92
Gorham, Derias	172	Green, Milton	225
Gorham, General Jackson	212	Green, Rachel C.	252
Gorham, John W	73	Green, Robert 1-2-7-8-10-11-18-	
Gorham, Leura	m43	21-22-28-37-46-47-49-68-72-87-	
Gorham, Mary E	293	92-105-106-122-126-132-134-136-	
Gorham, Martha V	289	144-145-148-151-157-174-191-235	
Gorham, Nancy C	352	237-326	
Gorham, P.	158-167	Green, Robert J.	192
Gorham, Richard	303	Green, Sally C	196
Gorham, Susan M.	223	Green, Susan C	295
Gorrell, Mary F	313	Green, Thomas L.	322
Gorrell, S. S.	158	Green, V. A.	189
Gossett, B. A.	156	Green, W. H.	191
Gossett, B. F.	314	Greer, A. M. 278-317-320- 337	
Gossett, Jackson	270	Greer, Ann R	63

Greer, Greenbery	64	Gunn, Martha P	83
Greer, Mary R	330	Gunn, Mary E	101
Gregory, Mary C	33	Gunn, Mary F	218
Greesam, M. F.	302	Gunn, Mary G	10
Griffin, James C	151	Gunn, Phebe G	54
Griffin, John A	37	Gunn, Rhoda A	138
Griffin, Margaret E	132	Gunn, Shadrick	27
Griffin, Mary Ann 335	335	Gunn, Susan	17
Griffin, Reuben	11	Gunn, Thomas 28-49-56-61-109-119	
Griffeth, Sarah	119	Gunn, W. T.	325
Grigsby, Wm. J	255		
Brimble, Elizabeth	77		
Grimes, F. M.	200		
Grimes, Jesse	24	H.	
Grimes, Mary F	284	Hacker, H. D.	308
Grimes, Rhapsy	36	Hackney, Margaret H	212
Grise, Ginsey	337	Hadett, H. S.L.	107
Grisham, John	2	Haggard, William H	41
Grover, Bennet	89	Halcomb, Julina	215
Grover, James	108	Hale, B. N.	282
Groves, Louisa	288	Haley, Agripa	64
Groves, L.A	159	Haley, Paschal	185
Grow, Martha	176	Haley, Susannah	38
Grow, William	278	Haley, Wm. 16-17-29-34-49	
Grubbs, E. P.	210	Hall, Corinaem	334
Grubbs, F. W.	175	Hall, Eliza J.	146
Grubbs, John W	290	Hall, James	33
Guest, Ebenezer	87	Hall, Jane T.	185
Guill, Barnet	260	Hall, Jesse B.	120
Guinn, David d	71	Hall, Jordan W.	89
Guinn, Ellen	315	Hall, Joshua	122-126
Gullage, James	98	Hall, J. T.	165
Gullage, Mary	84	Hall, Mary F.	312
Gullage, William F	65	Hall, Polly	6
Gunn, Barbary E	1	Hall, Sarah E	85
Gunn, E. M.	240	Hall, William A.	121
Gunn, E. W. 207-224-225		Hall, Willie	50
231-271-272-290-347		Hallum, James B.	1
Gunn, Elizabeth W	187	Haly, Carroll B	273
Gunn Francis	289	Ham, Susan	231
Gunn, G. M.	149	Hames, Susan	181
Gunn, G. R. 255-258-263-275-		Hammer, Perry	299
281-294-317-322-334		Hammond, E. W.	231
Gunn, Graves	149	Hammond M. D.	221
Gunn, Griffin	191	Hampton, Amanda	180
Gunn, Harriet	206	Hampton, Amanda E	274
Gunn, J. M. 2-10-12-15-24-		Hampton, G. H. M.	255
30-32-33-54-56-70-78-80-110-		Hampton, Isaiah	32
114-167-178-191-198-215-224-229		Hampton, Martha	166
Gunn, James 10-12-24-32-33-54		Hamson, Amanda	178
56-80-146-151		Hamson, M. M. M.	175
Gunn, Jane	70	Hanan, Paterick	317
Gunn, John A	268	Hancock, Eliza A	52
Gunn, Joseph	185-271	Hancock, Elizabeth A	212
Gunn, J. R.	245	Hancock, William	90
Gunn, Martha A	338	Hanes, Susan	181
		Hannam, Carline	110

Head, Sarah	197
Head, Willie H.	330
Head, Wm. H.	345
Healprin, John	281
Heath, L. M.	90
Heath, Margaret	301
Heath, William H.	58
Heatle, Nancy	34
Heiflin, Willie	66
Heitty James	310
Helterbran, Sarah	45
Helson, O. E.	208
Henderson Adeline	256
Hennderson, Harriet E.	125-136
Henderson, John	81
Henderson, Nancy C	349
Hendley, D. D.	316
Hendley, Mary K	307
Henley, Azariah	1
Henley, Martha A.	84
Henry, Alley	110
Henry, Cordelia	22
Henry, Daniel	151-163
Henry, David 193-194-196-207	
208-209-213-216-219-223-226-229	
231-235-237-247-248-250-253-254	
	255
Henry, E	143
Henry E. L. M.	192
Henry, Hugh	339
Henry, JWM. 151-154-163-167-172	
175-180-185-197	
Henry, John M.	72
Henry, Laura V	319
Henry, Lemuel J.	8
Henry, Leroy	264
Henry, Maranda	104
Henry, Matilda M.	65
Henry, Menerva	310
Henry R. S.	254
Henry, T. M.	206
Henry Z.	158
Hensle, William H.	254
Henson, Sarah	291
Herald, Polly	16
Hermans, Theodore	87
Herndon, Geo. T	104
Herndon, James W	104
Herndon, D. C.	230
Herndon, John B. Sr.	241
Herndon, M. J.	89
Herndon, P. E.	230
Herndon, Tho. M.	73
Herring, A. H.	176
Herring, Amsey C.	113
Herring, David 93-127-128-129	
208-209-214-216-220-225-237-238	
	239

Herring, Elizabeth	5
Herrington, Louisa	262
Herrington, M. W.	277
Herrington, P. J.	294
Herron, Eli T	172
Heysmith, Henry	249
Hickman, Nancy	298
Hickman, Polly Ann	313
Hickman, Rachel	35
Hickman W. P.	228
Hicks, J. Y.	291
Hicks, R. K.	63
Hide, Katherine	64
Higgs, Judith	120
Higgs, M. C.	344
Highsmith, J. R.	342
Highsmith, Sarah M	346
Hight, G. Ann	111
Hightower, Katherine	24
Hightower, Thomas I	35
Hill, E. C.	352
Hill, Eliza A.	100
Hill, J. T.	165
Hill, Mary E	357
Hill, Polly	342
Hilliard A. F.	314
Hindman, S. G.	320
Hines, Danl. C	298
Hingham, John	36
Hinkle, James M.	269
Hinkle, Jesse	292
Hinkle, Mary J	220
Hinkle, Nancy C	313
Hinkle, Peter 229-234-	290
Hinkle, Sarah 291-	277
Hiser, Martha	133
Hitt, James M.	310
Hitt, Mary	91
Hives, Danl. C.	298
Hodge, M.	233
Hodges, Alfred	78
Hockersmith, D. C.	251
Holeman, Geo. I	97
Holeman, James C	7
Holeman, Margaret G.	87
Holeman, Martha J	93
Holeman, M. P.	293
Holeman, Mary G.	117
Holens, Sarah	137
Holland, Ann	259
Holland, Bennett L.	138
Holland, Beersheba	59- 60
Holland, Benjamin F.	52
Holland, Daniel H.	121
Holland, D. L.	346
Holland, Elizabeth 132-174-275	
Holland, Eliza H.	302
Holland, Garrett	17

Holland, Jackson V.	241
Holland, James M	32
Holland, J. L.	40
Holland, John	19-230
Holland, Josephine	297
Holland, Martha	140-223
Holland, Mary	74
Holland, Mosely	107
Holland, M. M.	334
Holland, Nancy	33
Holland, Nancy B.	59-60
Holland, N. W.	220
Holland, P.B.	183
Holland, Presley	151
Holland, Rebecca	192
Holland, R. M. C.	234
Holland, Selcheat	118
Holland, Susan	80
Holland, Thomas	335-266
Holland, W.	4-9-10-12-35-59-60-
	65
Holland, Willie	11
Hillins, B. D.	330
Hollins, Elisha L.	228
Hollis, J. S.	212-214-224-242
251-264-272-275-290-330-344	
Hollis, James W.	354
Hollis, Malinda	299
Hollis, Malinda C	132
Hollis, Mary	270
Hollis, N. J.	169
Holloway, Chest	225
Holloway, John G	37
Holloway, William	9
Holman, D.D.	42
Holman, Elizabeth	41
Holman, Elizabeth P	236
Holman, George T	97
Holman, J. C.	196
Holman, James B.	336
Holmes, Angelina	227
Holmes, E.	155
Holmes, H. A.	146
Holmes, Huddah	19
Holmes, James C.	238
Holmes, James W	147
Holmes, Nancy A	289
Holmes, Tho. A	206
Holt, William	248
Holt, W. J.	280
Homes, Huldy	264
Homes, Margaret M.	281
Honeycutt, Preston	319
Honeycutt, T. W.	239
Hooper, Benjamin	172
Hooper, D. M.	123-167
Hooper, Dosha	199
Hooper, Elizabeth A	120

Hooper, Mary Ann	335
Hooper, Pleasant C.	99
Hope, L. I.	352
Hope, Patience	80
Hope, Susan	338
Hopkins, W. W.	207
Horton, Emily	323
Horton, John A	159
Horton, Samuel	69
Horton, Sarah	282-325
Horton, Z. D.	307
Host, Lewis	124-305-311-313
	316-318-319-322
House, Dempsy	27-255
House, Elisha	30
House, James A	224
House, James H.	88
House, Mary	245
Houston, Sarah	108
Houtchan, John	114
Howard, Charles	31-76
Howard, Ellen	348
Howard, Fannie E	255
Howard, James H.	308
Howard, John C	185
Howard, J. N.	142
Howard, Lucinda	42
Howard, Mary	166
Howard, Polly	1
Howard, Sarah Ann	32
Howell, Elizabeth	124-127
Howell, Thomas	87
Hubbard, James D.	186
Hubbard, Mary A	84
Hubbard, Nancy C	82
Huddleston, Agnes	88
Hudleston, J. A.	318
Huddleston, J. W.	272
Huddleston, Letta Y.	334
Huddleston, M. E.	203
Huddleston, R. E.	122
Huddleston, Robert	178
Huddleston, Susan	275
Huddleston, William	5-129
Huddleston, William C.	130
Huddleston, Wm. R.	196
Hudgins, W. H.	9
Hudgins, C. A.	207
Hudgins, Daniel	49
Hudgins, John	121
Hudgins, John F.	99
Hudgins, Martha A.	160
Hudgins, Nancy D.	186
Hudgins, Nancy H.	33
Hudgins, Nancy L.	136
Hudgins, Sampiar, L. F.	97
Hudson, William	299
Huduall, C. H.	357

Hudwall, W. L.	180
Hudwall, William S.	321
Huey, Aramanda	104
Huey, Carroll	334
Huey, M.A.	153
Huey, Nancy	25
Huffman, John D	170
Huffman, L.H.	263
Huffman, Robert	316
Huffman, W. A.	344
Huflin, Willie	66
Hughan, John	36
Hughes, Edmund W	61
Hughes, Ellen E	290
Hughes, John F	252
Hughes, Thomas W.	311
Hughey, Carrol	135
Hughlett, Eliza	246
Hughlett, Frances	247
Hughlett, J.H.	232
Hughlett, Nancy	163
Hughlett. T.	203
Hughlett, Toliver	247
Hull, J. H.	53
Hulsey, Barnet D.	264
Hulsey, James C.	183
Humphreys, James	85
Hunsacker, S. A.	155
Hunt, A. J.	198
Hunt, Benj. F	109
Hunt, DicyA	24
Hunt, Elena	64
Hunt, Elizabeth S	248
Hunt, Hannah	36
Hunt, J. W.	13-15-16-18-24-33
44-62-83-84-112-124-125-127-150	
151-154-155-161-163-176-177-	
186-211-212-214-215	
Hunt, James F.	213
Hunt, Martha J.	230
Hunt, Mary P.	14
Hunt, Mathew	97
Hunt, Nancy A	102
Hunt, Rhoda	200
Hunt, Thomas	44
Hunt, Wm.	163-354
Hunt. Wm. B.	102
Hunter, James	97
Hunter, Lydia	63
Hunter, Mary	354
Hunter, Nancy A	349
Hunter, Sherrod	63
Hurley, Paterick	326
Hurt, James F.	273
Hurt, Wm.	311-353
Huskey, Emily F.	258
Husky, Mary A. E.	120
Husky, Tho.	277
Hutcherson, Mary Ann	317

Hutcherson, Zelicha	123
Hutchins, Mary Ann	97
Hutchins, Nancy A	322
Hutchings, Dicy	148
Hutchings, Manuel	7
Hutchison, A.L.	119
Hutchison, Emily	323
Hutchison, John	20
Hutchison, P.A.	189
Hutchison, Tabitha J.	75
Hydo, A. F.	15
Hyde, A. P.	161
Hyde, Carroll W.	57
Hyde, David	241
Hyde, H. E.	347
Hyde, Mary	24
Hyde, Nancy	44
Hyde, Taywell	333
Hyde, Wesley H.	35
Hyde, Willis	20
Hysmith, James A	298
Hysmith, Susan E.	295
Hysmith, Sunthoa A	253
Hynnes, W. H.	254

I.

Ingram, Azariah	101
Ingram, M.VV.	336
Inman, Dorothy H	115
InMan, Lucinda	107
Inom, James W.	109
Inscore, Joseph	134
Inscore, Lewis	15
Ireland, M. A.	332
Ireland, Samuel S.	91-259
Irvin, Angeline	278
Irvine, Elizabeth	74
Irvine, Dorothy	195
Ivens, Mary	147
Ives, M. A.	179
Ivey, Anney	102
Ivey, John W.	157
Ivey, Mary J.	354
Ivey, Nancy	91
Ivey, Tho.	102
Ivey, Virginia	303
Ivy, Elizabeth	17
Ivy, Little J. W.	88
Izer, R. H.	

J.

Jacob, William J.	279
Jackson, A W	338
Jackson, Caroline	267
Jackson, Dabney	6

Jackson, E. M. P.	83	Johns, Reece		134
Jackson, Emily C.	230	Johns, Sarah Ann		133
Jackson, H.	199	Johnson, A. B.		165
Jackson, J. A.	91	Johnson, Anderson		40
Jackson, J.A.W.	281	Johnson E. A.	165 -280	
Jackson, Jessie W.	311	Johnson, Geo. H		65
Jackson, John B	192	Johnson, J. H.		341
Jackson, Lilburn M.	83	Johnson, James		269
Jackson, Miles A	76-145	Johnson, John		144
Jackson M. W.	313	Johnson, John K.		237
Jackson, Permilia L.	145	Johnson, L. M.		151
Jackson, Priscilla	230	Johnson, M. A.		214
Jackson, Rebecca J.	322	Johnson, Margaret H.		235
Jackson, Sol.	166	Johnson, Martha	68-237	
Jackson, Wilford J	78	Johnson Mary A		28
Jackson, W. M.	327	Johnson Mary E.		183
James, Caroline M.	152	Johnson Nancy	21 -62	
James, E.	112	Johnson, Nancy L.		220
James, Elizabeth	110	Johnson, Peliha		11
James, John W.	110	Johnson, Rachel		10
James, L.A.	147	Johnson, W. A.		161
James, L.B.	190	Johnson, William	67-216-291	
James, Lucy	124	Johnson, Willis		182
James, Martha E.	262	Johnston, David C		174
James, Mary F.	175	Johnston, D. L.		225
James, Mildred	106	Johnston, Francis		235
James, R.E.	205	Johnston, James M.		58
James, S. A.	147	Johnston, Martha J.		67
James, W. B.	256	Johnston, M.T.		174
James, W. H.	344	Johnston, Wm. W		140
Jamison, C. D.	267	Joice, Moleys		313
Jenkins, Manfield	54	Joiner, Sarah		84
Jenkins, George	219	Jones, Albert G.		89
Jenkins, Julia A	306	Jones, Alfred		28
Jenkins, Joel	25	Jones, Alfred P.		117
Jernigan, A. W.	169	Jones, Allen	94-245	
Jernigan, David M.	107	Jones, Annis		63
Jernigan, Eliza A	222	Jones, Anderson		306
Jernigan Eliza J.	313	Jones, Arch. D		3
Jernigan, James	107	Jones, Artamissa		297
Jernigan, J. W.	285	Jones, Calvin		274
Jernigan, Lucretia	315	Jones, Caroline		128
Jernigan, Lewis Parker	118	Jones, David	64-78-94-99-100-	
Jernigan, Malinda	39		104-106-108-137-290	
Jernigan, Marcus	144	Jones, Drusilla J.		286
Jernigan, Martha J.	159-255	Jones, Eli		247
Jernigan, N. A.	318	Jones, Eliz.	16 -66-92	
Jernigan, Purahan	12	Jones, Elizabeth	130-242-303	
Jernigan, Rhoda M.	309	Jones, Elizabeth H.		242
Jernigan, William P.	86	Jones, Elsey		166
Jernigan, Welsey M.	248	Jones, Emelia		94
Jernigan, W. F.	326	Jones, Frederick		176
Jernigan, Wm. E	285	Jones, Geo. E		297
Jewell, Harry	151	Jones, George S.		2
Johns, Daniel	192	Jones, Granberry B		106
Johns, P. B.	162	Jones, Hyram	265 -122	
Johns, Polly	47	Jones, James		2
Johns, Rebecca	75	Jones, James H.		295

Jones, James L.	105-102	Keller, Emily	141
Jones, C. C.	173	Keller, Emoline	232
Jones, J. L.	330	Keller, Henry	192
Jones, Joel M	97	Keller, Mathews	144
Jones, John	10	Keller, Samuel	346
Jones, John A	281-283	Keller, Sarah J	326
Jones, J.R.	210	Kelly, Benjamin W.	84
Jones, Josiah J	242	Kelly, Elizabeth G.	189
Jones, Josh M.	133	Kelly, Greenberry	63-66-74-76
Jones, Lucy	124	83-85-101-149-161-162-179-215-	
Jones, Lucy Ann	319	265-292-294-355	
Jones, Marcus L.	197	Kelly, Harrison	170
Jones, Mariah	68	Kelly, Lutindy	85
Jones, Martha	148-320	Kelly, Wm. B.	142-148-150-
Jones, Mary Amm	97-256	170-172-174-182-184-190-343	
Jones, Mary E.	263-324	Kelly, Paulina	30
Jones, M. H.	179	Kelton, James	26
Jones, M. L.	319	Kelton, John	123
Jones, M. P.	321	Kembrough, W L.	218
Jones, Nancy J.	307	Kenneddy, G.	348
Jones, Nancy W	273	Kenton, James M.	137
Jones, Rebecca	75	Keys, Robert F.	315
Jones, Richard	122-100	Kiger, Danl.	224
Jones, Sally Ely	2	Kiger, Henry	243
Jones, Sandy	154	Kiger, James L.	153
Jones, Sarah Ann	133	Kiger, Margaret	303
Jones, Stephen	144	Kiger, Martha P	223
Jones, Stephen A	307	Kiger, Mary	129
Jones, Stephen J.	274	Kiger, Mary A	341
Jones, Susan	310	Kiger, William	304
Jones, Susan E	255	Kilgore, Charles	16
Jones, S. V.	208	Killebrew, M. L.	258
Jones, Thomas F.	149	King, A. J.	311
Jones, Thomas J	258	King, Ann Eliza	284
Jones, W A.	207	King, B. F.	349
Jones, Waddy	153	King, Benj. F	340
Jones, W. H.	144	King, George H.	262
Jones, William	170	King, James A	158
Judkins, J. W.	26-37-38-66-82	King, Martha M.	279
95-112-126-129-142		King, Rosey M.	99
Judkins, Jordan T.	169	King, Samuel	136
Justen, Geo. W. L.	103	Kingly, George Q.	117
Justice, A.	6-35-36-47-51-66	Kirby, Francis	354
77-88-91-114-121-132-137		Kirby, J. L.	168
Justice, Armstead A	149	Kirby, Mary	147
Justice, E. F.	161	Kirby, Stephen	3
Justice, Eliza S.	265	Kirby, William	152
Justice, Haldah	22	Kirk, Joseph	89
Justice, Jack A	105	Kittly, James W	215
Justice, Nancy	41	Knight, Adaline	73
Justice, Susan M.	347	Knight, James	18
		Knight, Joseph F	103
		Knight Sarah P.	336
		Knight, Susan I	214
K.		Knox, Simon P	171
Keeler, Jacod	16	Knox, Turner E	179
Keith, Lewis	291	Koepf, Charles E	314
Keller, Abner	173	Krisel, Emeline	183
Keller, Emily	141		
Keller, Emoline	232		

Krisle, Amanda	260	Lawrence, N.	193
Krisle, John	127	Lawrence R. C.	197
Krisle, Louisa	60	Lawrence, Reuben	55
Krisle, Mary E	262	Lawrence Wm. J	144
Krisle, T	208	Leak, Saml.	108
Krisle, Wilson	299	Leake, James	32
		Leake, Marsha	273
		Leaton, P. M.	189
		Ledbetter, Asa	184
L.		Ledbetter, John	240
Lacy, Charlotte P.	312	Ledbetter, Mary L.	117
Lacy, Hyram	325	Ledbetter, William	236
Lacy, John H	136	Lee, James	86
Lamaster A	154	Lellan, Beady	28
Lamaster, John	27	Lemmons, Nancy D.	114
Lamb, James	161-168	Lemons, Nancy	29
Lamb, John A	303	Leonard, Gideon Franklin	188
Lambert, David	108	Leonard, Richard	275
Lanaster, Mills H.	122	LePrade, Melissa A	194
Lancaster James	150	Leptrick, Emeline	106
Lancaster, Minerva	114	Lett, Adeline	334
Landen, D. C.	76	Lett, Mary J.	278
Landeer, Mary A	134	Lett, Saml. J.	233
Landin, F. C. E.	112	Levell, George B.	301
Lands, Mary Ann	125	Lewis, Charlotte	9
Langanas, Mary Ann	129	Lewis, Elizabeth	314
Langen, Newton M.	126	Lewis, L.	265
Langford, A. J.	177	Lewis, Mary	338
Langford, A. W.	302	Lewis, Mary A	144
Langford, M. A.	104	Lewis, N. B.	139
Langford, Mary	8	Lewis, Wm.	87
Langford, Mary N	22	Ligon, Stephen M.	188
Langford, Susan	116	Ligon, W. H. F.	160
Langston, William A	306	Liles, Polly Ann	116
Langston, W. B.	234	Limenaugh, Mary E	33
Lankford, Tho. N.	106-160-220	Limmons, M. M.	123
LaPrade, Malcom A.	194	Limmons, Phebe	77
LaPrade V. E.	258	Linch, Amand	119
LaPrade, Victoria	287	Link, George K.	249
Larison, Walton	300	Link, John A	169
Larkin, H. C.	62	Link, Matilda	266
Larkin, Judith	134	Lipford, M.E.	344
Lassiter, Thimothy T.	182	Lipford, Lucy Ann	327
Late, Lucy Ann	278	Lipscomb, A. L.	104
Latimer, Daniel	137	Lipscomb, A Jackson	289
Latimer, William	273	Lipscomb, Henderson	112
Lawes, John	55	Lipscomb, James	337 -303
Lawler, James W.	20	Lipscomb, Louisa	132-337
Lawrason, Elizabeth	268	Lipscomb, Thomas W.	140
Lawrence, Ale	10	Lipscomb, Thos.	160
Lawrence Elijah L.	312	Lockard, Mary G	104
Lawrence, James E.	32-185	Lockert, Clayton	10
Lawrence J.	156-168-170-216	Logan, William	293
220-226-228-231-232-233-239-241		Long, A. E.	176
Lawrence, John F.	228	Long, E. J.	78
Lawrence Joseph	92	Long, Elizabeth	121
Lawrence Mary E.	141	Long, Elizabeth C.	225
		Long, Emily	108

Long, James,	240	Madden, Patrick	311
Long, Jesse	108	Madin, H.T	189
Long, J.H.	198	Maddox, Mary E	194
Long, John	157	Maddox, Nancy	120
Long, John R.	309	Maddrix, Matthew	323
Long, Mary	182	Madole, Richard B.	301
Long, Mary J.	10	Madox, L. D.	86
Long, Meredith	46-322	Mafford, Jacob	174
Long, M.M.	51	Magee, George W.	263
Long, Nancy	137	Magee, Marion	242
Long, Nancy M.	184	Maginnes, J. L.	89
Long, Sarah	232	Maguire, James	283
Long, William H.	216	Maguire, W. W.	233
Lorence, J.	197	Mahon, Barket	155
Loulbs, William A.	118	Maign, M. A.	169
Love, Emeline	57	Maize, Ephraim	116
Love, L.W.	281	Maize, Frances A	19
Love, Octavia	218	Majors, Benjamin	308
Lovel, George W.	36	Mall, Eliza J.	146
Lovell, James	306	Mallory, James H	252-329-331-349
Lowe, Alex	151	Mallory, M. F.	156
Lowe, Martha A	272	Mallory, John B	322
Lowe, Mary Elizabeth	97	Mallory Wm. L.	133
Loew, Rosanna A	322	Mangrund, Bedy A	263
Lowry, John J	187	Manletta, Lucretia	310
Lowry, Rhoda Ann	275	Manlove, A. A.	57
Loyd, Jonathan	281	Manlove, Christopher	253
Lucas, Amanda	250	Manlow, Sarah E. F.	151
Lucas, Angeline	351	Mann, W. W.	174
Lucas, C. F.	255-260	Manor, Aaron	84
Lucas, David M.	198	Mansker, John F	223
Lucas, G. H.	265	Mansker, Tennessee	323
Lucas, Louisa	242	Mansfield, Emily	183
Lucas, M.	200	Mantello, Lucretia	310
Lucas, Martha	170	Mantlo, Augusta	216
Lucas, M. M.	87	Mantlo, Linch T.	26
Lucas, William P	313	Mantlo, R. O.	209
Lucus, Elizabeth D. J.	271	Mantlo, Richd. W.	174
Ludus, Mary A	144	Mantlo, Sarah	74
Luie, M. M.	347	Mantlo, W. J.	331
Lunsford, A. J.	177	Marbary, M. F.	293
Luster, Isaac N.	215	March, Mary	30
Luter, Elisah	183-248	March, W. H.	193
Luter, Evaline N.	289	Marden, Thomas M.	55
Luter, F. M.	282	Markham, E. M.	339
Luter, Martha J.	272	Markham, Saml. P.	251
Luter, S. L.	295	Marklin, Augustus	125-127
Luton, James J.	267	Marlon, M. E.	120
Lydia, Woodall	211	Marshall, Amos B.	266
Lyle, Richard	324	Marshall, E. A.	248
Lynn, Pitts	52	Marshall, Josephus C.	56
Lyons, Abraham	85	Marshall, M.	95
		Marshall, ThomasB.	43
		Mart, Mary M.	73
		Mart, R. A.	239
M.		Martin, A	200
Mackafee, John	249	Martin Catherine	5
Mackey, A	323	Martin, G. W. 155-277-279-289
Mackey, Alex	353	297-301-302-304-342-343-349-351-
		352

Menees, Emma E.	281	Moore, A. B.	330
Menees, Nancy J.	334	Moore, A. L.	151
Menees, Nancy W	6	Moore, Frances	136
Menees, Sally A	262	Moore, Franklin	111
Menees, W. H.	262	Moore, Gracy J.	239
Merrett, John	100	Moore, Harriet	28
Merrett, Josephine	-297	Moore, J. F	233
Merrett, Lewis	6	Moore, Jeremiah	16
Merrett, William	80	Moore, Joel	137-171
Merryman, Lacky L.	103	Moore, John	102
Miles, Eliz.	29-68	Moore, John C.	293
Miles, Gilbert	29	Moore, John R.	302
Miles, Jacob	116	Moore, John P.	7
Miles, Mary A.	213	Moore, Leah A.	260
Miles, Polly L.	52	Moore, Lydia A	214
Miles, Q. R.	207	Moore, Macon	194
Miles, Syntha	32	Moore, Mary A. E.	212
Miles, William	38	Moore, Nancy	102
Millen, W. H.	354	Moore, Patrick	252
Miller, Bluford J.	160	Moore, Polly	224
Miller, Charles F.	52	Moore, Robert	36-330
Miller, Frances	147	Moore, Sally	16
Miller, Jesse S	123	Moore, Sally A	116
Miller, Mahala	77	Moore, Sampson	85
Miller, Nancy S.	302	Moore, Scina	212
Miller, Susan S	304	Moore, Susannah I.	30
Miller, William	136	Moore, William	101-272
Millican, Elias	170	Moreland, D. K.	341
Milliken, G. R.	284	Morgan, John	43
Milliken, J. K.	171	Morgan, Martha A	257
Milliken, Mary	302	Morgan, Mary	243
Mills, John	299	Morgan, Mary A	90-134
Mills, Wm.	85	Morgan, Melissa	111
Mimms, D. S. W.	222	Morgan, Nancy	1-144
Mimms, Mary E	263	Morgan, Thetis	2
Mimms, W. J.	222	Morris, Alexander	225
Minnick, John	33	Morris, Amanda	192
Mitchell, B. O.	318	Morris, A. J.	188
Mitchell, C. M.	321	Morris, Benjamin S.	312
Mitchell, Mary A. M.	63	Morris, Elizabeth	221
Mitchell, R. B.	29-30-35-50-51	Morris, George W.	188
Mitchell, Samuel M.	33	Morris, Gideon J.	292
Mitchell, Sarah	35	Morris, Isiah	205
Mize, Solomon B.	104	Morris, Jackson	127
Moake, G. W.	158-199	Morris, James B.	161
Moize, Ephriam	87-116	Morris, James H.	284
Moize, M. A.	169	Morris, John	260
Moody, R.	136	Morris, John A	131
Moon, A.	161	Morris, L. W.	313
Moon, Frances J.	136	Morris, Martha Ann	241
Moon, James	244	Morris, Mary	14-29-324
Moon, Jordan	172-179	Morris, Matthew	349
Moon, Louisa	179	Morris, M. T.	352
Moon, M. A.	151	Morris, N.	26-27
Moon, Martha	139	Morris, Nancy Jane	137
Moon, Matilda	147	Morris, Nathan	20-24
Moon, Rebecca	264	Morris, Priscilla	138

****

Morris, Rachel	137		Murphy, B. G.	202
Morris, Thomas E	244		Murphy, Byard B.	276
Morris, William	216		Murphy, Goe.	240
Morris, Wilson L.	315		Murphy, George W	282
Morris, Winny	141		Murphy, James H.	197
Morrison, Mary K.	228		Murphy, Mary Ann	242
Morrison, Margaret	216		Murphy, Priscilla	256
Morrison, Hugh	324		Murphy, Richard	246
Morrison, O.C	337		Murphy, Sally	194
Morrison, Rebecca	243		Murrah, Amelia	327
Morrow, O. H.	151-186-188-		Murrah, Charles	33
	204-238		Murrah Eliz,	161
Morrow, William	135		Murrah, Henry P.	247
Mosely, William H	67-74		Murrah, L.A.	309
Mosely, E. R.	259		Murrah, Margaret	116
Moss, Elinor L.	339		Murrah, Mary F.	265
Moss, Eliza	21		Murrah, Robt. B	243
Moss, James	35		Murray, Jane	123
Moas, James C.	269		Murray L. M.	203
Moss, Mary A. E.	273		Murray, N. A.	317
Moudy, Abraham	214		Murray, Samuel M	155
Moudy, John	352		Murray, William B.	210
Moulton, Frederick	267		Murray, Wm. G.	304
Moulton, John J	169		Musick, Elizabeth	39
Moulton, Suantha E.	290		Myers, Jacob	146
Moulton, Wesley W.	53		Myers, John M.	28
Mozee, Squire	80		Myers, Robert D.	151
Mullen, Sarah A	219			
Mulloy, Daniel	225-249		Mc.	
Mulloy, Mary	317		McCarley, Sarah	306
Murphey, Amanda	273		McCarley, Susan	246
Murphey, B. G.	202		McCarley, William	25
Murphey, Bridget	311		McCarty. M. A.	193
Murphey, E. G.	37		McCasland, James	70
Murphey, Eliz.	52		McCasland, M. A.	113
Murphey, Elizabeth E	311		McCause, Sarah	303
Murphey, Geo.	66		McCawley, Geo	164
Murphey, Geo. C.	13		McClaim, S. A.	163
Murphey, George W	282		McClaan, Donald	106
Murphy, Hiram	44		McClendon, Cyntha	88
Murphey, J. A. E.	299		McCloud, Nancy	73
Murphey, James H.	139-197		McCormack, Harriet J.	48
Murphey, James G.	42		McCormack, Phillip	125-126
Murphey, James P	279		McCormick, Smith	283
Murphey, John C	257		McCrary, J. N.	338
Murphey, Lucinda	332		McDaniel, James	91
Murphey, Martha	191-236		McDaniel, R.	125
Murphey, Mary	155		McDaniel, Rebecca J.	187
Murphey, Mary W	345		McDearman, John	305
Murphey, Robert	229		McDolan, James	91
Murphey, S.	176		McDonald, John	269
Murphey, Samuel, J.	174		McDoland, M. J.	202
Murphey, S. H.	177		McDole, Presley	323
Murphey, Thomas W.	264		McFaran, John M.	308
Murphey, W. H. C	257		McFarland, Catherine M.	274
Murphey, William D	286		McFarland, Martha	276

McFarland, Jesse	338	**N.**	
McFerrin, A. P.	346	Naive, Virginia T.	336
McGan, James L.	219	Naive, W. W.	335
McGoldrick, John C. M.	327	Nanny, Mary A	163
McGuire, E.	163	Nanny, Zelah	81
McGuire, Jos. E.	166	Nave, Frances V.	211
McGuire Wm.	83	Nave, James P.	312
McHaffy, James	305	Nave, Mary C	192
McHenry, E. L.	192	Nave, T. M.	180
McHenry, John M.	93	Nave, William	11
McHenry, Mandy	143	Neal, Napolean B.	70
McHenry, Susan	103	Neel, M. A.	108
McIntosh, Artimissa	285	Neel, Presley	89
McIntosh, Elija	120	Neely, D.	82
McIntosh John	154	Neely, L. J.	267
McIntosh J. W. R.	346	Neely, Susan	353
McIntosh, Susan	225	Neill, Amanda	101
McKay A.	323	Neill, G. F.	22
McKey, Huley	116	Neill, Galbreath F.	94
McKey, Thomas	88	Nelms, Berry F	120
McKissick, Wm. J.M.	85	Nelms, Martha	4
McLeland, L. W.	288	Nelms, Rebecca	92
McMillen, Emily K.	101	Nelson, Kindred	53
McMillin, E. I.	74	Nelson, William T.	119
McMillin, Evelin	244	Nevell, Sarah C	348
McMillin, George	340	Newland, James M.	250
McMillin, James N.	106	Newman, E	177
McMunn, Matilda	314	Newman Harriet	148
McMurdy, H.	151	Newman, J. H.	352
McMurray, Elizabeth	38	Newman, Jas. W.	314
McMurray, H.	163	Newman, Thomas	80
McMurray, J. E.	71	Newton, A. P.	242
McMurry, M.	176	Newton, Amanda	127
McMurry, A	238	Newton, Edward	70
McMurry, Caroline	122	Newton, Eliza	128
McMurry David	302	Newton, Elizabeth	246
McMurry, Eli	218	Newton, F. M.	221
McMurry, George W.	334	Newton, Henry	203
McMurry, Gandison	215	Newton, John W	22
McMurry, Jacob	93	Newton, Mary	354
McMurry, Jeremiah	100	Newton, Mary A	56
McMurry, Martha Ann	8	Newton, Olivia A	46
McMurry Mary F	343	Newton, Samantha	79
McMurry, Samuel	3	Newton, William R.	312
McMurry, Sarah	4	Newton, William W.	312
McMurry, Thos. E. J.	34-59	Newton, Wm.	46
McMurry, Thos. Jefferson	255	Nicholas, Martha A.	179
McNeal, Amanda	314	Nichols, Jane	181
McNeil, J. A.	329	Nichols, Martha C.	140
McNeill, Caroline C	76	Nichols, Mary Jane	164
McNeill, Lucena	30	Nicholls, L. B. M.	19
McNeily, Eliz.	42	Nicholls, Mary C.	26
McNelly, Geo.	13-15	Nicholls, William A	22
McPherson	23-322	Nicholls, William B.	24
		Nicholls, Willis	186
		Nicholson, A. H.	265
		Nicholson, Jesse D.	86
		Nicholson, Lucretia	255

Nicholson, M. A.	171		Osburn, James	341
Nicholson, Martha	221		Osburn, Saml.	214-275
Nicholson, Sarah A.	135		Overstreet, Jane	82
Night, Mary	182		Overstreet, Martha J.	66
Night, W. H.	224		Overstreet, Mary L	99
Night, William	234		Owen, Ambrose D.	77
Nimo, David	345		Owen, C. J.	336
Nimmo, Henr y	232		Owen, C. R.	276
Nimmo, James H.	247		Owen, Frances	332
Nimmo, Martha	42		Owen, John T.	299
Nippen, Richard C.	310		Owon, L.A.R.	188
Nipper, Ellis	183			
Nipper, R. C.	276			
Nipper, Thomas	214-245			
Noe, Gustin	41			
Noe, Peter	140		P.	
Noe, Susan	221		Pace, A. C.	27
Nolen, John M.	74-150-160-221		Pace, B. F.	327
	295		Pace, Emily	86
Norfleet, Mary E	252		Pace, John	62
Norfleet, L. L.	167		Pace, William H.	120
Norfleet, Willie L.	8		Pack, Mary R. B.	40
Norman, Frances	108		Page, Amanda	259
Norman, Harriet	149		Page, C. M.	348
Norman, J.	196		Page, Frances M.	261
Norris, C. J.	192		Page, John B.	325
Northington, M. L.	224		Page, J. N.	321
Northington, Saml. H.	120		Page, Leonard	161-136
Nowlin, J. C.	158		Page, M. A. L.	161
Nuckolds, Amelia F	261		Page, Mary E	257
Nuckolds, Tempe	286		Page, Samuel	232
Null, Galbreath F	94		Page, Saml. W.	168
			Page, Sarah A	308
			Palmer, Charles	335
			Pankey, Louisa	232
			Panson, Nancy	162
O.			Paraise, Richard	34
Oats, Joseph	313		Parham, M. P.	164
Odle, Adeline	308		Parker, A. A.	230
Odle, Louisa	338		Parker, Almarinda	332
Odle, Martha J	89		Parker, Catherine A	264
ODonnell, Bridget	336		Parker, Cyntha	193
Odonnell, Connell	336		Parker, David H.	320
Ogburn, Saml. D.	251-252-254-		Parker, G. W.	180
	256-257-259-262-330		Parker, Harriet A	344
Ogg, Maranda	350		Parker, J. W.	294
Ogg, Martha A	331		Parker, Julia	253
Ogg, M. E.	295		Parker, L. J.	206
Ogg, R.	156		Parker, M.B.	160
Ogg, Susan M.	308		Parker, M. E.	308
Ogg, Washington	150		Parker, Mariah	251
Oran, Ellen	341		Parker, Nancy E	286
Orand, Wm.	140		Parker, Sarah C.	219
Orman, McCarney A	186		Parker, Sarah E.	182
Ormand, Emily	295		Parker, Suntha C.	193
Orndorff, Eli	291		Parker, Wm. L.	97
Orndorff, H. H.	276-280-281-		Parkison, James W.	244
	282-284-288-290-291-292-297			
	299			

Parks, A. L.	328	Pepper, Julia	151
Parks, Anna	107	Pepper, Lemuel	243
Parks, M.	62	Pepper, Lucy	343
Parris, John L.	87	Pepper, Mary	356
Parrish, F.H.W.	332	Pepper, Nancy J.	236
Parsons, J. T.	213	Pepper, Sally	35
Parsons, John B.	30	Pepper, Susan A	328
Parsons, M.B.	305	Pepper, W. C.	190
Parsons, Polly	1	Pepper, W. W. 225-230-250- 265	
Parsons, Rachel C.	195	301-310-313-326-330-331-33-338-	
Paster, F. C.	241		343
Patten, Sarah A	104	Pepper, Westly W.	63
Patterson, Absolum	2	Pepper, Willis	143
Patterson, F.	154	Percise, Sue D.	335
Patterson, Robt. C.	38	Perkerson, George W.	55
Patterson, Teresa B.	302	Perry, Minerva	235
Patton, E. J.	70	Perry, William L. 119-120-121	
Patton, Louisa	299		131
Payne, Alice	288	Persise, E. B.	268
Payne, Ann	167	Persise, Martha W	222
Payne, Boliver	211	Person, Charles	46
Payne, C.	167	Pert, Martha F.	353
Payne, Cynthia	230	Pettie, O.E.	316
Payne, David	282	Peteway, Olive	328
Payne, Dpretha	336	Pettey, Amanda L.	307
Payne, Eliza	243	Petty, Alexander	14
Payne, Erastus	288	Phelps, G. W.	274
Payne, Henrietta	14	Phelps, John E	230
Payne, J.	204	Phelps, William	162
Payne, Joseph	295	Phepps, E.	181
Payne, Larkin	329	Phibbs, Elmore	245
Payne, Leuisa	137	Phillips, Elizabeth	272
Payne, Mahaly E.	261	Phillips, M.	162
Payne, P.	152	Phipps, Aiby	261
Payne, Permely	175	Phipps, Jackson	227
Payne, Sophia	264	Phipps, John	254
Payne, Susan	232	Phipps, Lwellyn	98
Payne, Thomas	56	Phipps, Mary	192
Payne, W. L. 39-40-42-52-56-		Phipps, Saley L.	118
59-64-69-71-75-85-86-87-89- 211		Phipps, Lewellyn	120
Payne, Wm.D.	95	Phipps, Susan	153
Payne, Wm. H.	213	Phipps, William	288-301
Peacher, C. E.	207	Pickard, W E.	314
Pearson, Carter	173	Picking, William	121
Peck, Jacob	335	Pike, James M.	171
Peck, Sarah V.	213	Pike, James W.	251
Peck, William L.	223	Pike, Julia A	275
Peesly, Perry M.	78	Pike, Mary A	331
Pence, G. W.	318	Pike, Matilda	70
Pence, John Ellen	341	Pike, Nancy M.	329
Pennington, Berry	31	Pike, Thomas	126-129
Pennington, Martha J.	65	Pike, W. A.	338
Pennington, R.	114	Pike, William	80
Pentecost, Hiram W.	337	Pilant, Jepthah	112
Pentecost, Mary Matilda	342	Pilant, Martha L.	35
Pepper, Emily	100	Pince, Mary Jane 226	226
Pepper, Harriet	340	Piles, Jo.	145
Pepper, John	9-66	Pill, H. M.	189

Pince, Mary Jane	226	Pool, Lucretia	173
Pince, Robert	221	Pool, Mary	171
Pitman, J.B.	276	Pool, Nancy Ann	263
Pitman, James E.	216	Pool, Norfleet	110-224
Pitman, M. B.	228	Pool, Reason	125-219
Pitman, Sarah E. F.	241	Poor, Bowling L	75
Pitron, J.M.	32	Poor, Carroll	269
Pitt, Almerina	137	Poor, R. A.	231
Pitt, Bartlett	140	Poor, Robt. A.	187
Pitt, Elvina	271	Pope, Ann	282
Pitt, Geo. W.	217	Pope, James W.	311
Pitt, H.	142	Pope, Martha	78
Pitt, Jacob	313	Pope, S	160
Pitt, James B.	253	Pope, Sally A. L.	8
Pitt, Jeremiah	235	Pope, Sarah	292
Pitt, Joseph	124-286	Pope, William	194
Pitt, Levi	172	Pope, William J.	310
Pitt, M.	208	Pope, Wm. H.	113
Pitt, Martha	226	Pope, W. R.	331
Pitt, Mary	253	Porter, Adeline	245
Pitt, Mary J.	352	Porter, Amanda	17-249
Pitt, Vincent W.	190	Porter, Ambrose	149
Pitt, Will L.	206	Porter, B	208
Pitt, Wilson	4	Porter, B. F.	207
Pitmen, James	216	Porter, Edwin	22
Pittman, Piety	329	Porter, Eliza M.	287
Pitts, Alvis	33	Porter, Elizabeth B.	123
Pitts, Delana	82	Porter, Henry	95
Pitts, J.B.	34-43-52-54	Porter, James A.	79
Pitts, Margarett	135	Porter, John	138
Pitts, Martha	192	Porter, John A	262
Pitts, Randolph R.	123	Porter, Joseph	188
Pitts, W. M.	79-80	Porter, Lucy Ann	271
Pitts, Warren M	23-33- 72	Porter, Manerva	216
Plaster, F. C. 197-230-234-238		Porter, Martha	144
244-252-256-257-258-261-264-279		Porter, Mary Ann	4
283-284-286-287-289-297-304-305		Porter, Mary Jane	341
312-314-325-327-328-329-344-346		Porter, Nancy	287
349-356		Porter, P.E.	190
Plasters, Flemming C.	12	Porter, Reason L.	70
Polk, James K.	218	Porter, Richd.	216
Polk, L.A.	192	Porter, Sarah J.	229
Polk, M.A.	244	Porter, Susan 117-240-265	
Polk, Mary A.	42	Porter, William B.	46
Polk, Mary R. B.	40	Porter, William C.	213
Polk, Sallie A.	287	Posey, William H.	35
Polk, S. E.	159	Powell, Baxter	216
Polk, Tho. B.	176	Powell, D.	238
Pollock, P. N.	304	Powell, Dewit W.	308
Pollock, William M.	318	Powell, Edney	324
Pond, Elinor	147	Powell, Eliza J.	198
Pond, Elizabeth	217	Powell, James W.	145
Pond, Lucy	173	Powell, Lewis	59-65
Ponds, Benj.	329	Powell, M. 100-195-196-202	
Ponds, Joice	294	Powell, Margaret	225
Ponds, Sarah	305	Powell, Mary	264 -189
Pool, H.	11-159	Powell, Mary A	273
Pool, Lewis	316	Powell, Mary Ann	260

Powell, Mary J.   59-60-65-346
Powell, Meredith   268-328
Powell, Nancy   209-240-292
Powell, Rich.   237
Powell, Pamelia Adeline   117
Powell, Sarah   80-217
Powell, Sarah H.   187
Powell, Susan   40
Powell, Syntha A   30
Powell, William   204-217-299
Preston, S. B.   309
Price, Amanda   78
Price, Andrew F.   257
Price, Avery G.   31
Price, E   207
Price, Harriet   203
Price, Mary   27-204
Price, Mary E.   75
Price, Nancy D.   133
Price, Saml.   157
Price, Walter J.   256
Price, Warren   193
Price, Wm.   111
Pride, Frances   114
Pride, James L.   190
Pride, J. E.   239
Pride, Martha J.   325
Pride, W. F.   314-342-345-346-
                            348-354
Prince, Margaret   293
Prince, W. A.   338
Prine C.   206
Purtle, Sarah   254
Purherson V.   162

Q.
Guinn, Dorothy   195

R.
Radford, William T   344
Ragsdale, Burwell   23
Ragsdale H. L.   204
Ragsdale, J. E.   116
Ragsdale, J. F.   138
Ragsdale, L. J.   348
Ragsdale, M. A.   204
Ragsdale, Piety Ann   114
Ragsdale, S. E.   116
Ragsdale, Thomas   307-33
Ragland, Leroy   314
Randolph B.   169
Raines, J. A.   318
Rainey, James M.   277
Rainey, Milton   54
Rainwater, Wm.   187

Raley, Phillip S.   35
Ramer, J. A.   318
Ramey, Milton   156-158
Ramey, W.   150
Randolph, A. B.   151-164-169-
171-174-175-178-179-185-186-187
206
Randolph, Elizabeth   185
Randolph, George B.   260
Randolph, Geo. W.   275
Randolph, Harriet   172
Randolph, John   172
Randolph, James   66
Randolph, L.S.   255
Randolph, Martha   169
Randolph, Mary.   26
Randolph, N.   300
Randolph, Permelia   26
Randolph, Sycrugus   338
Randolph, Thomas   83-156
Randolph, William   148
Rany, Milton   42-43
Ratcliff, America   315
Rawls, Almeda E.   243
Rawls, Benj.   6-44-52-55-56-57
84-97-110-121-130-169-170-171-
172-179-184-190-203-206-215-217
219-223-224-229-234-235-245-252
256-261-277-279-287-295-301-319-
                320-328-353-355
Rawls, Charles E.   277
Rawls, David   276
Rawls, Harriet   240
Rawls, James H.   230
Rawls, James   151
Rawls, Jesse   184
Rawls, Jesse J.   234
Rawls, J. W.   354
Rawls, John H.   220
Rawls, Joseph   256
Rawls, Lydia A   328
Rawls, M. A.   337
Rawls, Mary A   170
Rawls, Mary J.   279
Rawls, W. U.   329-341-342
Rawls, William C   57
Ray, Genetta   241
Ray, Jamina   212
Ray, Lucy   160
Ray, Tellman   50
Rayson, Pernicy   175
Read, Hugh   123
Read, John H.   1
Read, W. D.   310
Readfern, C.   142
Readfern, Patsy   58
Readfern Townley   131

Reasing, Nancy	36	Richmond, W. B.	134
Reason, Chas.	241	Richmond, W. C 98-98-99-119-	137
Reason, Jesse	50	Riddle, Elizabeth F.	269
Reaves, Eli	57	Riddle, Greeberry	176
Redding, Elizabeth	214	Rife, W. H. 256-173-180-185-	
Redding, Geo. R	215	192-197-218-227-236	
Redding, Moresty E.	287	Riggan, William H.	255
Redding, Nancy A.C.	273	Riggen, Luther	177
Redding, Saml. F.	289	Riggins, W. H.	274
Redding, Sarah A	170	Rigsbee, Eliza E.	225
Redfern, A. H.	74	Rigsbee, George	245
Redfern, Eliz.	60	Rigsbee, George J.	269
Redfern, Hanzey	148	Rigsby, Martha	152
Redfern, Nancy	56	Riley, Saml.	244
Redfern, William	182	Ring, Nicholas T.	28
Redford, R. A.	206	Ring, Rebecca	156
Redford, Susan	88	Ring, Robert	95
Redman, Harriet	318	Rippy, Simon	272
Reed, B. F.	213	Ritter, Martha	188
Reed, Elizabeth	242	Roach, B. B.	297
Reed, John	262	Roach, Emily A	55
Reed, John T.	30	Roach, Frances, T.	298
Reed, John E.	65	Roach, John H.	298
Reed, Martha E.	341	Robb, Alfred	95
Reed, Mary	63	Robertson Carter	202
Reed, Melinda J.	111	Roberts, E.	167
Reeder, Clayhorn	31	Roberts, Edmund L.	159
Reeder, Elizabeth	325	Roberts, Eliz.	120
Reeder, Mary Ann	250	Roberts, Elizabeth	2
Reeks, Benjamin F.	261	Roberts, Jabos, L.	120
Reeks, J. B.	295	Roberts, James E.	163
Reener, H.	200	Roberts, John	31
Reeves, John D.	211	Roberts, Jesse	47
Reeves, Jonathan J.	212	Roberts, Martha W.	186
Reley, James	132	Roberts, Nancy	46
Reilly, William	121	Roberts, P.B.	104
Reaner, James	83	Roberts, Pleasant B.	285
Renfro, William	128	Roberts, Rachel	46
Repetol, Wm.	197	Roberts, Sophrona	267
Reynold, E. M.	110	Roberts, Stephen	30
Reynold, Mary	102	Roberts, Susan	224
Reynolds, Nancy	183	Robertson, Alex	242
Rhinehart, Andrew	120	Robertson, Alexander	253
Rhinehart, Andrew J.	93	Robertson, Angeline	141
Rhinehart, Joseph	321	Robertson Almira	325
Rice, Hiram	29-83-90	Robertson, Elizabeth	121
Rice, James	104	Robertson, E.	120
Rice, Jeremiah	137	Robertson, H. P.	154
Rice, Marthy	38	Robertson, Isaac	66
Rice, William	81	Robertson, James	254
Richard, John C.	101	Robertson, Jesse	98
Richard, R. D.	209	Robertson, Meredith T.	331
Richards, Ed. M.	175	Robertson M. T.	258
Richerson, E. W.	201	Robertson, Oliva	241
Richerson, L.	199	Robertson, Sarah	29
Richeson Eliz.	64	Robertson, William	166
Richeson, Susan	79	Robertson, William A.	322
Richmond, J. B.	323	Robertson, W. J.	87

Rock, H. A.	160	Rosson, J. S.	213
Robins, Eliz	98	Rosson, James	134
Robins, Highly	3	Rosson, Lucinda	317
Robins, John	303	Rosson, Mary	148
Robins, Mahalia	37	Rosson, Nancy	120
Robins, Samuel H.	303	Rosson, Tabitha	149
Robins, Susan	259	Roundtree, Armildrice	92
Robinson, Isaac	66	Rowe, Louisa	66
Roby, W. W.	347	Rowe, Moses J.	77
Rodden, Stephen	77	Roy, James V.	75
Roderick, Wm.	179	Ruffin, Elizabeth	312
Rodgers, William	20-320	Ruffin Emeline E	95
Roe, Harriet E	325	Ruffin, J. E.	248
Roe, H. E.	209	Ruffin, Martha J.	54
Roe, Leroy	280	Ruffin, Nancy	147
Roe, Malind	208	Ruffin, R. E.	233
Roe, R. M.	141	Ruffin, Thos. W. 62-82-91-130	
Rogers, Albert	250	133-138-156-165-175-189-190-205	
Rogers, Edny F.	280		217
Rogers, George S.	280	Ruskin, P. W.	129
Rogers, Henry	298	Russell, Ann E	278
Rogers, Jane	302	Russell, Benjamin	132
Rogers, Mary E	322	Russell, Frances	136
Rolin, Caroline	28	Russell, G. B.	304
Roland, Nancy	49	Russell, Mary	78
Roland, Wm. T	30	Russell, Nathaniel	4
Roney, Eliz.	56	Russell, Robert	9
Roney, Josephine	285	Russell, William	148
Roney, M. J.	337	Rust, Chesterfield	254
Rose, A. 186-209-236-245-258		Rust, Isaac W.	234
261-262-264-273-274-275-283-291		Rust, Jackson	54
296-298-300-307-310-314-315-318		Rust, Lucy Ann	217
320-322-324		Rust, Lucy S.	325
Rose, Alfred J.	191	Rust, M. F.	205
Rose, E. R.18	189	Rust, Thos. M.	346
Rose, Elizabeth	64-222	Rust, William D	253
Rose, Henry M.	8	Rust, W. H.	350
Rose, James	76	Rutherford, Josiah	110
Rose, James B.	148	Ryan, Alexander E.	82
Rose, James R.	177	Ryan Alomzo	349
Rose, John	69	Ryan Darby	195
Rose, Martha J.	312	Ryan Eliza J.	226
Rose, Mary A.	132	Ryan, Elizabeth A	291
Rose, Michael W.		Ryan George L.	289
Rose, M. W.	189	Ryan, James	14-230
Rose, Nancy	170	Ryan, John	312
Rose, Penine	298	Ryan W. H.	120
Rose, R. B. 106-116-117-123-			
	138-139		
Rose, Redick	54		
Rose, Richard B.	59-269	S.	
Rose, Temperance	11	Sadler, Jesse	24
Rose, Vincent D.	94	Sadler, Sarah	24
Rose, William H.	224	Sadler, Thomas F.	324
Roslan, Nancy	148	Sadler W. R. 243-259-261- 272	
Ross, Elizabeth G.	221	278-302-303-310-331-335-348	
Ross, John	69	Sadler, William R.	138
Rosson, Ann	206	Sale, James M.	264

Sales, Samuel	91	Sellers, Martha	312
Sales, Wm. P	185	Sellers, John	246
Samaper, Frances	138	Sellers, Mark	184
Sams, Jane	244	Sellers, Martha	312
Samuel, M.J.	181	Sellers, Mary	183
Samuel, R. I.	202	Sellers, Wilmouth	217
Samuel, Susan	189	Sewall, James	179
Sand, Elizabeth	10	Senner, Katherine Jane	118
Sand, Mary A	10	Senter, Mark	192
Sandefur, E. T.	162	Seymore, Mary A	78
Sandefur, Minerva M.	133	Shackelford, A. M.	306
Sandefur, William A.	133	Shackleford, Ann E.	70
Sanders, D. C.	76	Shackleford, Mary	311
Sanders, David	164	Shanklin, Sophia	2
Sanders, David V.	38	Shannon, A. L.	182
Sanders, Elizabeth	198	Shannon, Allen J.	134
Sanders, John	113	Shannon, Elizabeth A	341
Sanders, Mary	48	Shannon, J. A.	295
Sanders, Phebe	113	Shannon, Jane	102
Sanders, Robert	200	Shannon, J. C.	159
Sanders, Wm. C.	200	Shannon, Jesse	298-312
Sanderson, Sarah	288	Shannon, John L.	90
Sandford, A. W.	302	Shannon, Kelly	242
Sandford, George	315	Shannon, Martha Ann	125-126
Sandford, J. B.	281	Shannon, Martha S.	286
Sandford, G.M.Jackson	293	Shannon, Mary	325
Sandford, Robert	300	Shannon, Rebecca J.	320
Satterfield, John	69	Shannon, Richard	252
Saunders, Giles, A	77	Shannon, Robert S.	300
Saunders, John	68	Shannon, William A.	243
Saunders, Nancy	68	Shannon, Wm. C	193
Sartin, Frances E.	112	Shark, Eliza M.	85
Savage, Amanda	292	Sharp, C. A.	204
Savage, L.	208	Sharp, David F.	228
Savage, Mary	51	Sharp, Hannah	101
Savage, Robert	143	Sharp, Silas H.	283
Savage, thomas	14	Sharp, William C.	115
Sawyer, Maleda	109	Shaw, Edmund H.	19
Sawyer, Newton M.	136	Shaw, Guinae	20
Sawyers, Jesse	66	Shaw, G. W.	24
Sawyers, Wm. T.	210	Shaw, H. B.	113
Sayers, A. B.	159-168-173	Shaw, Hepsey B.	69
Sayle, M.	202	Shaw, Henry	68
Sayles, Eliza Ann	249	Shaw, James	37
Sayles, John	268	Shaw, Lucinda	20
Schenck, John B.	65	Shaw, Marina	20
Scoggin, Elizabeth	4	Shaw, Nancy A.	170
Scott, A. J.	308	Shaw, Nancy F	69
Scott, Elizabeth	186	Shaw, Tho. J.	80
Scott, S. W. D.	45	Shaw, William	19-36-67-69
Scruder, Mary	303	Shaw, William S.	211
Seal, Mary E.	1	Shearing, Burgess	131
Seal, Sall Ann	57	Shelly, Carline	159
Seal, W.	55-61-66	Shelly, Susan	100
Seal, Wm. R.	78	Shelton, Hanton	293
Sears, M. J.	147	Shelton, James C.	351
Seat, Sarah	265	Shelton, James L.	51
Sellars, Beady	28	Shelton, James M.	45-334-104

Shelton, Mary	234	Simmons, William P	271
Shelton, Nancy	127	Simmons, William S.	222
Shelton, Virginia	350	Simmons, Xenophon	336
Shepherd, G. R.	267	Simpson, Charles	38
Shepherd, James D.	311	Sisk, Harrison D.	21
Shepherd, John	105	Sisk, Lucinda S.	181
Shepherd, Katherine	23	Sivols, Spiva	105
Shepherd, Mary J.	154	Slack, J. M.	251
Shepherd, Morgan	239	Slack, James W.	356
Shepherd, W. H.	179	Slack, Saml.	239
Shepherd, Wm. R.	203	Slater, Call C.	47
Sherain, Sterling W	80	Small, E. S.	165
Sherrick, James	311	Small, M. C.	139
Sherrill, John	5	Small, Permelia	12
Sherrodd, Caroline	258	Smart, J. M.	339
Sherrod, Harriet E.	65	Smelsar, Emaline	218
Sherrodd, James W	222	Smelser, J. B.	236
Sherrod, John	298	Smelser, James	237
Sherrod, Martha	9	Smelser, Lucinda J.	284
Sherrod, Mary J. E.	300	Smelser, Stephen	187
Sherrod, Saml. W.	181	Smiley, Carline	166
Sherrod, Sarah J.	297	Smiley, D.	120
Sherrod, William	63	Smiley, Elizabeth	244
Sherron, Elizabeth	87	Smiley, Hugh	194
Sherron, Martha A	68	Smiley, Mary	91
Sherron, James W.	164	Smiley, Sarah	34
Sherron, Joseph J.	213	Smith, AL. L.	51
Shoecroft, Fanny	234	Smith, Dicy A.	277
Shoemaker, Henry	268	Smith, E.	206
Shoemaker, John	145	Smith, Eliz.	57-69-168
Shoemaker, Russell	162	Smith, Eliz. B	185
Short, George E.	300	Smith, F. B.	151
Shettan, James L.	51	Smith George A	10-271
Shreve, Eliza Jane	266	Smith, Geo. H.	281
Shrives, Mary A.	42	Smith, Geo. W	181
Shrives, Susan,	44	Smith, James	110-114
Shrives, Wm. M.	110	Smith, James H.	23
Shuman, Jesse	263	Smith, J.H.	160
Shurron, Sally	239	Smith, John	317
Shy, Elizabeth	339	Smith, John F.	337
Simpson, Charles	38	Smith, John W. 267-270-278- 279	
Simpson, James B	95	284-289-293-294-299-305-321- 322	
Simmons, Amelia	348	323-324-327-333-334-335-336-337	
Simmons, Cive	287	338-341-345-346-349-350-353	
Simmons, Daniel H.	302	Smith, Levy	244
Simmons, Finula	321	Smith, Louis	65
Simmons, George W	188	Smith, Martha	75-88
Simmons, J. I. A	341	Smith, Martha A.	116
Simmonsm John T	26	Smith, Mary	196-305
Simmons, L.	142	Smith, Mary Ann	216
Simmons, Lucy	143	Smith, Mary E. M.	254
Simmons, M.M.	123	Smith, N. J.	203
Simmons, Martha W.	228	Smith, Olive	238
Simmons, Mary	262	Smith, O.W.	348
Simmons, Mary 1	197	Smith, Richd. B	107
Simmons, Nancy	29	Smith, Rich. L.	236
Simmons, S.	142	Smith, Richd. W.	167
Simmons, S. S.	220		
Simmons, Wesley	323		

Smith, Robert A.	281
Smith, R. S.	278
Smith, Samuel	38
Smith Viney	138
Smith, W. A.	237
Smith, W. C.	255
Smith, W. F.	321
Smith, William	107
Smith, Wilmouth B.	148
Smith, W. J.	236
Smith, W. L.	233
Smith, Wm. H.	83-183
Smith, W. T.	258
Smith, Wich E. A.	159
Sneed, G. W.	83-88
Sneed, Jane	149
Sneed, Martha	61
Sneed, Phillip	309
Sneed, Saml.	110
Snowdy, George	131
Soloman, Amanda	276
Solomon, Elizabeth	119
Solomon, F. F.	323
Solomon, John R,	207
Solomon, Loretta	247
Solomon, Olivia	318
Solomon, Polly A	189
Solomon, William	221
Sommerville, Phoebe	274
Sory, Frances	144
Sory, George B.	281
Sory, Robt.	44-340
Sory, Susan	37
Sory, Thos. W	267
Southland, John	355
Soward, John L.	307
Soyars, A. B. 196-209-210-214	
Soyars, James A.	297
Spain, Frances	319
Spain, James	250
Spain, Juanita	56
Spain, Thomas	181
Spayne, Catherine	244
Spears, J. G.	155
Spears, Sarah	761
Speer, J. M. 329-331-340	
342-254	
Spright, Jesse M	62
Sprouse, Goe. B.	81
Sprouse, H. P.	235
Sprouse, James 2-3-4-11-13-14	
51-61-62-66-67-71-76-91-92-97-	
100-109-112-117-118-124-125-127	
135-137-143-144-152-154-165-168	
169-173-182-192-205-213-215-223	
224-226-227-242	
Sprouse, Martha J	24
Sprouse, Richard S.	182
Sprouse, Thos. G.	44
Stack, L. F.	305
Stack, Wm. W	15
Stainback, Edwin	138
Stainback, Mary	259
Staley, Geo. L.	314
Staley, Thos.	163
Standley, James	308
Standley, Mary E	308
Standfield, John	286
Standfield, Silas, L.	261
Stanley, Anny	80
Stanley, Barbary A	196
Stanley, Keziah	3
Stanley, M.	176
Stanley, Moses	168
Stanley, Peter	6
Stanley, Thos. 103-109-111-118	
Stanley, William	316
Stanley, William J.	283
Stanley, Serena	3
Stark, Benj. 307-185-354	
Stark, Britton	138
Stark, Cyrene	53
Stark, Elizabeth	24-19
Stark, Elizabeth W.	266
Stark, Fielding	34
Stark, Franklin	226
Stark, Harriet	340
Stark, James Atlas	310
Stark, John W. 260-356-225	
Stark, J.P.	201
Stark, Lucinda	324
Stark, Malvina	94
Stark, Mary A	61
Stark, Mary Ann	6
Stark, M.E.	345
Stark, Meredith	78
Stark, M.J.	87
Stark, M. O. C.	177
Stark, Myran	133
Stark, Myram (Mary)	128
Stake, Nancy	226
Stark, Pantha A	187
Stark, Rebecca A.	307
Stark, Sally	79
Stark, Sally A	50
Stark, Sarah	174
Stark, Samnes	325
Stark, Susan	140
Stark, Thomas	81
Stark, Virginia F	292
Stark, W. J.	351
Stark, William	280
Stark, William H.	318
Steel, Caroline	74

Steel, Harriet	73
Steel, Isaac	2-27-31-32-42-64
77-81-87-88-89-90-95-132-133-	
146-147-166-181-202-209-217-222	
228-230-243-249-262-265-268-274	
285-288-301-308-315-316-338-341	
348-349-351-355	
Steel, J.	209
Steel, Mary M.	150
Steele. Emily	213
Stemmons, J. M.	104-152- 153
	179-218
Stephen, William L.	194
Stephens, B. M.	235-241
Stephens, D. C.	152
Stephens, *	
Sterry, William	160
Stevens, D. C.	135
Stewart, Benj. F	165
Stewart, J.	201
Stewart, John	185
Stewart, James	29
Stewart Jo A.	89
Stewart, Martha D	47
Stinson, James A	89
Stelts B. F.	169
Stolts, E. T.	155
Stoltz, Louisa	258
Stoltz, Martha	214
Stoltz, Mary C	301
Stoltz, Miranda	100
Stoltz, S. R.	157
Stoltz, Susan A	344
Stone, Eliza A	6.
Stone, George W	53.
Stone, Henry	70.
Stone, James C	246.
Stone, Lucinda Elizabeth	334.
Stone, Martha	258-230.
Stone, M.E.	356
Stone, Missippi	189.
Stone, Nicholas	21.
Stone, Obadiah	79.
Stone Winny	81.
Stone, Wm. K.	181.
Stother, Luoisa Y	21
Stout, Emily	109
Stout, Lucy	280
Stoval, Wesley	151
Stoval, William H.	29- 60
Stovall, Lourena	240
Strain, H.	108
Strain, M. J.	142
Strange, E. G.	334
Strater, Carline	117
Stratton, E	156

Stratton, Jane	248
Stratton, John	88
Stratton, John W	98
Stratton, Lewis	153
Stratton, Meredith	308
Stratton, William	260
Straughn, Juliet	45
Straughn, John L.	118
Street, Sarah	277
Strickland, Alice J.	263
Strickland, Croffard	108
Strickland, Mary J	339
Strickland, L.H.	210
Stricklin, Debby S.	107
Stricklin, James L.	25
Stricklin, Jessie	103
Strickling, John A	19
Srticklin, John R	45
Stringer, Sarah	166
Stringer, William	211
Stroder, Thomas	220
Strother, John B.	347
Strother, Lydia K.	227
Stroud, James M.	43
Stroud, William	120
Suddah, Benjamin	226
Sudith, Susan Ann	125
Sugg, J. B.	289
Sugg, Virgini. C	297
Sutton, Wm. F.	101
Sulam, Nancy	40
Sullivan, J	168
Sullivan, Moody Ann	268
Summer, Malinda	31
Summer, E. T.	347
Summers, Wm.	181
Summerville, E. F.	176
Summerville, James M.	327
Summerville, Mary J.	339
Summerville, Phillip D.	351
Summerville, Pheobe	274
Summons, Rebecca	119
Sumpter, Elizabeth	136
Surpt. L. J.	198
Suter, Martha A	106
Suter, Mary	27
Suter, J. M.	197
Sutton, David L. S.	306
Sutton, Wm. F.	101
Swann, B. N.	236
Swann, James W	159
Swann, John	339
Swann, John A	37
Swann, John F.	169
Swann, R.	203

****

Swift, Catherine	323	Terrill, James H.	6
Swift, Catherine W.	269	Terry, B. E. P.	218
Swift, James	274	Terry, Rachel	18
Swift, Martha	271	Thaxton, F. M.	199
Swift, Matilda	317	Thaxton, Thomas W.	324
Swift, Milly	92	Thomas, Archer	321
Swift, Richd.	29	Thomas, Chrissie	346
Swift, Sarah	304	Thomas, Elizabeth A. T.	13
Swift, Sarah J.	326	Thomas, George Ann	229
Swift, William	259	Thomas, Geo. E.	188
		Thomas, John A	147
		Thomas, Letitia M.	250
T.		Thomas, Lewis	5-74-171
Talley, Henry	32	Thomas, Mary J.	188-328
Tally, Sarah J.	335	Thomas, Matilda	310
Tanner, Eliza	55	Thomaa, Sally H.	316
Tanner, G. A.	149	Thomas, Silas M.	115
Tarpley, T. O.	340-350-354	Thomas, Virginia	192
Tate, Lucy Ann	278	Thomas, W. A.	168
Tate, Margaret N.	128	Thomas, Walter M.	115
Tate, Mary M. R.	124	Thomas, Wm. W	75
Tate, Nancy	94	Thomas, Wilmouth Ann	168
Tate, Robert C.	92	Thompson, Eliz.	288-59
Tate, Robert L.	159	Thompson Eliza J.	147
Tate, William	105	Thompson, Emaline	274
Tatum, Absolum	184	Thompson, James B.	95
Tatum, William	128-186	Thompson, Mary	146
Taylor, Alice N.	343	Thompson, N. A.	318
Taylor, Carline	151	Thompson, Nancy	305
Taylor, Emeline	71	Thompson, Robert W	275
Taylor, Hugh	133	Thompson, R. W.	46
Taylor, Jane	145	Thompson, Virginia	88
Taylor, Joseph T.	61	Thompson, W. H.	294
Taylor, L. M.	169	Thompson, William	258
Taylor, M. A.	162	Thornhill, J. N.	339
Taylor, Martha	76	Thurman, Mitchell G.	76
Taylor, Mary Ann Elizabeth	309	Thurman, Sarah	345
Taylor, M. D.	345	Tiller, L. A.	311
Taylor, Melissa D,	346	Tinson, Selia	120
Taylor, N. G.	342	Tisdale, Susan	31
Taylor, Penelope	76	Todd, Francis	349
Taylor, Richard D.	266	Todd, Wm. H.	349
Taylor, Sarah	33-281	Toler, A. M. N.	140
Taylor, Susan	43-21	Toler, Josiah	276
Taylor, Thomas W.	253	Toler, Maranda	276
Taylor, V. J.	294	Tollerson, E. A.	341
Taylor, William W	293	Toliver, Nancy A	292
Teasley, John W.	135	Toliver, William M.	336
Teasley, Plumer W	68	Tollison, John P.	317
Tellart, Larnice	209	Tomerline, John	113
Teller, L. A.	311	Tomerline, John L.	285
Tennison G.	237	Tomerline, Martha J.	285
Tennison, H. A. A.	337	Tooley, Martha	25
Tenson, Celia	120	Touman, W. E.	233
Teragen, Thos.	12	Townly, Elizabeth B.	6
		Townsend, Benjamin T.	104

Townsend, J. L.	276-346		Tucker, L. M.	211
Townsend, James M.	79		Tucker, Mary	150
Townsend, Nancy	33		Tucker, O. G.	24
Townsend. William L.	282		Tucker, Samuel	66
Trainnum, S. E.	325		Tucker, Silas	91
Trauber, Sally	174		Tucker, Susan I	226
Traughber, Alexander	119		Tucker, William G	150
Traughber, Alfred	284		Turner, Dosha	142
Thraughber, Amanda	236		Turner, Eliza	95
Thraughber, Amanda E.	83		Turner, Eliza Ann	32
Traughber, Anna	148		Truner, Elizabeth E	290
Thraughber Arness W.	119		Turner, Elijah	147
Thraughber E. A.	206		Turner, Henry	59-60
Thraghber Eliza	174-233		Turner, Jack E	150
Traughber, Eliza J.	337		Turner, James	78
Thraughber, Emanuel	119		Turner, Jane E.	88
Traughber, F. G.	147		Turner, John R	329
Traughber harriett	322		Turner, Joseph	179
Thraughber, Harvey	223		Turner, Josha W.	279
Traughber, Henry	279		Turner, Josiah	228
Traughber, Hiram	92		Turner, Nancy F.	185
Traughber, Joseph	267		Turner, Newton L.	998
Traughber, James	249		Turner, Prudence	168
Traughber, Lafayette	305		Turner, W. R	136
Traughber, Lydia	73		Turner, William	79
Traughber, M. A.	188		Turner, William K.	145
Traughber, M. E.	140		Turus, Carline	153
Traughber, Meredith	349		Tyner, William	78
Traughber, Milly	340			
Traughber, Richard	283			
Traughber, Rose Ann	283		U.	
Traughber, Sally	34-174		Underwood, John I.	328
Traughber, Sarah	54		Usry, Nathan	300
Traughber, Sarah J.	327			
Traughber, Thomas	91			
Traughber, Williams	131-238			
Traughber, William P.	271		V.	
Travathan, D. W.	287		Vance, Absolum	183
Travis, James	304		Vance, David	90
Travis, John	164		Vance, Elizabeth	12
Treadway, Isham	170		Vance, Nancy	216
Trenary, Geo. W	353-355		Vanhook, Lucretia	134
Trevathan, Priscilla	93		Vanhook, Mary A	85
Trice, Martha Ann	99		Vanhook, Maranda R	278
Trice, Henry	288		Vanhook, Richard	230
Trimble, Amand	278		Vannester Wm. C.	157
Trimble, Elizabeth	77		Vantress, James	239
Trimble, Margaret	105		Vaughn, Eli	115
Trimble, Nancy	177		Vaughn, James	226
Trimble, Robert F.	251		Vaughn, Joel	82
True, Martha M.	99		Vaughn, Lucy L.	289
True, Octavia	218		Vaughn, Martha E.	215
True, Sarah J	72		Vaughn, Mary E	326
Truman, H. E.	233		Vaughn William	62
Truman, L. J.	65		Vaughon B. W. L.	290
Tucker, Amanda	143		Vaught, Elizabeth	275
Tucker, Harriet	4		Vaught, J. E.	34
Tucker, Joseph A	66		Vaught, Larkin	266

Veal, Sally A	80	Walker, Paul L.H.	315
Venable. S.I.	230	Walker, Sterling	135
Ventress, Amanda	172	Walker, Thomas	245
Ventress, Lucy	1	Walker, W. J.	254
Ventress, Weathly I.	52	Walon, William J.	121
Verham, William	27	Walton, Andrew D.	252
Vestal, John M.	156-160-163	Walton, Carline	135
Vick, Elias V.	143	Walton, E. P.	33
Vick, Henrietta	82	Walton, J. B.	234-239-241- 251
Vick, James C.	257		287-296
Vick, John	79	Walton, Isaac B.	163
Vick, William E.	230	Walton, Lucy C.	299
Villines E. A.	151	Walton, M. B.	171
Villines, Ellen	180	Walton, Martha	53
Villines, James W.	227	Walton, Martha B.	178
Villines, Robt. M.	215	Walton, Martha F.	104
Villines, Susan E.	228	Walton, Parile	275
Villines, W. H.	317	Walton, Washington	253
Vilott, Elizabeth	212	Ward, F. F. D	33
Violet, Ann	153	Ward, John W.	229
Violett, Samuel	349	Ward, Martha A	158
Voloy, W. P.	318	Ward, Mary	257
Volver, Elias	168	Ward, William	304 -221
Volver, Samuel	155	Warden, Martha A	138
Volner, Wm.	173	Warden, Rachel	54
		Warford, M.J.	219
		Warmath, Martha	329
		Warner, Jesse	261
W.		Warner, Saml.	160
Wade, Mary A	146	Warner, Rosabell	276
Wade, Saml. M.	300	Warren, Allen	111
Waggoner, Harriet E.	262	Warren, C	210
Wall, May A	197	Warren, Catherine	347
Wall, Sally	105	Warren, Drury	100
Wall, Washington	164	Warren, Drewery	332
Wall, W. W.	112	Warren, E.P.	232
Wallace, Charity E.	226	Warren, Elijah	351-252
Wallace, James	179	Warren, Eliz.	167
Wallace, Martha J.	223	Warren, Elizabeth Jane	321
Walls, Mary A	73	Warren, Fielden	302
Walker, A. H.	214	Warren, Franklin	72
Walker, Anna	86	Warren, Henry	98
Walker, Benj. F.	112	Warren, Hiram 302-309-310-311-
Walker, Dicy J.	196	322-325-33-348-356
Walker, Elizabeth	87	Warren, Isiah 5-6-7-19-35-38-
Walker, E	206		41-72
Walker, G. W.	316	Warren, J. A.	320
Walker, Geo.	114	Warren, Jas.	46
Walker, Geo. W	315	Warren, John	166
Walker, Harriet	164	Warren John W.	93-343
Walker, James W.	137	Warren, Leethy	175
Walker, John	167	Warren, Lemuel	13
Walker, John J	59	Warren, Lewis	186
Walker, John V.	280	Warren, Martha	6
Walker, John W	121	Warren, Martha Ann	135
Walker. M.J.	154	Warren, Mary J.	168-320
Walker, Noah S.	279	Warren, Nancy A	300

Warren, Nancy J.	274	Wells, G. A.	189
Warren, N. W.	345	Wells, Henry	113-133
Warren, R. A.	175	Wells, John	153
Warren, Rachel	54	Wells, Josephine	341
Warren, Rhoda	193	Wells, Levi	259
Warren, Robert F.	236	Wells, Martha A	234
Warren, Roland	265	Wells, Mary A	73
Warren, Russel	125	Wells, Milton	128
Warren, Samuel	118	Wells, Thomas	116
Warren, Saraphine	288	West, Albert	175
Warren, Susan	229	West, Andrew	19
Warren, Thomas	225	West, A. W.	295
Warren, William	273	West, Benj.	100
Warren, W. P.	169	West, David	21
Washburn, Cyrus W,	316	West, James A	355
Wate, Elizabeth A. J.	12	West, James H.	85
Watson, Choischana	120	West, Mary	223
Watson, Elizabeth A	184	West, Rachel K.	211
Watson, Elizabeth	209	West, Sandford	164
Watson, Jane A	117	West, Sarah	219-253
Watson, John	158	West, Tabitha J.	340
Watson, L. C.	280	West, Thomas, 108-115-152-163-	
Watson, Mary A.	97	176-183-203-216-219-223-232-248	
Watson, Mary J.	184	253-269-274-277-280-295-310-316	
Watson, M. C.	164	314-339	
Watson, Mildred V.	345-288	West, Thomas. L.	85-278
Watson, P. B.	214	Westen, Harry	244
Watson, Robert	165-318	Wheat, Thos.	64
Watson, S.	165	Wheeler, E. J.	187
Watson, Sarah	236	Wheeler, Millie	64
Watson, W. A.	240	Whetter, Julia A. L.	174
Watson Wilmouth A	50	White, A. J.	19
Watson, William	248	White, Ann C. F.	232
Watts, Henry J.	219	White, Catherine	321
Watts, James H.	312	White, Christopher	42
Watts, Joseph W	196	White, Dosha	151
Watts, N. C.	310	White, ELL.	149
Watts, Thomas 142-188-194-352		White, Henry F.	177
Watts, Wesley W.	276	White, Iredell	137
Wautland, W. W.	353	White, J,B.	260
Webb, Eleanor	313	White, Jesse W.	86
Webb, John	227	White, John G	152-98
Webb, Lucinda	97	White, Julia A. M.	36
Webb, Mary F.	339	White, Lewis	271
Webb, Melissa A	345	White, M. A.	204
Webb, Nancy J.	186	White, M. E.	315
Webb, Parthena	125-127	White, Martha A	326
Webb, Sylvester F.	246	White, Rebecca	103
Webster, Benjamin F.	317	White, Rebecca F.	66
Webster, James 187-305-215		White, Tennessee	232
Welburn James W.	187	White, William	287
Welch, F. M.	302	White, William D.	257
Wells, Armstead B.	103	White, William Sr.	106
Wells, Carline	183	Whitehead, Frances	121
Wells, David M. 133-137-140-143		Whitehead, Geo. H	82
144-156-183-194-216-217-222		Whitehead, John L.	127

Whitehead, J. S.	125	Williams, Joannah	81
Whitehead, Louisa	17	Williams, J.K.	171
Whitehead, Mary V.	265	Williams, John A	72
Whitehead, Nancy A	131	Williams, John F.	
Whitehead, William H.	337	Williams, John W.	212
Whitemore, Elizabeth	50	Williams, Joseph	108
Whiten, William	274	Williams, Josephus	339
Whitescarver, Charles	23	Williams, L. L.	42
Whiteside, William	221	Williams, M. A.	205
Whitfield, James H.	282	Williams, Martha	252
Whitfield, Susan M.	51	Williams, Martha A.	104
Whiting, Archer	113	Williams, Mary E.	350
Whiting, Elisha	153	Williams, M. D. K.	77
Whitinghill, Elijah H.	85	Williams, Melissa	285
Whitmer, Milly	270	Williams, Nancy G.	37
Whitemore, Semantha	291	Williams, P.A.	252
Whitscarver, S. M.	73	Williams, Patterson	131
Whitten, Joel W.	67-71-324	Williams, Penelope	113
Widick, J. L.	353	Williams, Pernice	40
Wildon, Mary E	259	Williams, R. H.	123
Wilkerson, John L.	301	Williams, Rebecca	15-83-140
Wilkerson, Mary J.	237	Williams, Richd.	305
Wilkins, Rebecca	293	Williams, Robt.	6-8-12- 24-28-
Wilks, Edwards	279	37-55-65-91-124-134-148-149-150	
Wilks, David M.	144-156	167-184-206-207-213-217-224-225	
Wilks, Thos. J.	305	227-230-236-238-239-240-244-246	
Willard, Monroe	525	247-249250-254-257-260-265-267-	
Willhelm, Marshall D.	291	276-295	
Williams, A	172	Williams, Sally A	134
Williams, A. J.	106	Williams, Sarah	72-109
Williams, Alex H.	170	Williams, Sarah C.	291
Williams, Amanda	249	Williams, Sarenda	181
Williams, Benj. E.	132	Williams, Sol.	216
Williams, C. B.	169	Williams, Virginia	339
Williams, C. C.	161	Williams, Virginia F.	254
Williams, C. I.	210	Williams, W. A.	326
Williams, David	1	Williams, Washington J.	174
Williams, E. A.	13	Williams, Wm.	280
Williams, E. J.	12-21	Williamson, Alexander L.	101
Williams, Edwin B.	210	Williamson, Nancy	275
Williams, Elbert	15	Williamson, Virginia	321
Williams, E. R.	233	Williams, W. W.	70-86-87-110
Williams, E. R. H.	217	112-113-114-117-121-135-137-164	
Williams, Elizabeth S.	279	165-206-211-213-221-245-255-256	
Williams, Elizabeth	47-115-247	263-265	
Williams, F. V.	342	Willis, E. A.	190
Williams, George W.	345	Willis, Elijah	262
Williams, H	318	Willis, Elisha W.	182
Williams, Harriet	16-77	Willis, Elizabeth	95
Williams, Henry G.	6	Willis, Joseph	190-192-193-203-
Williams, Henry W.	350	204-206-207-211-213	
Williams, Jackson	306	Willis, Larkin W.	7
Williams, James	12	Willis, L.W.	344
Williams, James A.	175	Willis, Maryett	25
Williams, James S.	224	Willis, Mary K.	7
Williams, James T.	74	Willis, Martha	216
Williams, James W.	61	Willis, M. R.	205-322

Willis, Nancy P.	159	
Willis, Richd.	161	
Willis, Sarah H.	121	
Willis, S. E.	166	
Willis, Susan	213	
Willis, Thomas	80	
Willis, Thomas J.	305	
Willis, W. F.	335	
Willis, W. H.	228	
Willis, W. M.	356	
Willis, William	232	
Wills, Henry	133	
Wills, S. H.	165	
Wilson, Berry	40	
Wilson, Calvin	181	
Wilson, Caroline	191-236	
Wilson, Drury	189	
Wilson, E. W.	201	
Wilson, James J.	26	
Wilson, James S.	288	
Wilson, John	307	
Wilson, Joseph	172-178	
Wilson, L.J.	316	
Wilson, Lutitia	176	
Wilson, Martha	169	
Wilson, Martha Ann	229	
Wilson, Mary	281-355	
Wilson, Nancy	167	
Wilson Nancy E	227	
Wilson, R.E.	209	
Wilson, Robert G.	277	
Wilson, Robert P.	236	
Wilson, S.	238	
Wilson, Sally	35	
Wilson, Sarah	316-354	
Wilson, Susan P.	236	
Wilson, Terry	71	
Wilson, W. H.	236	
Wilson, W. P.	162	
Wimberly, Araminta	12	
Wimberly, E. A.	252	
Wimberly, Eugenia	289	
Wines, J. M.	190	
Winfield, Almyra	25	
Winfield, Cordelia	336	
Winfield, J. E.	177	
Winfield, Lemuel	279	
Winfield, N. E.	356	
Winfield, Susan J.	327	
Winfield, William	332	
Winger, Jacob B.	270	
Wingo, Allen H.	69	
Wings, Aisley S	169	
Winn, Amanda	169	
Winn, Charity	160	
Winn, James	199	
Winn, Jane	94	
Winn, J.M.	293	

Winn, L. M. J.	70	
Winn, Lucy Jane	331	
Winn, Mary F.	348	
Winn, Rebecca J.	99	
Winn, Richd. M.	185	
Winn, Richd. P.	64	
Winn, Sarah A	169- 191	
Winn, W. J.	266	
Winsett, Amanda	304	
Winns, Thos.	185	
Winset, Alfred	231	
Winters, Caroline	182	
Winters, Frances	251	
Winters, Harry B	72	
Winters, Isaac L.	245	
Winters, James N.	246	
Winters, J. C.	238	
Winters, John A	125-129	
Winters, M. W. 301-321-327-333		
335-336-337-342-345		
Winters, Martha M.	152	
Winters, Mary	98	
Winters, Mary M.	115	
Winters, Melissa A	66	
Winters, Nancy	47	
Winters, Nancy M.	250	
Winters, Zachariah	265	
Withers, Eliz. A	89	
Withers, Louisa A	279	
Witt, Asbury	146	
Wittson, A. Eliza	89	
Woldron, Thos.	266	
Wolf, Elizabeth	326	
Wolf, Malvina C	262	
Wood, William	301	
Woodall, C.	67-71- 90	
Woodall, Frances	45	
Woodall, James R	115-119	
Woodall, John W	40	
Woodall, Lydia	211	
Woodall, Rachel	21	
Woodard, Arthur	6	
Woodard Carline	105	
Woodard, Catharine	237-280	
Woodard, Drusilla	51	
Woodard, E.	208	
Woodard, Elbert	28	
Woodard, Elizabeth	337	
Woodard, F. M.	237	
Woodard, Harriet B.	72	
Woodard, James 4-8-9-16-17-19-		
24-26-33-41-43-46-47-52-60-61-66		
76-80-83-90-93-94-103-104-109-		
113-125-128-129-131-314-135-155-		
138-139-140-142-147-148-149-155-		
157-158-160-161-162-163-172-187-		
188-212-215-218-219-220-221-223-		
243-244-247-251-259-265-268-273-		
284-301-304-306-313-318-328-257		

Robertson Co., TN - Marriage Records - Volume 1 - 1839 - 1861   195

****

www.ingramcontent.com/pod-product-compliance
Lightning Source LLC
Chambersburg PA
CBHW080238270326
41926CB00020B/4294